Dimensions Math Textbook 4A

Authors and Reviewers
Bill Jackson
Jenny Kempe
Cassandra Turner
Allison Coates
Tricia Salerno

Consultant
Dr. Richard Askey

Singapore Math Inc.

Published by Singapore Math Inc.

19535 SW 129th Avenue
Tualatin, OR 97062
www.singaporemath.com

Dimensions Math® Textbook 4A
ISBN 978-1-947226-10-4

First published 2019
Reprinted 2020 (twice)

Printed in China

Acknowledgments

Editing by the Singapore Math Inc. team.
Design and illustration by Cameron Wray with Carli Fronius.

Preface

The Dimensions Math® Pre-Kindergarten to Grade 5 series is based on the pedagogy and methodology of math education in Singapore. The curriculum develops concepts in increasing levels of abstraction, emphasizing the three pedagogical stages: Concrete, Pictorial, and Abstract. Each topic is introduced, then thoughtfully developed through the use of problem solving, student discourse, and opportunities for mastery of skills.

Features and Lesson Components

Students work through the lessons with the help of five friends: Emma, Alex, Sofia, Dion, and Mei. The characters appear throughout the series and help students develop metacognitive reasoning through questions, hints, and ideas.

The colored boxes and blank lines in the textbook lessons are used to facilitate student discussion. Rather than writing in the textbooks, students can use whiteboards or notebooks to record their ideas, methods, and solutions.

Chapter Opener

Each chapter begins with an engaging scenario that stimulates student curiosity in new concepts. This scenario also provides teachers an opportunity to review skills.

Think

Students, with guidance from teachers, solve a problem using a variety of methods.

Learn

One or more solutions to the problem in **Think** are presented, along with definitions and other information to consolidate the concepts introduced in **Think**.

Do

A variety of practice problems allow teachers to lead discussion or encourage independent mastery. These activities solidify and deepen student understanding of the concepts.

Exercise

A pencil icon at the end of the lesson links to additional practice problems in the workbook.

Practice

Periodic practice provides teachers with opportunities for consolidation, remediation, and assessment.

Review

Cumulative reviews provide ongoing practice of concepts and skills.

Contents

Chapter 1

Numbers to One Million

Where have you seen large numbers around you?

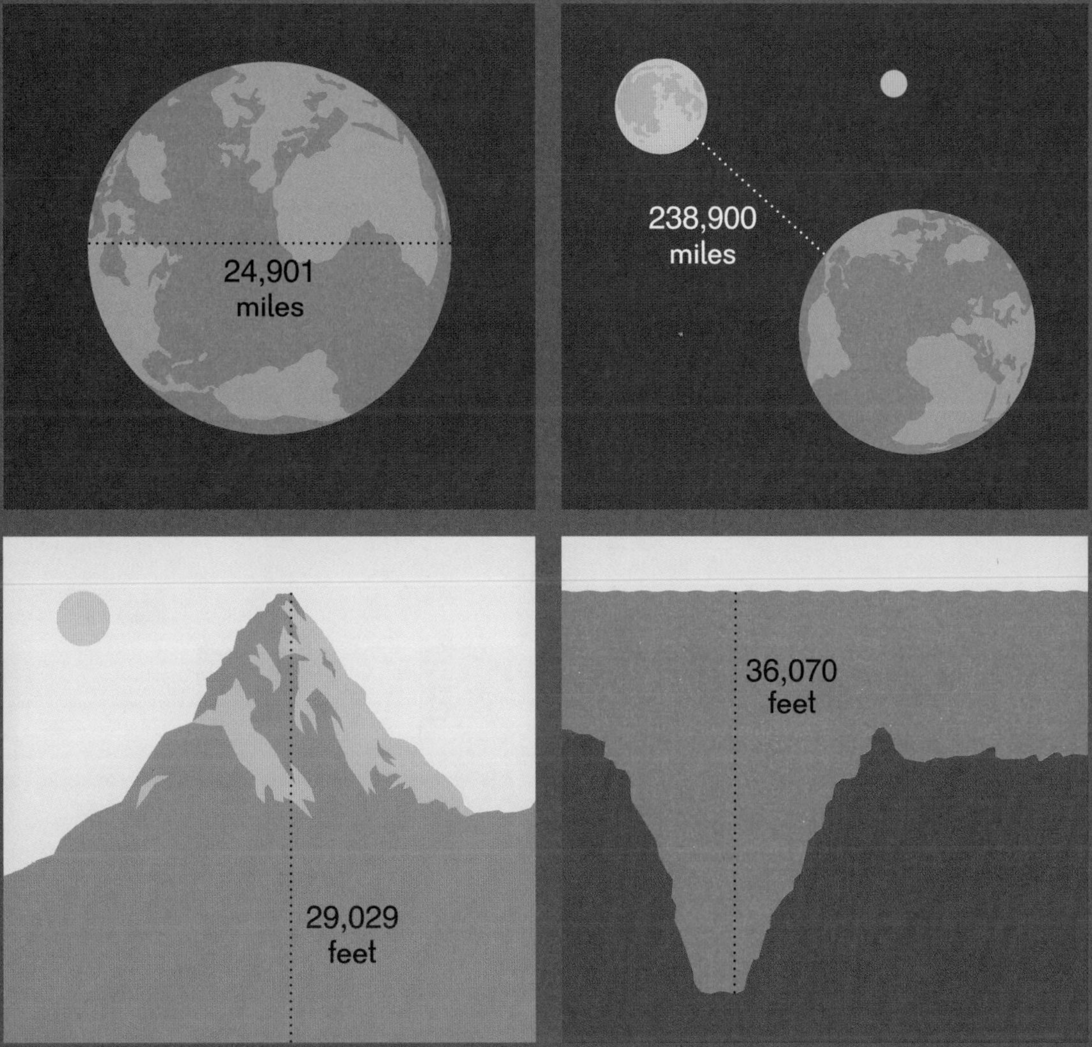

I wonder what the numbers mean.

I wonder how you say those numbers.

Lesson 1
Numbers to 100,000

1

Think

Some jars of beads are in the art room. How many beads are there?

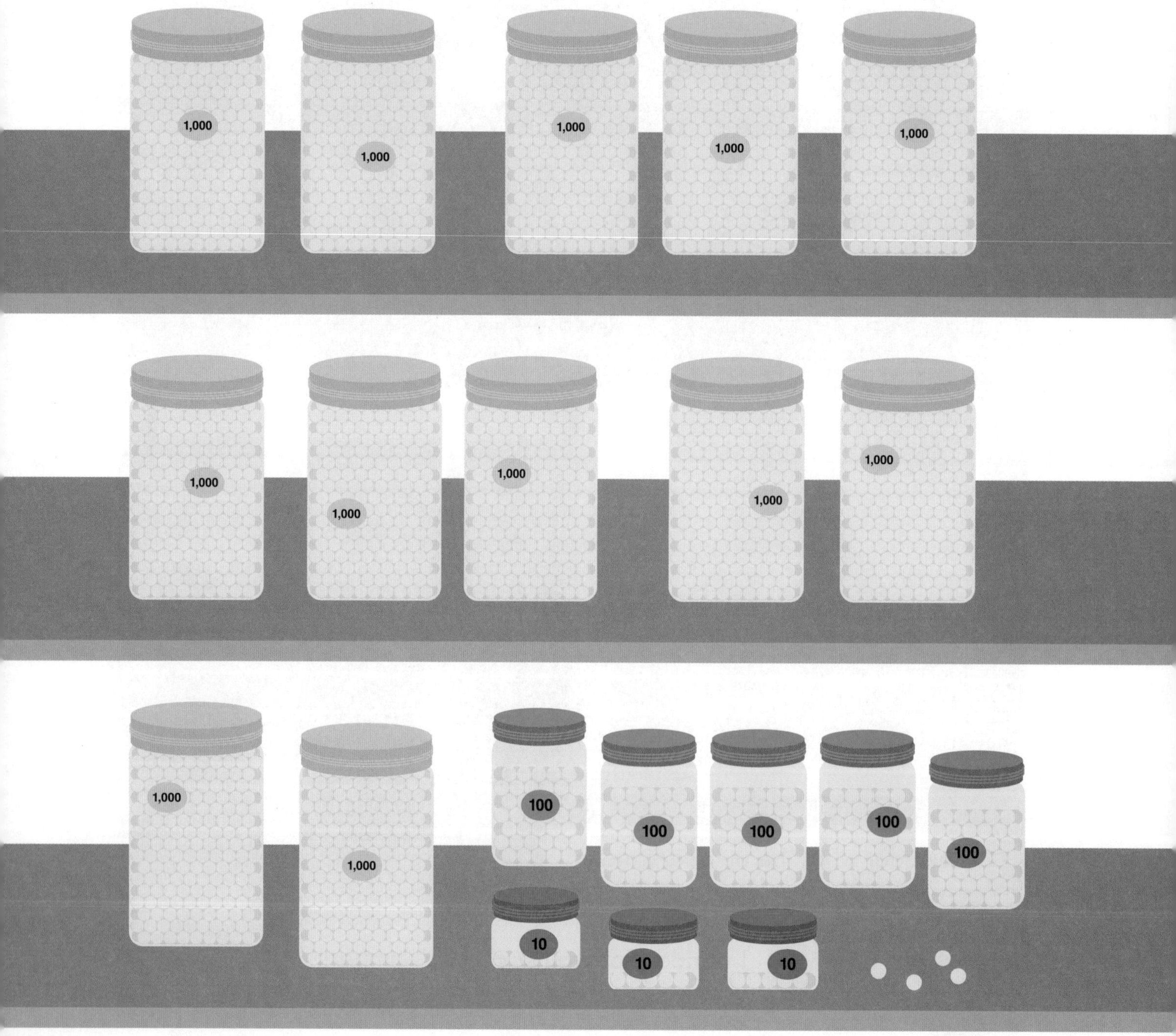

Learn

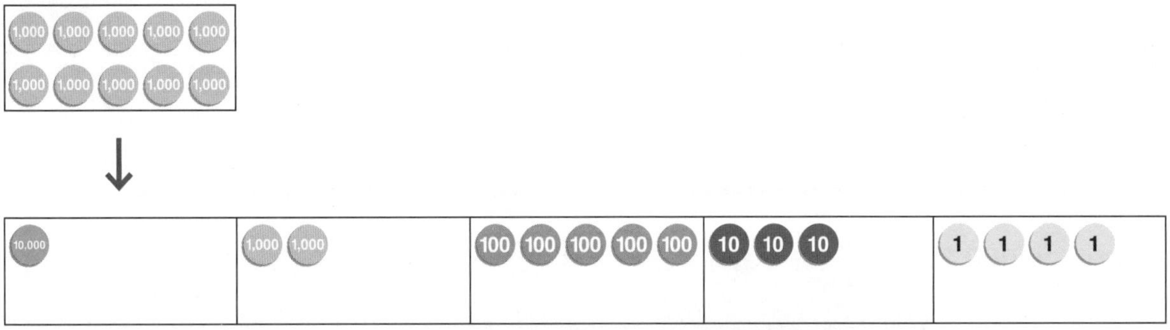

Ten Thousands	Thousands	Hundreds	Tens	Ones
1	2	5	3	4

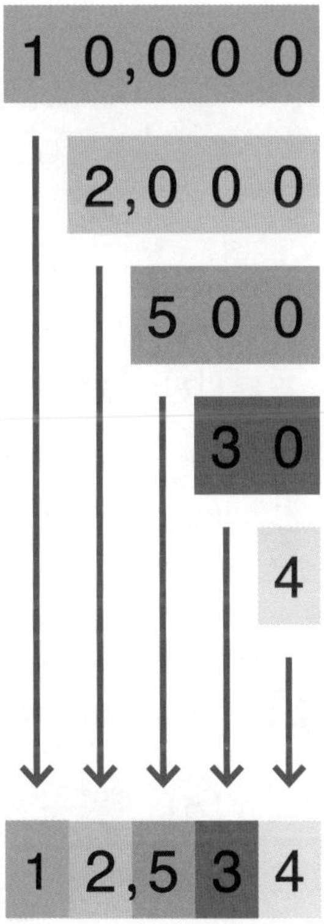

There are 12,534 beads. We read and write 12,534 as **twelve thousand, five hundred thirty-four.**

The digit 1 stands for 1 ten thousand. Its value is **10,000**.

The digit 2 stands for 2 thousands. Its value is ______.

What do each of the other digits stand for and what is each of their values?

A number written as the sum of the values of each digit is called the **expanded form** of the number.

12,534 = 10,000 + 2,000 + 500 + 30 + 4

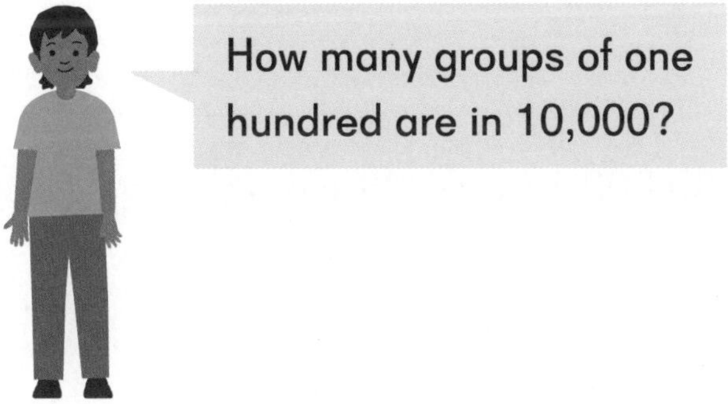

Do

1 Count by ten thousands from 0 to 90,000.

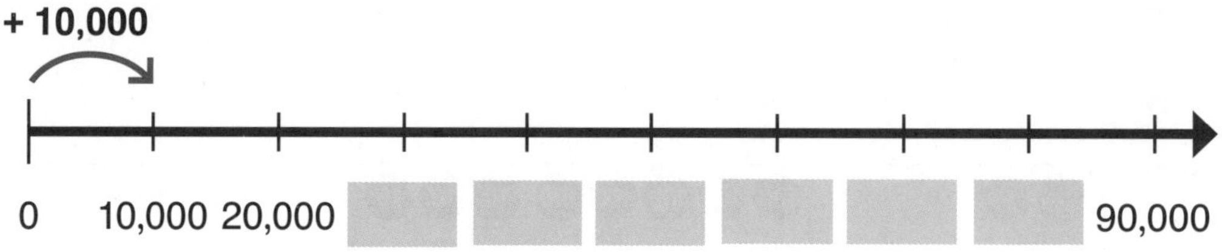

2 (a) What number is shown below?

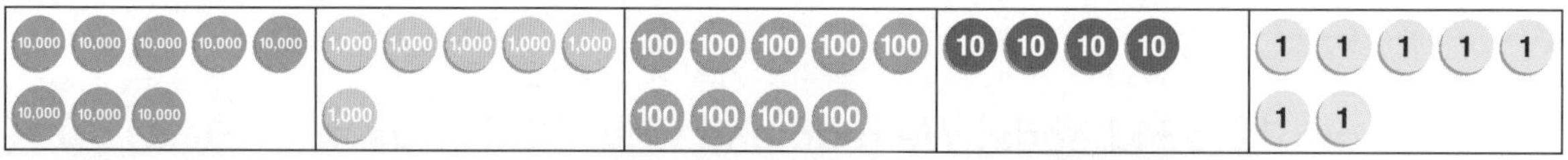

Ten Thousands	Thousands	Hundreds	Tens	Ones

(b) Write the number in numerals, in words, and in expanded form.

(c) What does each digit stand for and what is the value of each digit?

3 What number is shown by the place-value cards?

(a)

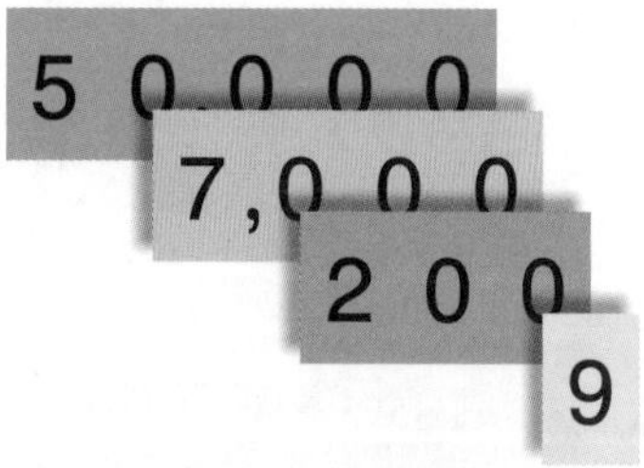

50,000 + 7,000 + 200 + 9 = ____

(b)

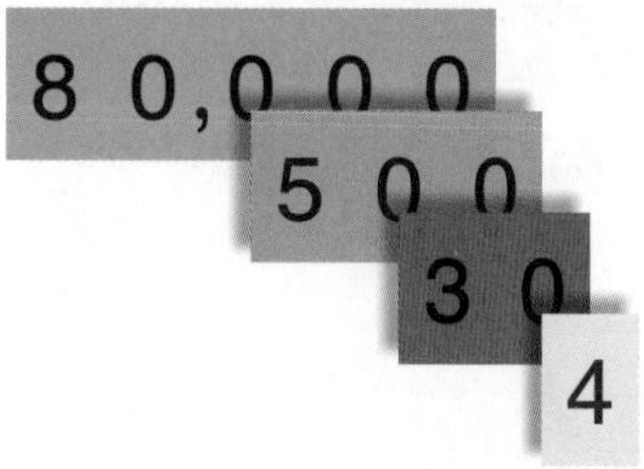

80,000 + 500 + 30 + 4 = ____

4 30,052 | 57,026 | 60,205 | 32,580 | 25,346

(a) Make each number with place-value cards.

(b) Read and write each number in words.

(c) What is the value of the digit 2 in each number?

(d) What does the digit 5 stand for in each number?

(e) In 57,026, the digit 0 stands for 0 ________. Its value is ____.

(f) Write each number in expanded form.

5 (a) 50,000 + 200 + 9 = ____

(b) 70,000 + 6,000 + 2 = ____

(c) 20,000 + 250 = ____

(d) 300 + 7 + 90 + 6,000 + 10,000 = ____

(e) 8 + 30,000 = ____

6 (a) 23,572 = ____ + 3,000 + 500 + 70 + 2

(b) 75,089 = 75,000 + ____

(c) 10,953 = ____ + 10,000 + 53

7 (a) ___ thousands = 20,000

(b) ___ hundreds = 20,000

(c) ___ tens = 20,000

(d) ___ hundreds = 41,000

(e) ___ tens = 41,000

(f) 700 hundreds = ___

(g) 350 hundreds = ___

(h) 9,200 tens = ___

8 The students in an art class used 30,000 beads to make necklaces, 700 beads to make pictures, 5,000 beads to make bracelets, and 58 beads to make bookmarks. How many beads did they use altogether?

9 There are 320 cherries in one box. How many cherries are in 100 boxes?

Exercise 1 • page 1

Think

A school has a supply of 15 stacks of 10,000 sheets of green paper, 2 stacks of 1,000 sheets of yellow paper, 4 stacks of 100 sheets of orange paper, 3 stacks of 10 sheets of red paper, and 6 sheets of white paper.

Learn

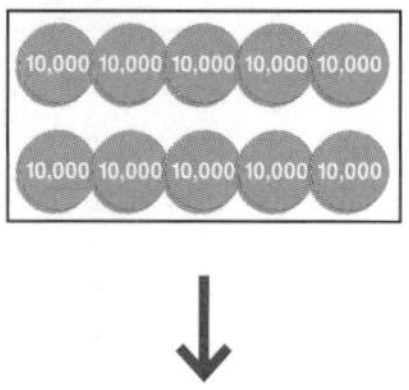

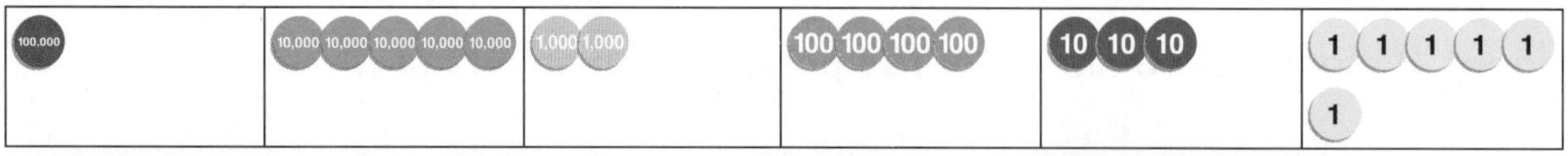

Hundred Thousands	Ten Thousands	Thousands	Hundreds	Tens	Ones
1	5	2	4	3	6

There are 152,436 sheets of paper.

We read and write 152,436 as
one hundred fifty-two thousand, four hundred thirty-six.

The digit 1 stands for 1 hundred thousand. Its value is **100,000**.

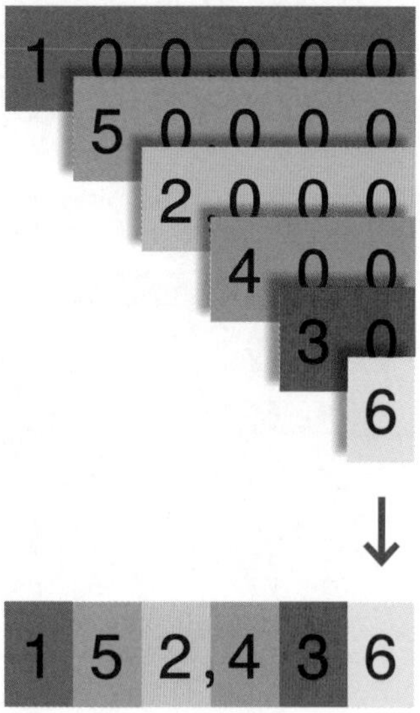

100,000 + 50,000 + 2,000 + 400 + 30 + 6 =

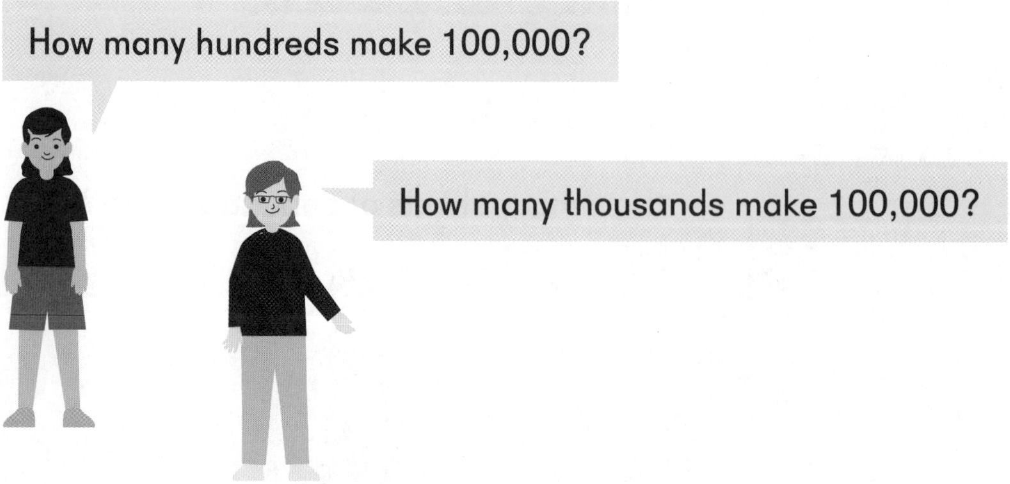

Do

1

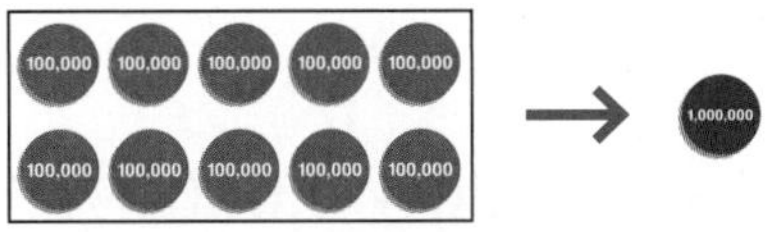

1,000,000 is **one million.**

1 million is ______ hundred thousands.

1 million is 1,000 thousands.

How many ten thousands make one million?

2 Count by hundred thousands from 0 to 1,000,000.

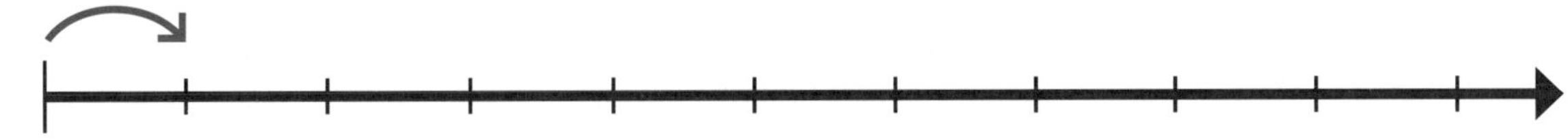

0 100,000 200,000 ______ ______ ______ ______ ______ ______ ______ 1,000,000

3 Write the number shown below in numerals, words, and expanded form.

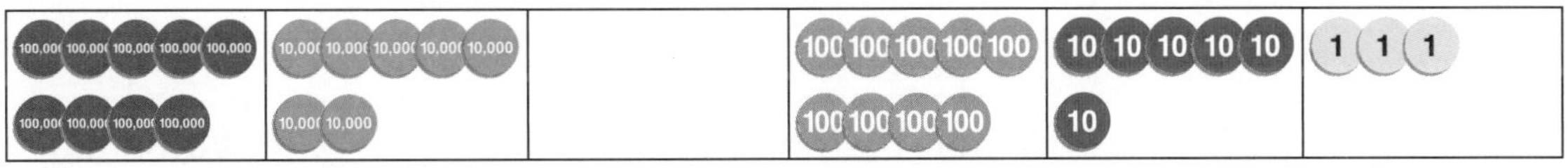

Hundred Thousands	Ten Thousands	Thousands	Hundreds	Tens	Ones
☐	☐	☐	☐	☐	☐

4 What number is shown by the place-value cards?

(a) 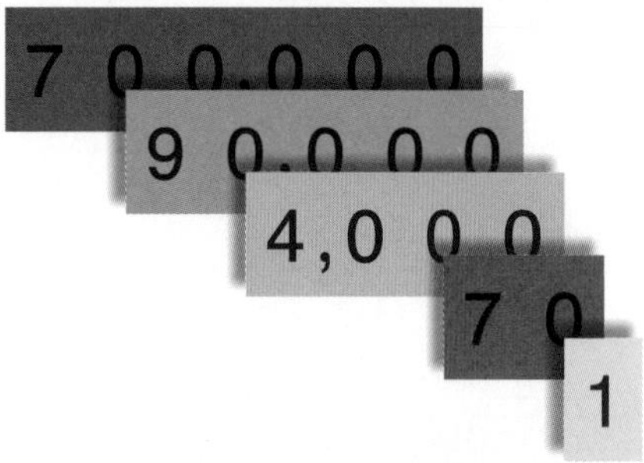

700,000 + 90,000 + 4,000 + 70 + 1

= ______

(b) 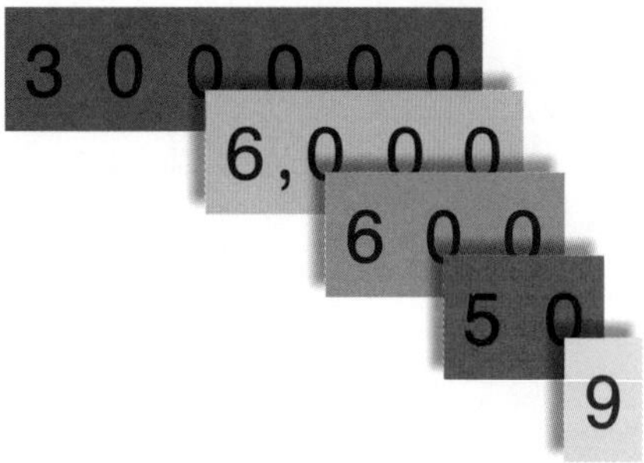

300,000 + 6,000 + 600 + 50 + 9

= ______

5 875,431 | 480,277 | 748,010 | 700,840 | 611,084 | 304,008

(a) Make each number with place-value cards.

(b) Read and write each number in words.

(c) What is the value of the digit 8 in each number?

(d) What does the digit 4 in each number stand for?

(e) In 480,277, the digit 0 stands for 0 ___________. Its value is ______.

(f) Write each number in expanded form.

6 (a) 500,000 + 60,000 + 4,000 + 200 + 7 =

(b) 200 + 3 + 400,000 + 6,000 + 50,000 + 90 =

(c) 600,000 + 20,000 =

(d) 1,000 + 30 + 40,000 =

(e) 351,200 = 350,000 +

(f) 80 + 300,000 + 7,000 =

7 (a) 20 ten thousands =

(b) 4,000 hundreds =

(c) 97,000 tens =

(d) 100 ten thousands =

8

A school ordered 100,000 red streamers and 70,000 green streamers. To thank the school for the large order, the company also sent 200 silver streamers as a gift. How many streamers did the school receive in all?

9 How many sheets of paper are in one thousand packs of 750 sheets?

Exercise 2 • page 4

Lesson 3
Number Patterns

3

Think

(a)

Ten Thousands	Thousands	Hundreds	Tens	Ones
2	9	9	5	8

Show the number in the place-value chart with place-value discs.

What number is 10,000 more than this number?

What number is 1,000 more than this number?

What number is 100 more than this number?

(b)

Ten Thousands	Thousands	Hundreds	Tens	Ones
6	0	0	8	2

Show the number in the place-value chart with place-value discs.

What number is 10,000 less than this number?

What number is 1,000 less than this number?

What number is 100 less than this number?

Learn

(a) Twenty-nine thousand, nine hundred fifty-eight

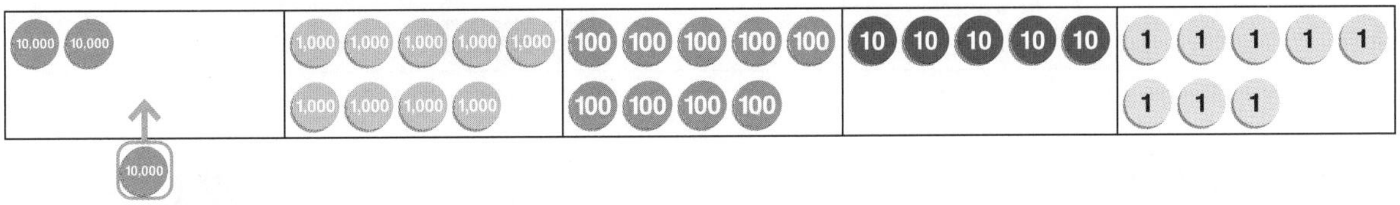

29,958 + 10,000 =

2 ten thousands + 1 ten thousand = ? ten thousands

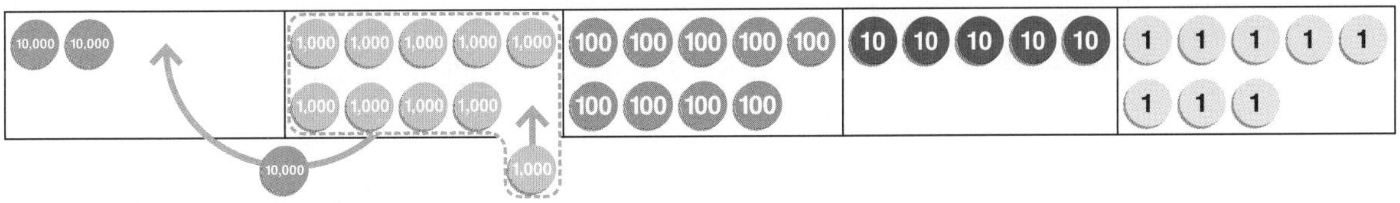

29,958 + 1,000 =

29 thousands + 1 thousand = ? thousands

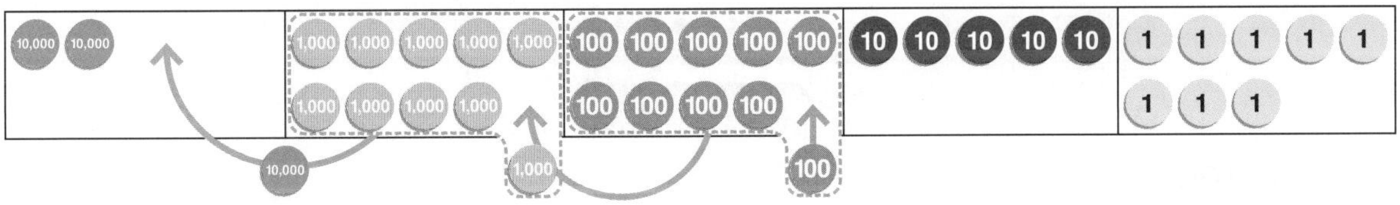

29,958 + 100 =

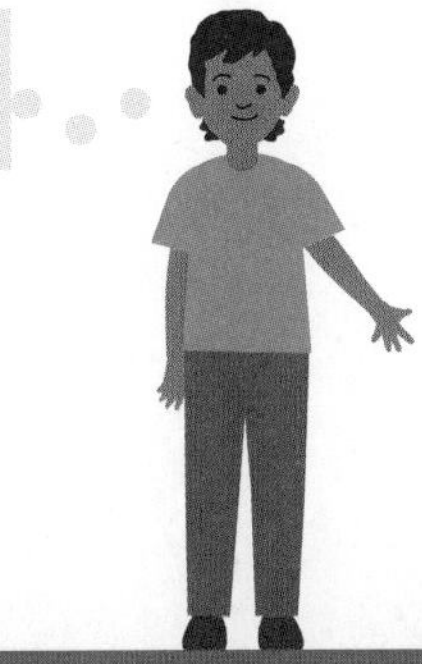

299 hundreds + 1 hundred = ? hundreds

(b) Sixty thousand, eighty-two

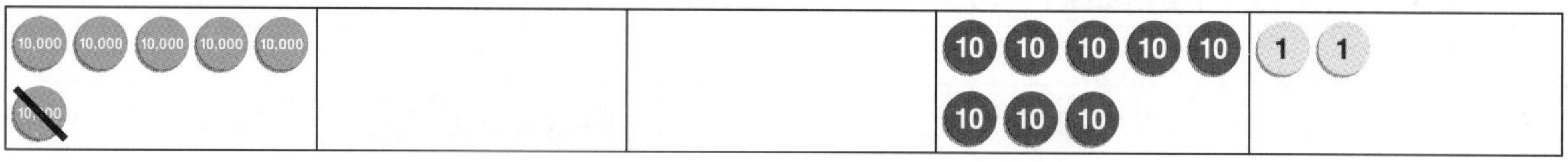

60,082 – **1**0,000 =

6 ten thousands – 1 ten thousand = ? ten thousands

60,082 – **1**,000 =

60 thousands – 1 thousand = ? thousands

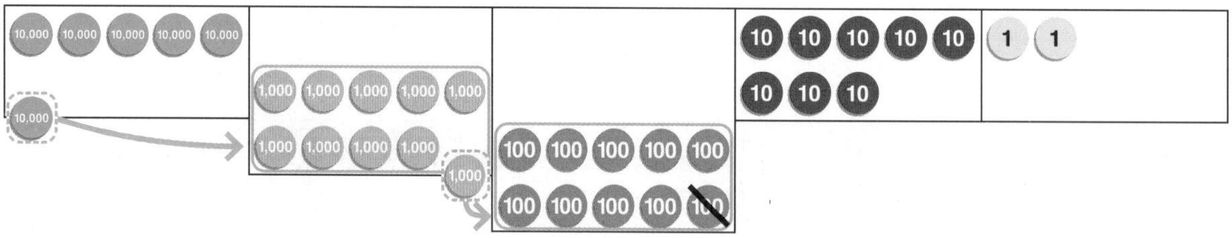

60,082 – **1**00 =

600 hundreds – 1 hundred = ? hundreds

Do

1 Use place-value cards to show what happens when we add 10,000, 1,000, 100, 10, or 1 to 63,547.

(a) 63,547 + 10,000 = ____

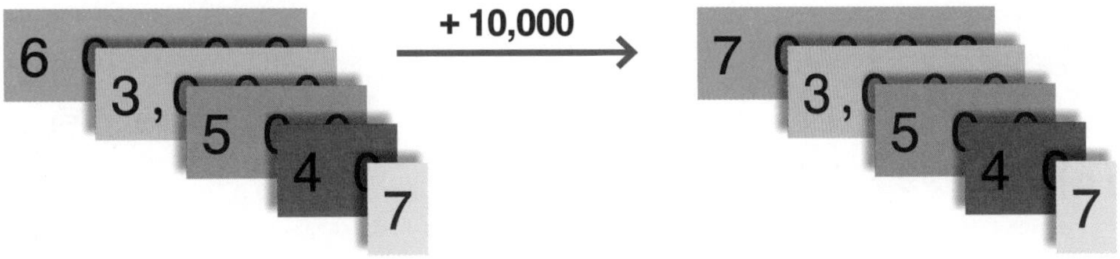

(b) 63,547 + 1,000 = ____

(c) 63,547 + 100 = ____

(d) 63,547 + 10 = ____

(e) 63,547 + 1 = ____

2 Use place-value cards to show what happens when we subtract 10,000, 1,000, 100, 10, or 1 from 49,386.

(a) 49,386 – 10,000 = ____

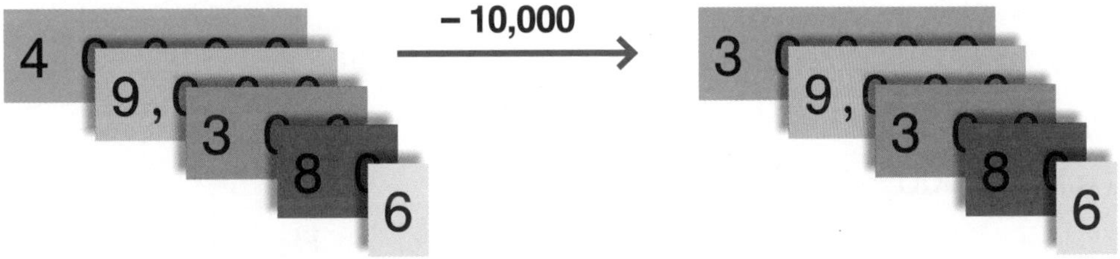

(b) 49,386 – 1,000 = ____

(c) 49,386 – 100 = ____

(d) 49,386 – 10 = ____

(e) 49,386 – 1 = ____

3 Use place-value discs to show what happens when we add 10,000, 1,000, 100, 10, or 1 to 59,999.

10,000 10,000 10,000 10,000 10,000	1,000 1,000 1,000 1,000 1,000 1,000 1,000 1,000 1,000	100 100 100 100 100 100 100 100 100	10 10 10 10 10 10 10 10 10	1 1 1 1 1 1 1 1 1

(a) 59,999 + 10,000 = ▭

(b) 59,999 + 1,000 = ▭

(c) 59,999 + 100 = ▭

(d) 59,999 + 10 = ▭

(e) 59,999 + 1 = ▭

What will happen when we add 1 more in each place?

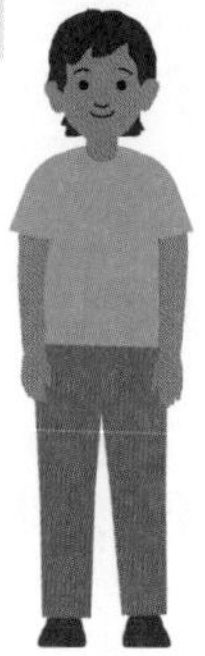

4 Use place-value discs to show what happens when we subtract 10,000, 1,000, 100, 10, or 1 from 60,000.

10,000 10,000 10,000 10,000 10,000 10,000				

(a) 60,000 − 10,000 = ▭

(b) 60,000 − 1,000 = ▭

(c) 60,000 − 100 = ▭

(d) 60,000 − 10 = ▭

(e) 60,000 − 1 = ▭

How do we regroup the place-value discs in order to subtract in (b) to (e)?

5 Complete the number patterns.

(a)	53,280	43,280	33,280			
(b)				46,590	46,580	46,570
(c)		27,700	27,800	27,900		
(d)	13,285		11,285	10,285		
(e)	35,320	35,220				34,820
(f)	19,980	19,990			20,020	
(g)	40,003	40,002	40,001			

6 (a) 99,999 + 1 = ______

(b) 999,999 + 1 = ______

(c) 90,000 + ______ = 100,000

(d) ______ + 1,000 = 100,000

(e) 99,900 + ______ = 100,000

(f) 100,000 – 10 = ______

(g) 1,000,000 – ______ = 999,900

Exercise 3 • page 7

Lesson 4
Comparing and Ordering Numbers

4

Think

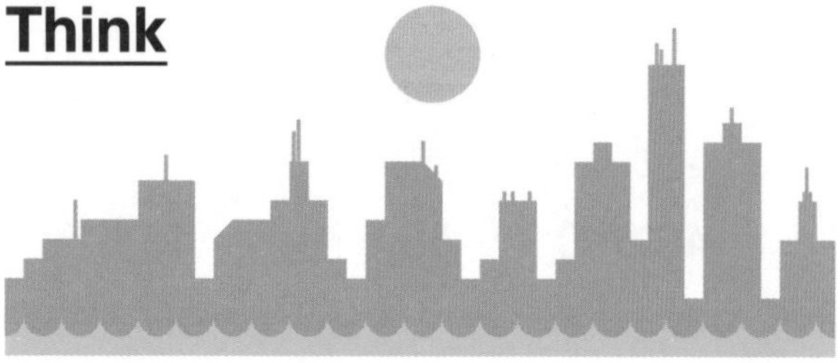

East City
146,298 people

West City
147,132 people

Which city has the greater population?

Learn

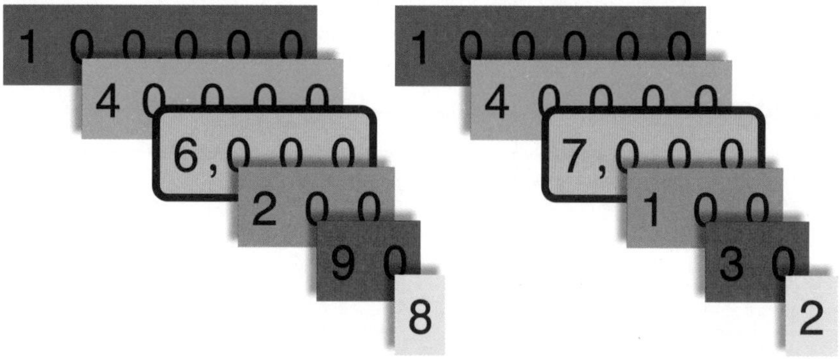

Start by comparing the digits in the highest place first.

Both numbers have the same digits in the hundred thousands and ten thousands places, so compare the digits in the thousands place.

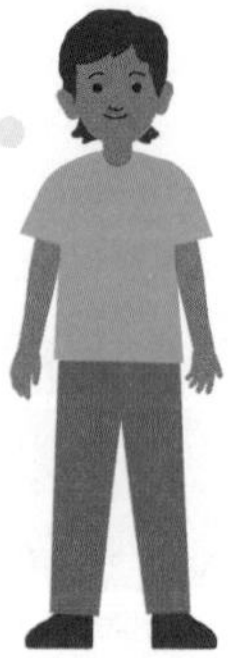

146,298 ◯ 147,132

__________ has the greater population.

Do

1 Compare 197,685 and 205,783.

Hundred Thousands	Ten Thousands	Thousands	Hundreds	Tens	Ones
1	9	7	6	8	5
2	0	5	7	8	3

197,685 ◯ 205,783

The digits in the hundred thousands place are different.

2 Compare 112,200 and 98,986.

Hundred Thousands	Ten Thousands	Thousands	Hundreds	Tens	Ones
1	1	2	2	0	0
	9	8	9	8	6

112,200 ◯ 98,986

There are no hundred thousands in 98,986.

3 Compare 374,108 and 350,990.

Hundred Thousands	Ten Thousands	Thousands	Hundreds	Tens	Ones
3	7	4	1	0	8
3	5	0	9	9	0

374,108 ◯ 350,990

Both have 3 in the hundred thousands place.

4 Compare 422,588 and 422,600.

Hundred Thousands	Ten Thousands	Thousands	Hundreds	Tens	Ones
4	2	2	5	8	8
4	2	2	6	0	0

422,588 ◯ 422,600

Which digits are the same?
Which digits should we compare?

5 What sign, > or <, goes in each ◯?

(a) 63,130 ◯ 56,130

(b) 40,411 ◯ 40,389

(c) 85,992 ◯ 102,000

(d) 440,200 ◯ 439,869

(e) 677,321 ◯ 670,877

(f) 64,985 ◯ 60,000 + 4,000 + 1,000

(g) 8 + 4,000 + 80,000 + 30 ◯ 78,438

(h) 9,000 + 20,000 + 700 ◯ 80 + 500 + 4,000 + 9

6 Arrange the following numbers in increasing order.

(a) 53,280 38,025 58,320 50,820 35,802

(b) 324,179 342,917 342,719 342,971 321,719

(c) 89,008 800,809 890,000 809,000 898,000

7 The table shows the distance by air from New York City to other cities in kilometers.

City	Distance from New York City (km)
Bangkok	13,951
Cape Town	12,551
Manila	13,676
Calcutta	12,743
Hong Kong	12,961

(a) Arrange the distances from least to greatest.

(b) Which city is farthest from New York City?

(c) Which city is closest to New York City?

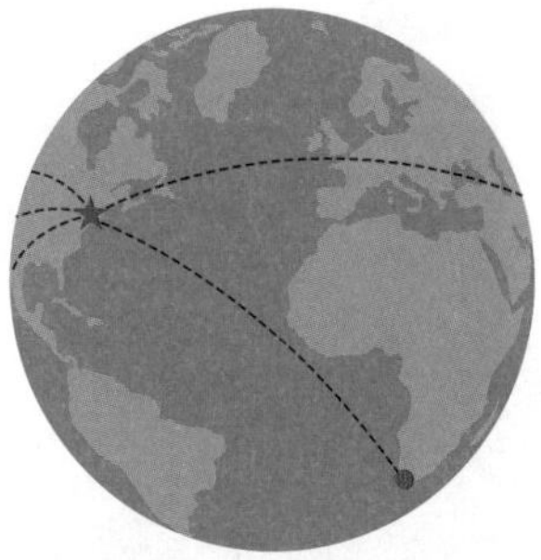

Exercise 4 • page 10

Lesson 5
Rounding 5-Digit Numbers

5

Think

The table shows the height in feet of some tall mountains.

Mountain	Height (ft)
Mount Everest	29,029
K12	24,370
Kamet	25,446

About how high is each mountain to the nearest 10,000 ft?

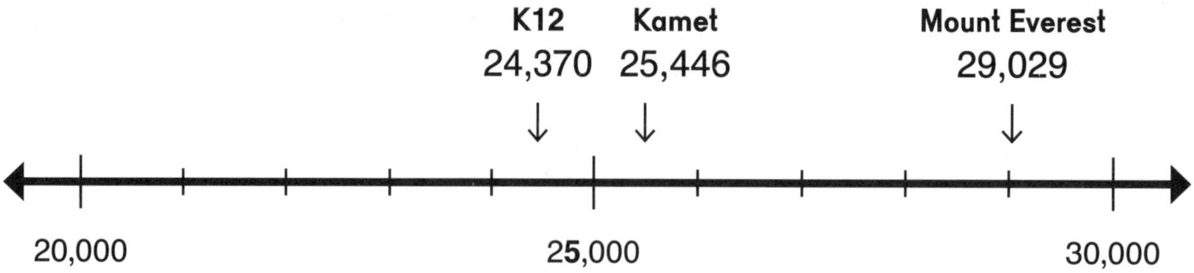

Learn

Mount Everest: 2**9**,029 ft

> The digit 9 in the thousands place is greater than 5. 2**9**,029 is nearer to 30,000 than to 20,000.

2**9**,029 is 30,000 when rounded to the nearest ten thousand.

The height of Mount Everest is about ______ ft.

K12: 2**4**,370 ft

> The digit 4 in the thousands place is less than 5. 24,370 is nearer to 20,000 than to 30,000.

2**4**,370 is ______ when rounded to the nearest ten thousand.

The height of K12 is about ______ ft.

Kamet: 2**5**,446 ft

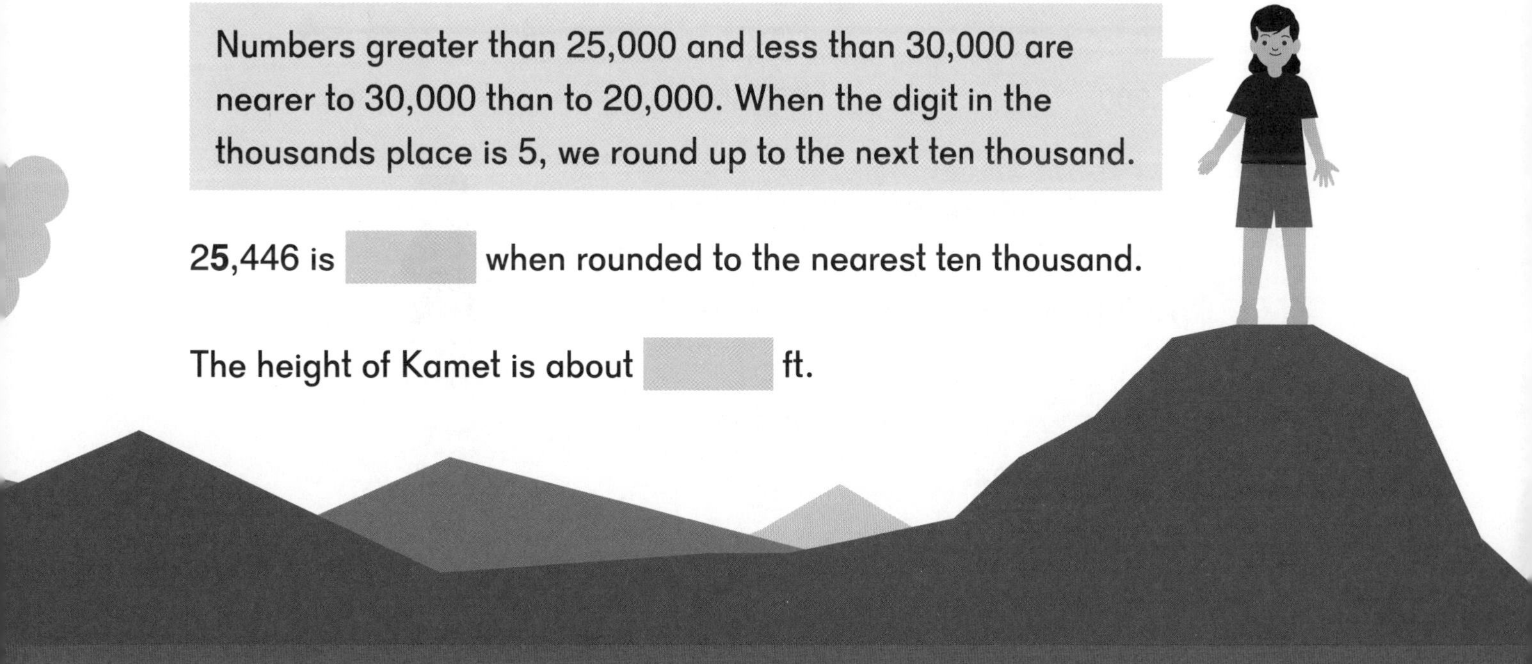

> Numbers greater than 25,000 and less than 30,000 are nearer to 30,000 than to 20,000. When the digit in the thousands place is 5, we round up to the next ten thousand.

2**5**,446 is ______ when rounded to the nearest ten thousand.

The height of Kamet is about ______ ft.

Do

1 (a) Round 62,952 to the nearest ten thousand.

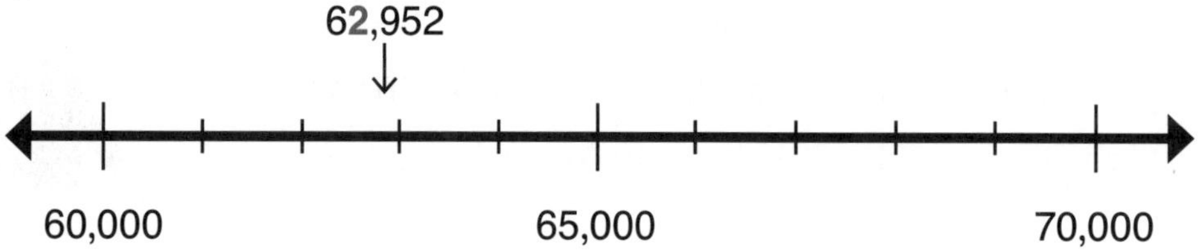

62,952 is ______ when rounded to the nearest ten thousand.

(b) Round 62,952 to the nearest thousand.

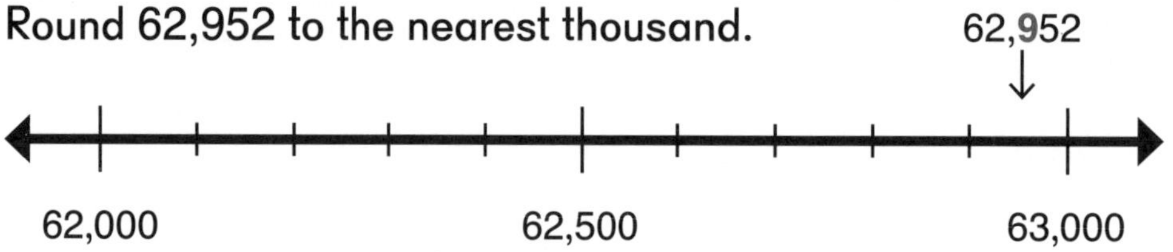

62,952 is ______ when rounded to the nearest thousand.

(c) Round 62,952 to the nearest hundred.

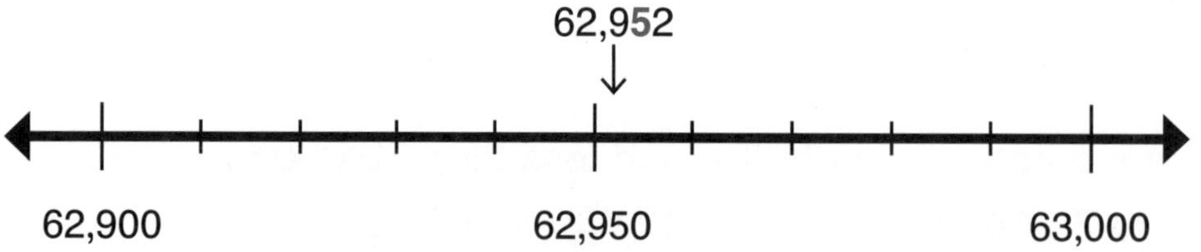

62,952 is ______ when rounded to the nearest hundred.

2 Round 12,030 to the nearest hundred.

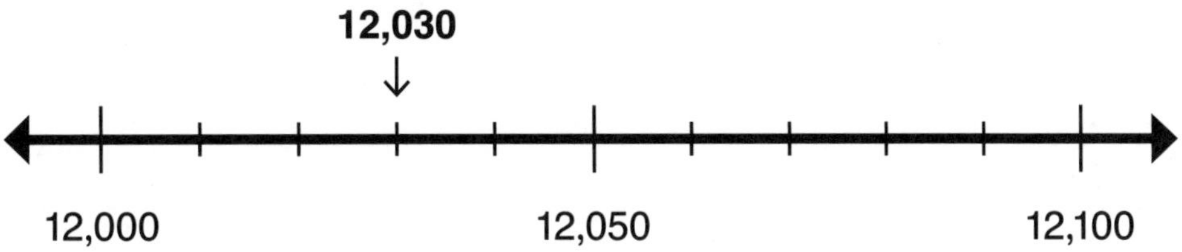

3 Round 96,223 to the nearest ten thousand.

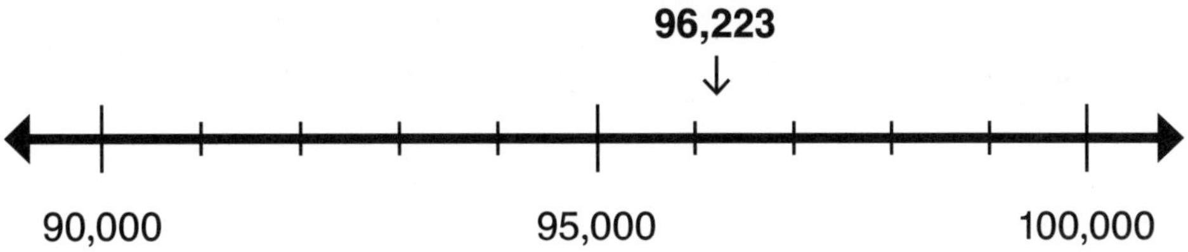

4 Round each number to the nearest thousand.

(a) 65,891 (b) 8,311 (c) 49,500

5 The table shows the weight in pounds of some different types of vehicles. Copy and complete the table.

Truck	Weight (lb)	Weight to the nearest		
		10,000 lb	1,000 lb	100 lb
Delivery van	10,975			
School bus	23,721			
Dump truck	57,704			
Fire truck	85,204			
Semi truck	99,993			

Exercise 5 • page 13

Lesson 6
Rounding 6-Digit Numbers

6

Think

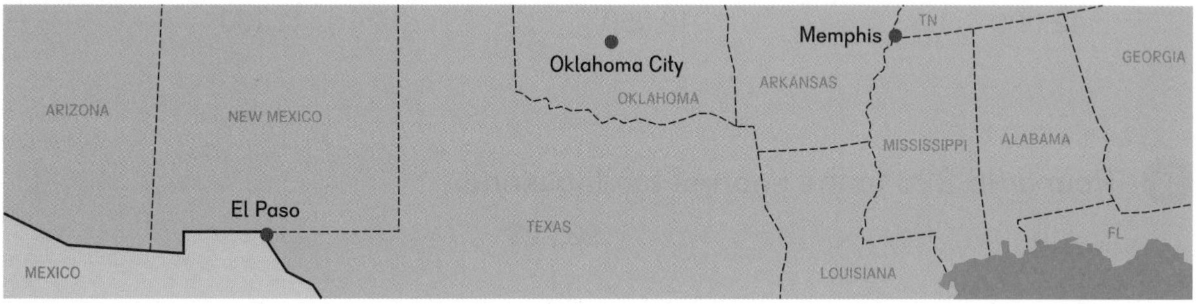

This table shows the population of some cities.

City	Population (Number of people)
Oklahoma City	631,346
El Paso	681,124
Memphis	655,770

What is the population of each city to the nearest hundred thousand?

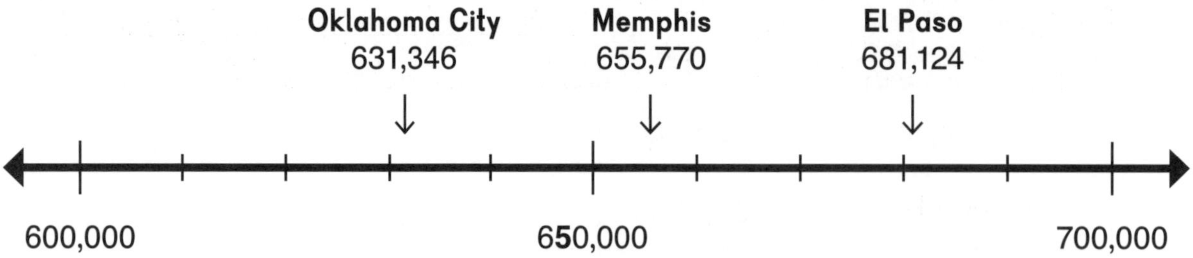

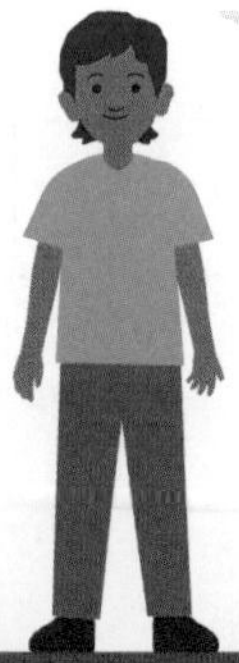

The digit 5 in the ten thousands place of 650,000 tells us that 650,000 is halfway between 600,000 and 700,000.

Learn

Oklahoma City: 6**3**1,346

The digit 3 in the ten thousands place is less than 5.

6**3**1,346 is 600,000 when rounded
to the nearest hundred thousand.

The population of Oklahoma City is about ______ people.

El Paso: 6**8**1,124

The digit 8 in the ten thousands place is greater than 5.

6**8**1,124 is 700,000 when rounded
to the nearest hundred thousand.

The population of El Paso is about ______ people.

Memphis: 6**5**5,770

The digit in the ten thousands place is 5.
We round up to the next hundred thousand.

6**5**5,770 is ______ when rounded to the nearest hundred thousand.

The population of Memphis is about ______ people.

Do

1 (a) Round 748,500 to the nearest hundred thousand.

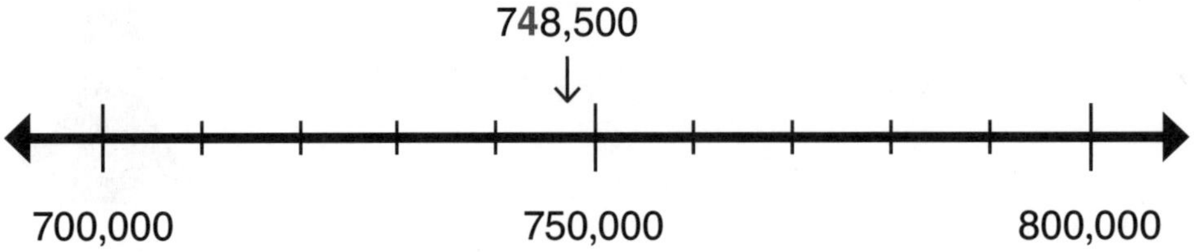

748,500 is ______ when rounded to the nearest hundred thousand.

(b) Round 748,500 to the nearest ten thousand.

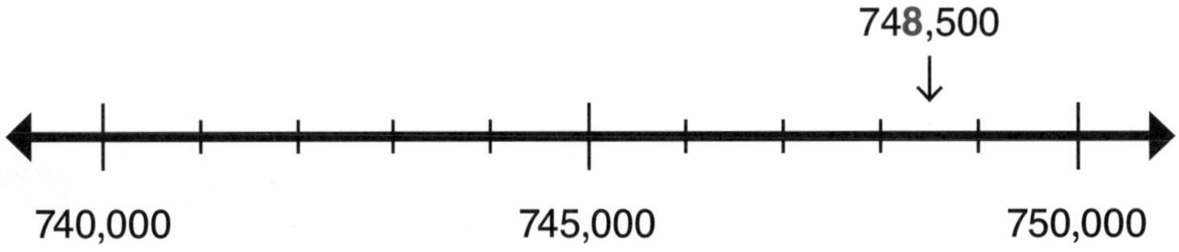

748,500 is ______ when rounded to the nearest ten thousand.

(c) Round 748,500 to the nearest thousand.

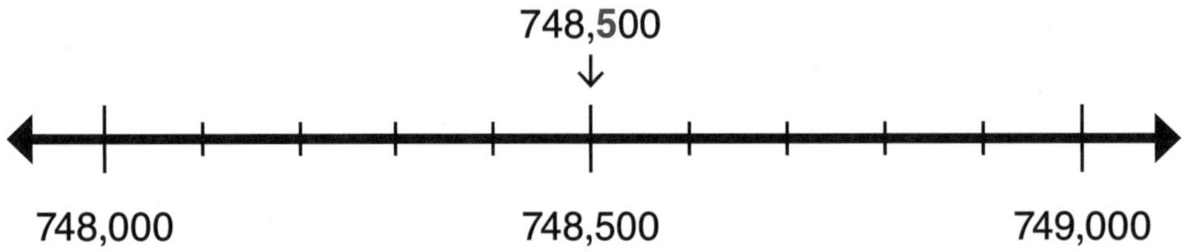

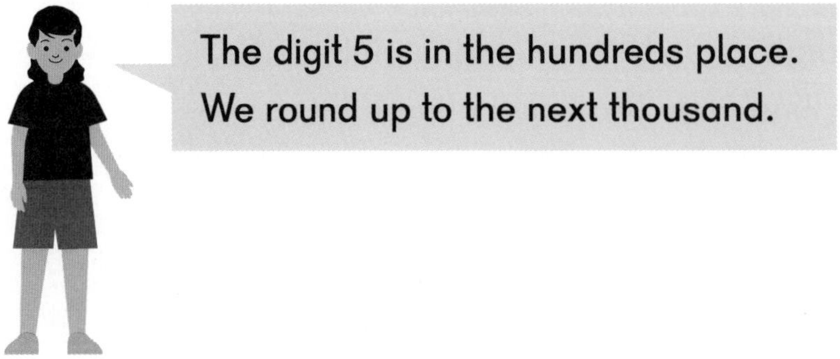

748,500 is ______ when rounded to the nearest thousand.

2 Round each number to the nearest hundred thousand.

(a) 485,000 (b) 130,498 (c) 150,873

3 Round each number to the nearest ten thousand.

(a) 285,000 (b) 160,498 (c) 827,055

4 Round each number to the nearest thousand.

(a) 640,989 (b) 345,500 (c) 297,368

5 The table shows the weight in tons of some different types of cruise ships. Copy and complete the table.

Ship	Weight (tons)	Weight to the nearest		
		100,000 tons	10,000 tons	1,000 tons
Oasis of the Seas	225,282			
Ovation of the Seas	168,666			
Queen Mary 2	149,215			
Navigator of the Seas	139,570			
Celebrity Eclipse	121,878			

A ton is a unit of weight equal to 2,000 pounds.
We use tons to express the weight of heavy objects.

Exercise 6 • page 16

Lesson 7
Calculations and Place Value

7

Think

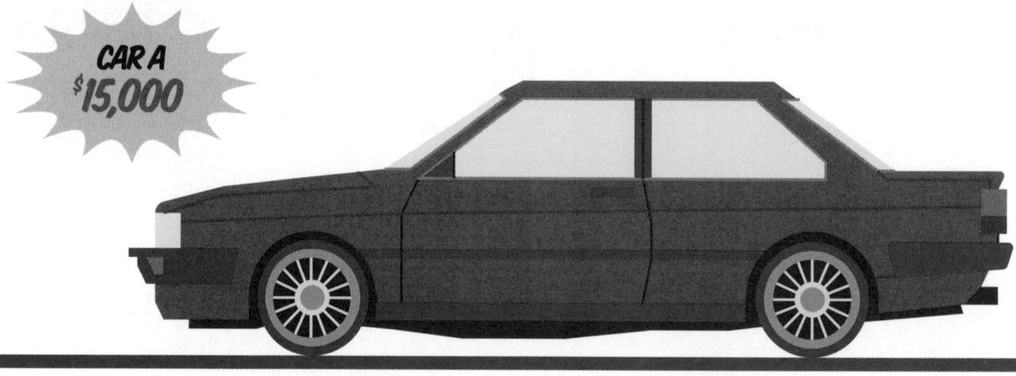

Which car costs more money? How much more money?

Learn

Car A

Car B

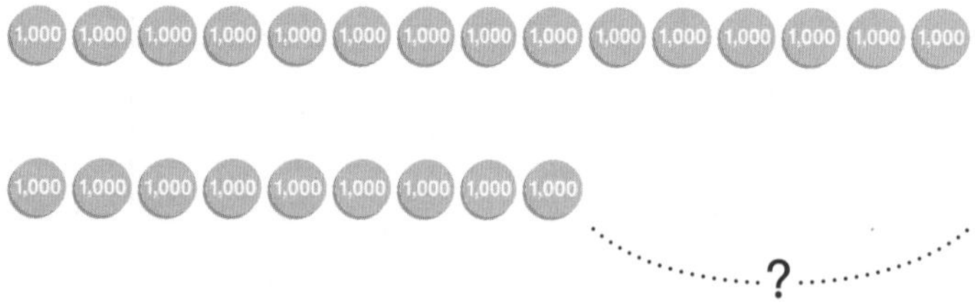

15 thousands – 9 thousands = ? thousands

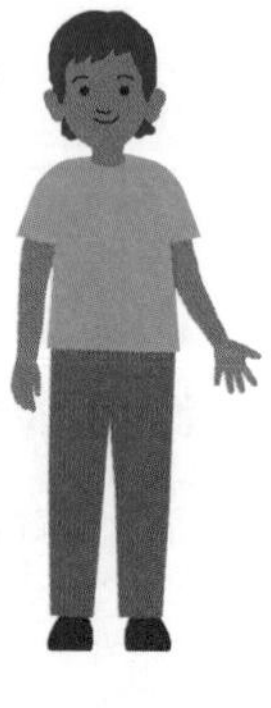

15,000 – 9,000 = ______

Car A costs $______ more than Car B.

Do

1 Find the sum of **17**0,000 and **8**0,000.

17 ten thousands + 8 ten thousands = ? ten thousands

170,000 + 80,000 = ☐

2 Multiply **3**,000 by 4.

3 thousands × 4 = ? thousands

3,000 × 4 = ☐

3 Divide **9**0,000 by 3.

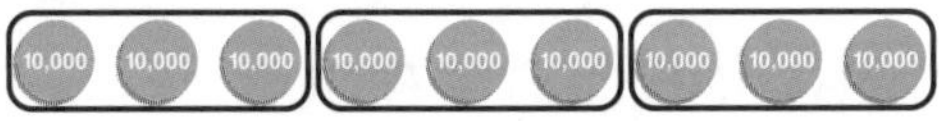

9 ten thousands ÷ 3 = ? ten thousands

90,000 ÷ 3 = ☐

4 Divide **12**,000 by 4.

12 thousands ÷ 4 = ? thousands

12,000 ÷ 4 = ▭

5 Find the product of 8 and **5**,000.

5 thousands × 8 = ? thousands

5,000 × 8 = ▭

6 Find the quotient of **2,0**00 divided by 5.

2,000 ÷ 5 = ▭

20 hundreds ÷ 5 = ? hundreds

7 Find the values.

(a) 7,000 + 8,000

(b) 35,000 + 6,000

(c) 120,000 – 40,000

(d) 41,000 – 5,000

(e) 80,000 × 3

(f) 6 × 5,000

(g) 400,000 ÷ 8

(h) 54,000 ÷ 9

Exercise 7 • page 19

1 | 89,200 | 95,002 | 20,900 | 908,420 |

(a) Read and write each number in words.

(b) What is the value of the digit 9 in each number?

(c) What does the digit 2 stand for in each number?

(d) Write each number in expanded form.

2 (a) 70,000 + 500 + 6 = ____

(b) 54 + 55,700 = ____

(c) 600 + 200,000 + 50,000 + ____ = 250,608

(d) 9 + 500,000 + 600 + 30,000 + 1,000 = ____

3 (a) 99,990 + ____ = 100,000

(b) 38,056 − ____ = 37,056

(c) ____ + 100 = 45,682

(d) ____ − 10,000 = 987,600

4 Arrange the numbers in increasing order.

(a) 7,658 | 27,580 | 189,758 | 72,980

(b) 40,308 | 43,803 | 40,380 | 50,083

(c) 139,509 | 153,990 | 135,099 | 153,909

5 Complete the number patterns.

(a) 6,274 | 6,174 | ___ | ___ | ___ | 5,774

(b) 43,850 | 43,950 | ___ | ___ | ___ | 44,350

(c) 50,075 | 40,075 | 30,075 | ___ | ___ | ___

6 (a) ___ ten thousands = 450,000

(b) ___ thousands = 450,000

(c) ___ hundreds = 450,000

7 (a) Which arrow on the number line corresponds to each of these numbers?

979,590 | **959,168** | **937,820**

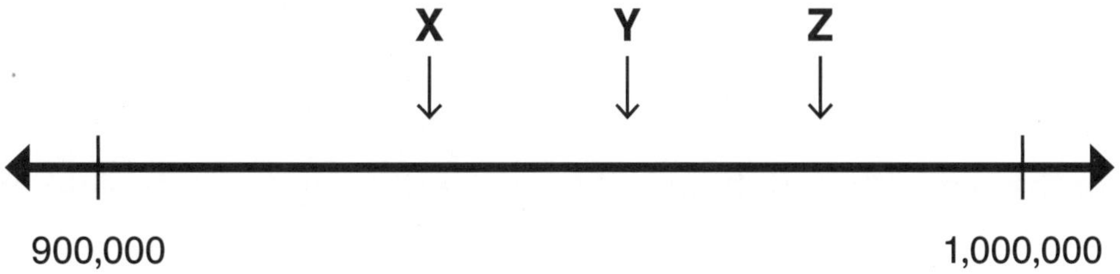

(b) Round each number to the nearest ten thousand.

(c) Round each number to the nearest thousand.

8 What sign, >, <, or =, goes in each ◯?

(a) 133,795 + 10,000 ◯ 40,000 + 100,000 + 70 + 900 + 5

(b) 98,978 + 100 ◯ 90,000 + 8,000 + 700 + 9

(c) 7 + 90 + 2,000 ◯ 3,000 – 1

(d) 40,009 – 1,000 ◯ 30,000 + 9 + 9,000

9 (a) 7,000 tens + 62 tens = ______

(b) 7 hundreds + 62 thousands = ______

(c) 70 ten thousands + 62 hundreds = ______

10 Find the values.

(a) 46,000 + 7,000

(b) 250,000 – 8,000

(c) 9,000 × 3

(d) 36,000 ÷ 9

11 Use the digits 4, 7, 0, 6, and 2 to make the greatest possible odd number.

12 A whole number is rounded to 687,000 when rounded to the nearest thousand. What is the least whole number and what is the greatest whole number it could be?

13 A whole number is rounded to 32,000 when rounded to the nearest hundred. What is the least whole number and what is the greatest whole number it could be?

14 A car costs 3 times as much as a motorcycle. If the car costs $18,000, how much does the motorcycle cost?

15 Mrs. Bahtia saved $15,000. She spent $4,000 on a dining room set and $8,000 on a living room set. How much money does she have left?

16 A sofa costs $5,000 and a recliner costs $3,000. How much do 5 sofas and 4 recliners cost?

Exercise 8 • page 22

Chapter 2

Addition and Subtraction

Emma's family is trying to conserve water.

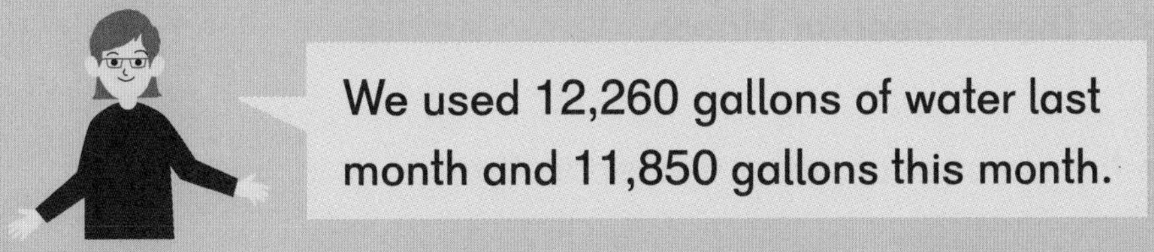

About how many gallons of water did Emma's family use altogether?

Think

In March, a car wash used 95,617 gallons of water. In April, it used 25,186 more gallons of water than it used in March.

(a) Estimate the amount of water it used in April.

(b) Find the actual amount of water it used in April.

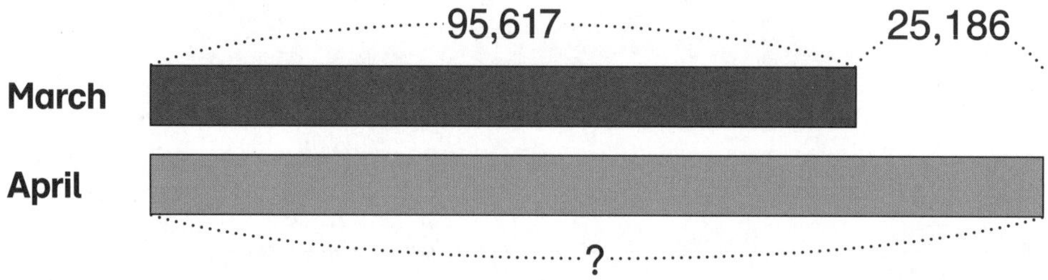

Learn

95,617 + 25,186

(a) To find an estimate, use numbers that are easy to add mentally.

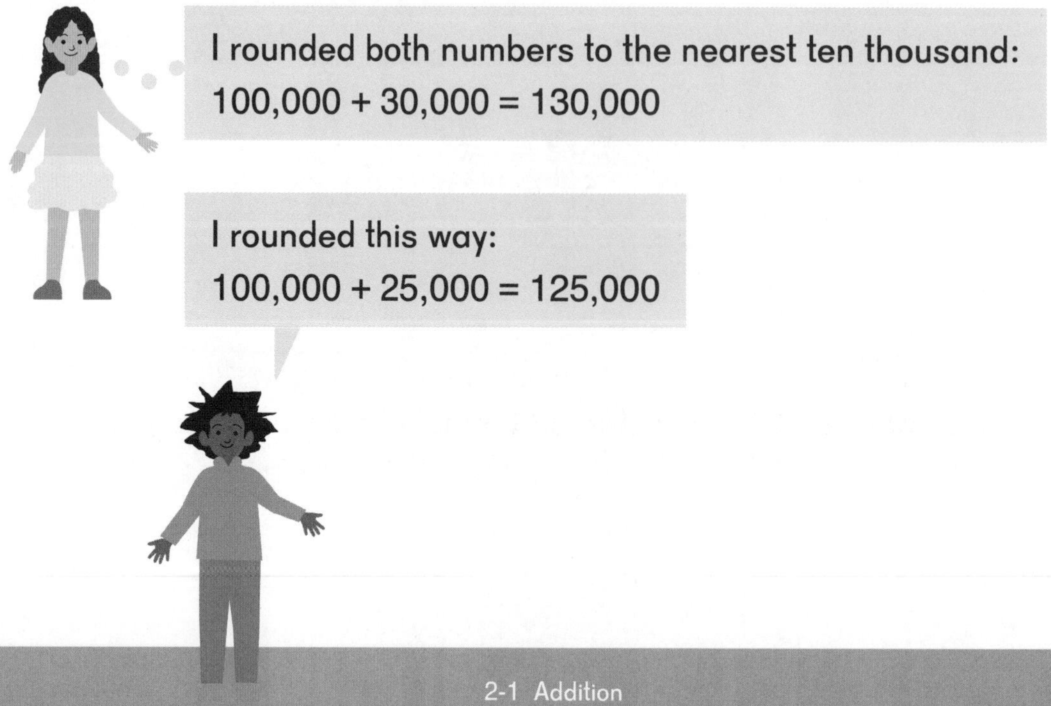

95,617 + 25,186 ≈ ____

Which estimate will be closer to the actual sum?

≈ stands for **is approximately equal to** or **is about.**

(b) Add the ones first, then the tens, then the hundreds, and so on, regrouping when needed.

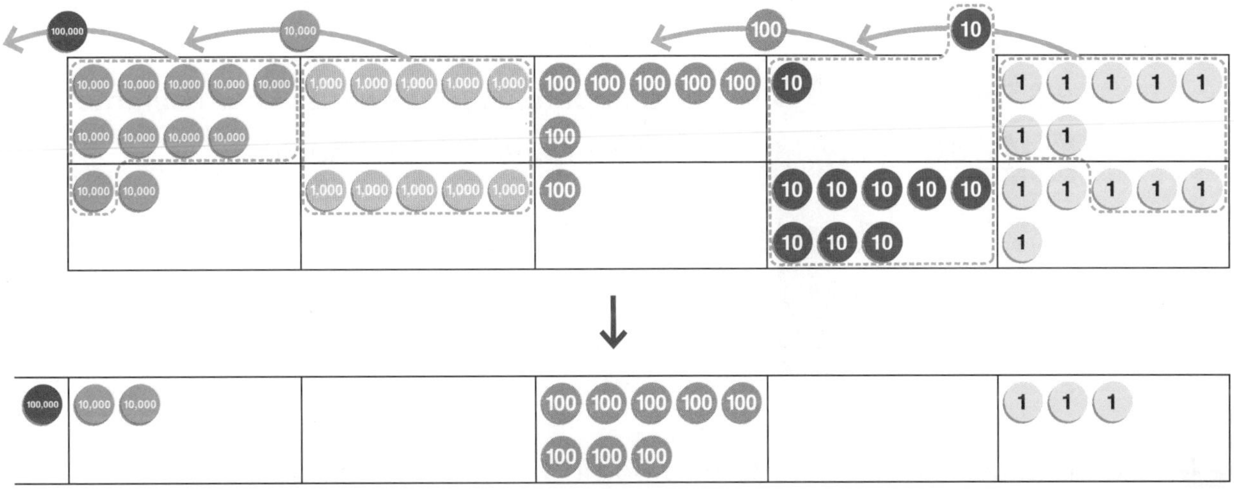

	1	1		1	1	
		9	5,	6	1	7
+		2	5,	1	8	6
	1	2	0,	8	0	3

In which places did we have to regroup?

The car wash used ____ gallons of water in April.

Do

1 (a) Estimate the sum of 37,839 and 4,203.

37,839 + 4,203 ≈ ______

(b) Find the sum of 37,839 and 4,203.

$$\begin{array}{r} 37{,}839 \\ +\ \ 4{,}203 \\ \hline \square \end{array}$$

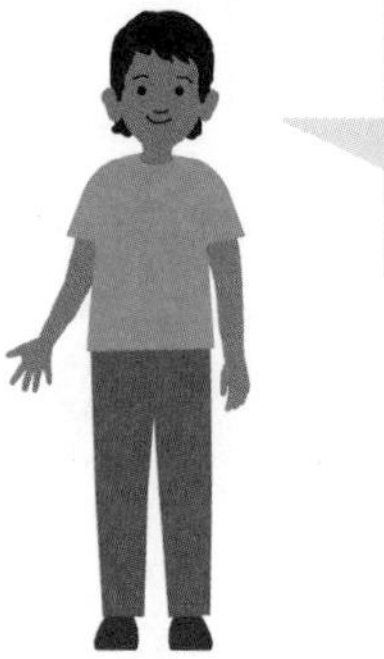

2 Estimate the sum of 73,583 and 84,968. Then find the actual sum.

(a) 73,583 + 84,968
↓ ↓
______ + ______ = ______

(b)

$$\begin{array}{r} 73{,}583 \\ +\ 84{,}968 \\ \hline \square \end{array}$$

3 Estimate the sum of 75,583, 26,986, and 4,987. Then find the actual sum.

(a) 75,583 + 26,986 + 4,987 ≈ ______

I used these numbers: 75,000, 25,000, and 5,000, because they are easy to add.

(b)
$$\begin{array}{r} 75,583 \\ 26,986 \\ +\quad 4,987 \\ \hline \end{array}$$

4 Estimate the sums. Then find the actual sums.

(a) 62,387 + 698

(b) 8,421 + 43,875

(c) 75,284 + 6,396

(d) 82,087 + 29,903

(e) 62,805 + 86,102

(f) 148,135 + 52,009

(g) 459,242 + 240,989

(h) 3,895 + 987 + 9,213

5 15,285 people went to the ballet in September, 12,378 people went in October, and 13,698 people went in November.

(a) About how many people went to the ballet in all three months?

(b) Exactly how many people went to the ballet in all three months?

Exercise 1 • page 25

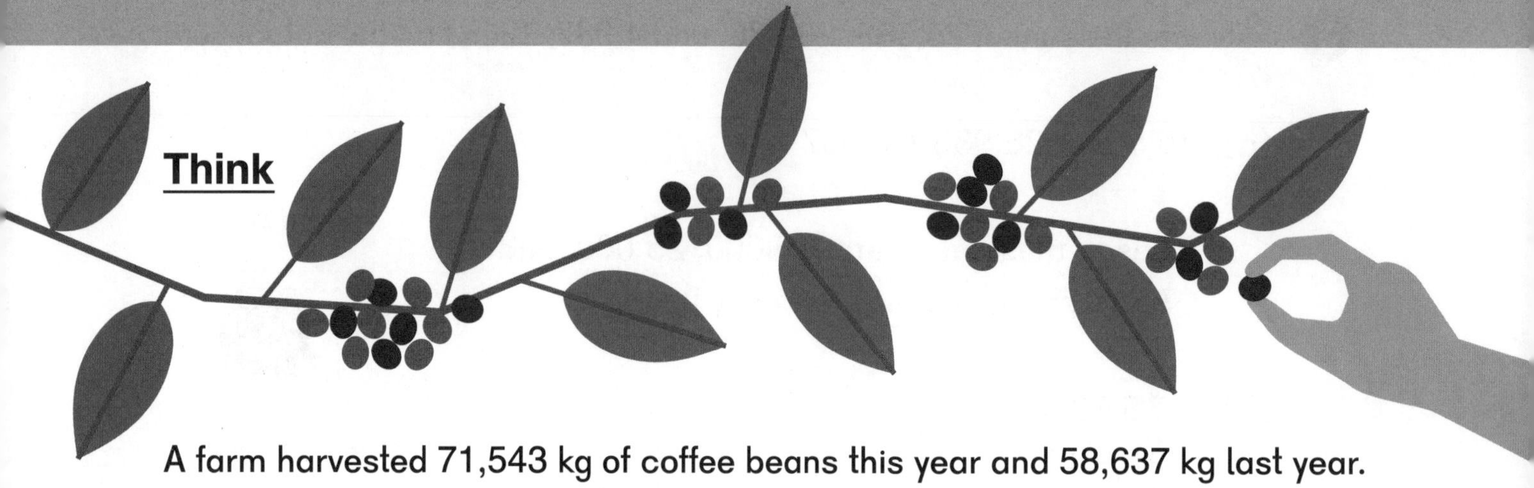

Think

A farm harvested 71,543 kg of coffee beans this year and 58,637 kg last year.

(a) Estimate how much more coffee was harvested this year than last year.

(b) Find how much more coffee was harvested this year than last year.

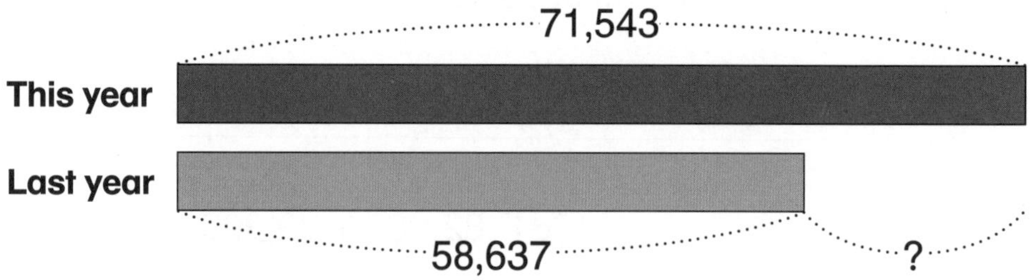

Learn

71,543 – 58,637

(a) To estimate the difference, use numbers that are easy to subtract mentally.

71,543 – 58,637
↓ ↓
70,000 – 60,000 = 10,000

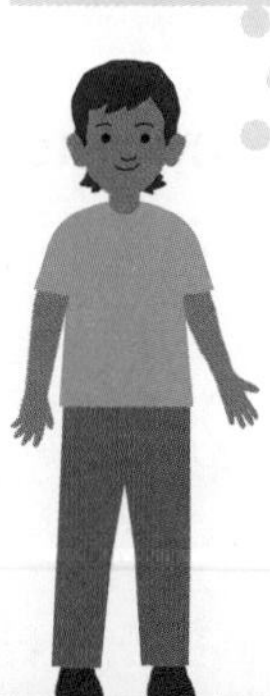

71,543 – 58,637
↓ ↓
72,000 – 60,000 = 12,000

71,543 – 58,637 ≈ ______

Which estimate will be closer to the actual difference?

(b) Subtract the ones first, then the tens, then the hundreds, and so on, regrouping when needed.

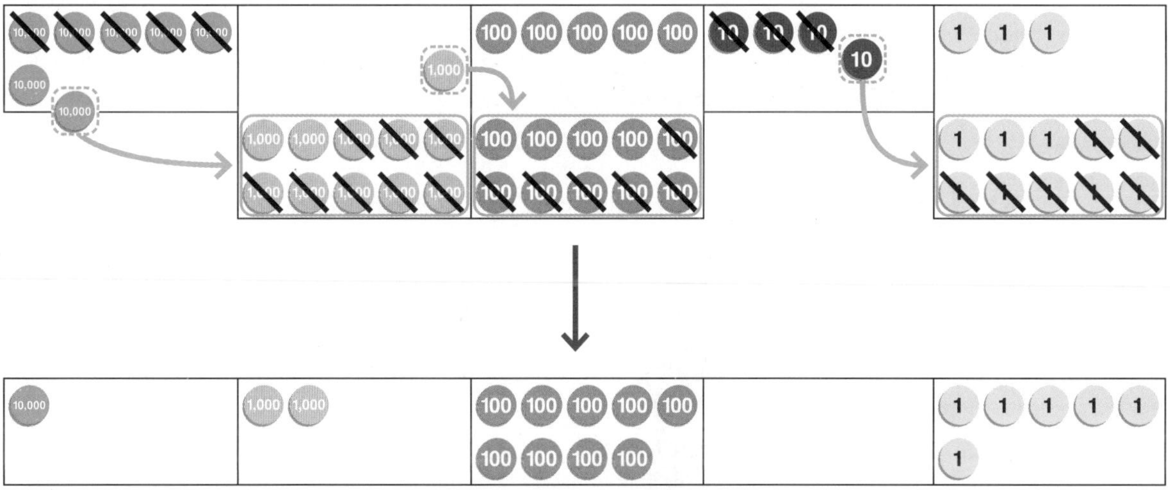

In which places did we have to regroup?

$$
\begin{array}{r}
\scriptstyle 6\ \ 10\ \ 15\ \ 3\ \ 13 \\
\not{7}\ \not{1},\not{5}\ \not{4}\ \not{3} \\
-\ 5\ \ 8,6\ \ 3\ \ 7 \\
\hline
1\ \ 2,9\ \ 0\ \ 6
\end{array}
$$

______ kg more coffee was harvested this year than last year.

Do

1 (a) Estimate the difference between 34,027 and 6,518.

34,027 – 6,518
↓ ↓
30,000 – 7,000 = ?

34,027 – 6,518
↓ ↓
34,000 – 7,000 = ?

34,027 – 6,518 ≈ ____

(b) Find the difference between 34,027 and 6,518.

$$\begin{array}{r} 34{,}027 \\ -\ \ 6{,}518 \\ \hline \end{array}$$

Compare your answer to your estimate. Is your answer reasonable?

2 Estimate the difference between 26,509 and 80,043. Then find the actual difference.

(a) 80,043 – 26,509
↓ ↓
____ – ____ = ____

(b)

$$\begin{array}{r} 80{,}043 \\ -\ 26{,}509 \\ \hline \end{array}$$

3 Estimate the difference between 65,045 and 783. Then find the actual difference.

(a) 65,045 – 783 ≈ ______ (b) 65,045 – 783 = ______

4 Estimate the differences. Then find the actual differences.

(a) 87,569 – 498 (b) 46,304 – 8,291

(c) 70,503 – 9,840 (d) 30,002 – 5,226

(e) 67,583 – 34,070 (f) 51,082 – 37,124

(g) 140,087 – 79,293 (h) 569,950 – 82,486

5 A store owner had \$50,000. She spent \$15,925 on office furniture and \$5,289 on computer equipment.

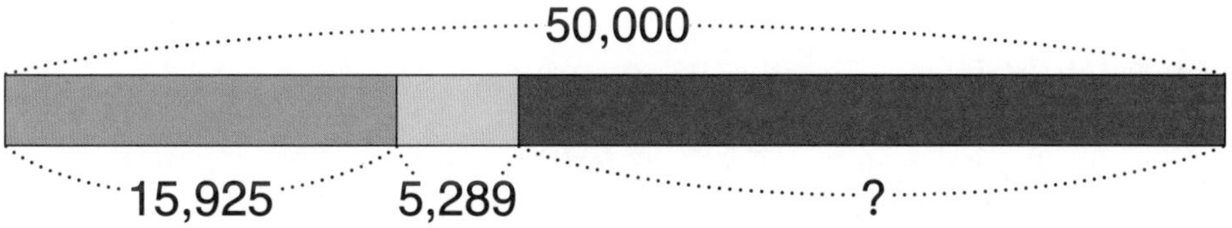

(a) About how much money does she have left?

(b) Exactly how much money does she have left?

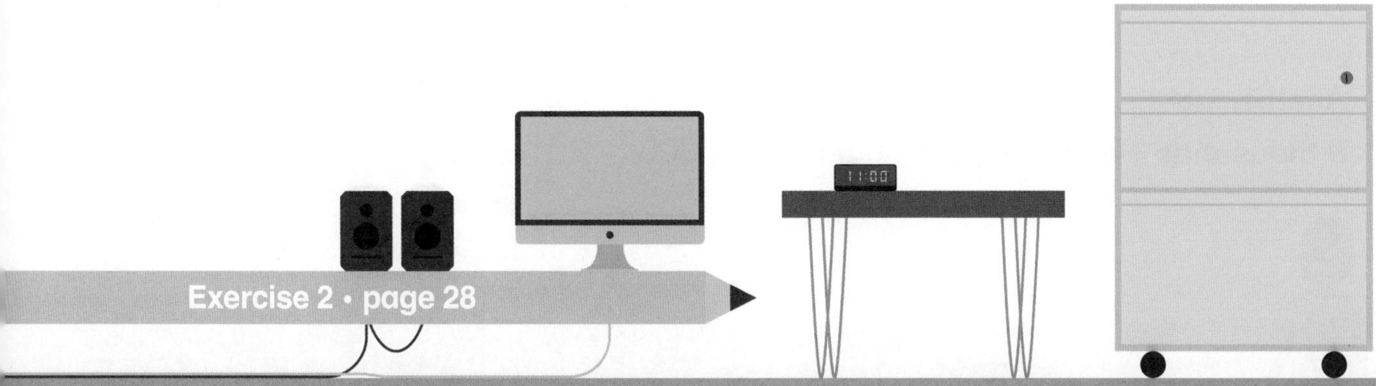

Exercise 2 • page 28

Think

Find pairs of numbers that make 10,000.

5,736	**1,560**	**5,207**	**1,086**	**6,800**
8,440	**8,914**	**4,264**	**3,200**	**4,793**

Learn

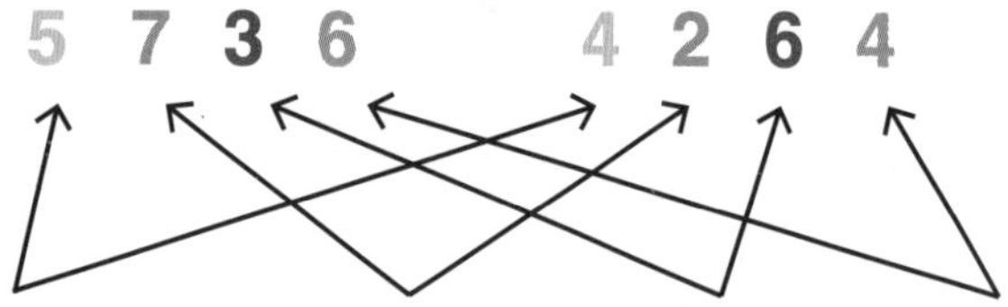

9 thousands + **9 hundreds** + **9 tens** + 10 ones = 10,000

5,736 + 4,264 = 10,000

5,736 and 4,264 is one pair. Two more pairs are 5,207 and 4,793, and 1,086 and 8,914.

Another pair is 6,800 and 3,200 since 9 thousands + 10 hundreds = 10,000.

Another pair is 1,560 and 8,440 since 9 thousands + 9 hundreds + 10 tens = 10,000.

Do

1 Find the difference between 5,672 and 10,000.

	5 thousands	6 hundreds	7 tens	2 ones
+	? thousands	? hundreds	? tens	? ones
	9 thousands	9 hundreds	9 tens	10 ones

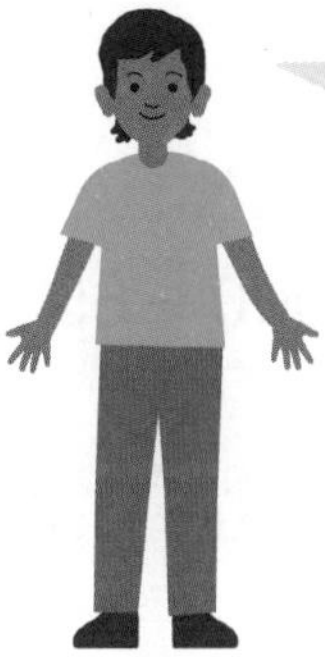

How is the mental calculation similar to this method?

		9	9	9	10
	~~1~~	~~0~~,	~~0~~	~~0~~	~~0~~
−		5,	6	7	2
		?,	?	?	?

10,000 – 5,672 =

2 Subtract.

(a) 100 – 3 (b) 1,000 – 3 (c) 10,000 – 3

(d) 100 – 42 (e) 1,000 – 42 (f) 10,000 – 42

(g) 1,000 – 671 (h) 10,000 – 671 (i) 10,000 – 771

(j) 10,000 – 5,209 (k) 10,000 – 1,337 (l) 10,000 – 8,002

(m) 100 – 80 (n) 10,000 – 880 (o) 10,000 – 8,880

3 Subtract 4,530 from 70,000.

70,000 – 4,530 = ______

70,000 – 4,530
60,000 10,000

4 Subtract 62 from 8,500.

8,500 – 62 = ______

8,500 – 62
8,400 100

5 Subtract.

(a) 500 – 65 (b) 5,000 – 65 (c) 50,000 – 65

(d) 9,000 – 372 (e) 90,000 – 372 (f) 90,000 – 3,720

(g) 3,200 – 35 (h) 32,000 – 35 (i) 32,000 – 350

(j) 1,500 – 140 (k) 15,000 – 140 (l) 17,000 – 226

6 A farm needs to deliver 10,000 kg of coffee beans. So far it has delivered 3,608 kg of coffee beans. How many more kilograms of coffee beans does it need to deliver?

Exercise 3 • page 31

Lesson 4
Other Ways to Add and Subtract — Part 2

4

Think

The upholstered bed frame costs $1,745. The platform bed frame costs $998. How much do both bed frames cost altogether?

Learn

1,745 + 998

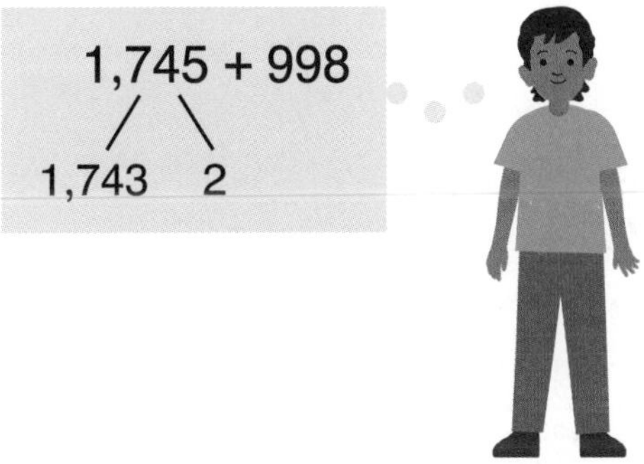

Method 1

998 + 2 = 1,000
1,743 + 1,000 = 2,743

Method 2

$1{,}745 \xrightarrow{+1{,}000} 2{,}745 \xrightarrow{-2} 2{,}743$

Method 3

$$\begin{array}{r} {\scriptstyle 1\ 1\ 1\ \ } \\ 1{,}745 \\ +\ \ 998 \\ \hline 2{,}743 \end{array}$$

Altogether, they cost $______.

Do

1 Subtract 998 from 3,221.

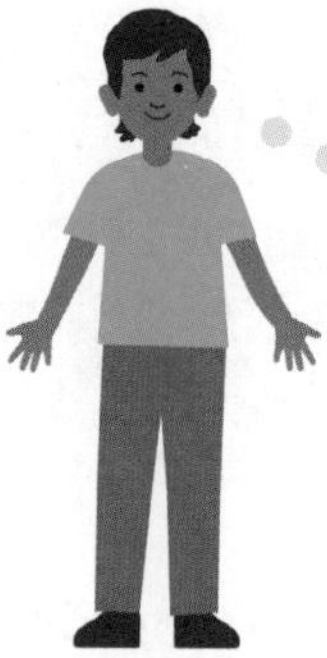

3,221 − 998

2,221 1,000

1,000 − 998 = 2

2,221 + 2 = ?

```
  2  11 11 11
  3, 2  2  1
−     9  9  8
-------------
```

$3{,}221 \xrightarrow{-1{,}000} ? \xrightarrow{+2} ?$

3,221 − 998 = ____

2 Find the values.

(a) 7,536 + 9 (b) 7,536 + 99 (c) 7,536 + 999

(d) 7,536 − 9 (e) 7,536 − 99 (f) 7,536 − 999

(g) 623 + 98 (h) 623 + 198 (i) 623 + 298

(j) 623 − 98 (k) 623 − 198 (l) 623 − 298

3 Add 846 and 58.

846 + 58

844   2

58 + 2 = 60

844 + 60 = ?

```
  1 1
  8 4 6
+   5 8
-------
```

846 + 58 = ☐

4 Subtract 39 from 703.

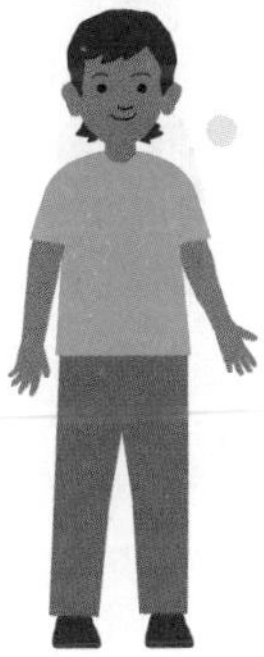

703 − 39

663   40

40 − 39 = 1

663 + 1 = ?

```
  6 9 13
  7 0 3   (crossed out)
−   3 9
-------
```

703 − 39 = ☐

5 Find the values.

(a) 27 + 49	(b) 327 + 49	(c) 6,327 + 49
(d) 82 − 28	(e) 782 − 28	(f) 3,782 − 28

Exercise 4 • page 34

Lesson 5
Word Problems

5

Think

38,000 people went to the tulip festival last year. 12,870 of them were women. There were 4,200 more men than women. The rest were children. How many children went to the tulip festival?

Learn

I drew this model. I can see that I need to find the number of men first.

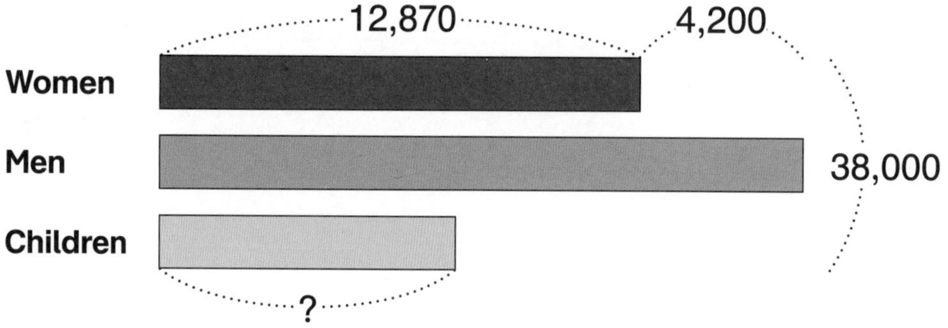

Number of men: 12,870 + 4,200 = 17,070

Number of men and women: 12,870 + 17,070 = 29,940

Number of children: 38,000 − 29,940 = ______

Check your answer. Is the sum of the number of women, men, and children 38,000?

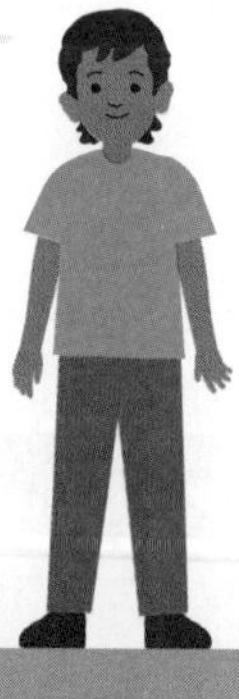

______ children went to the tulip festival.

Do

1 An orchard harvested 3,300 pounds of Honeycrisp and Gala apples altogether, and 4,600 pounds of Gala and Fuji apples altogether. It harvested 1,900 pounds of Honeycrisp apples. How many more pounds of Fuji apples than Gala apples were harvested?

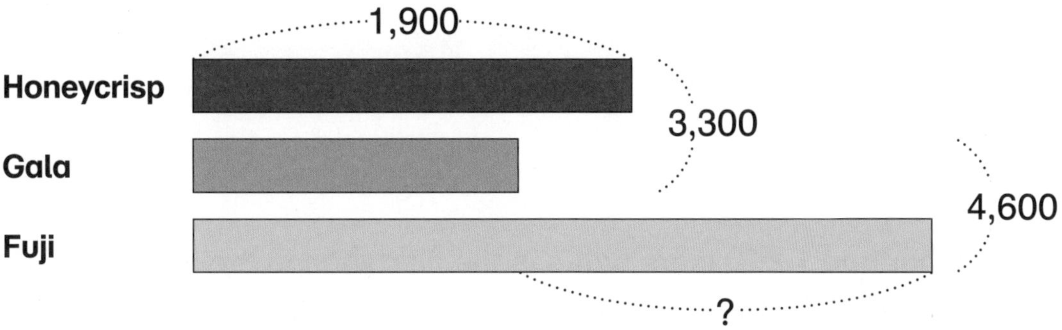

2 A school raised $30,000. It used $13,700 to buy playground equipment and $9,500 to buy sports equipment. They gave the rest to the clubs. How much more was spent on playground equipment than on the clubs?

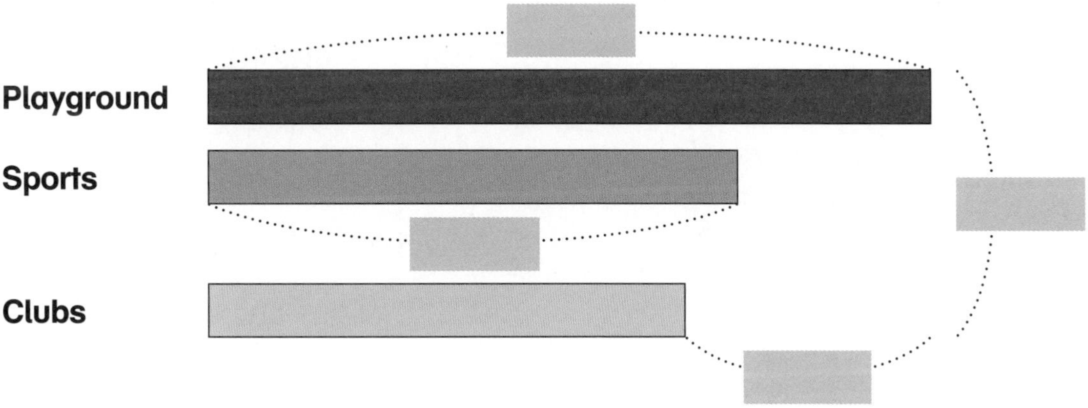

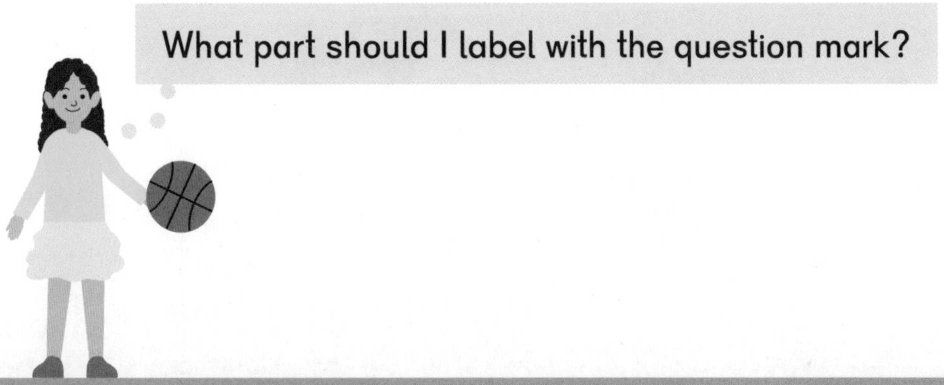

3 A truck costs \$45,000. A motorcycle costs \$27,950 less than the truck. A car costs \$14,500 more than the motorcycle. How much do the three vehicles cost altogether?

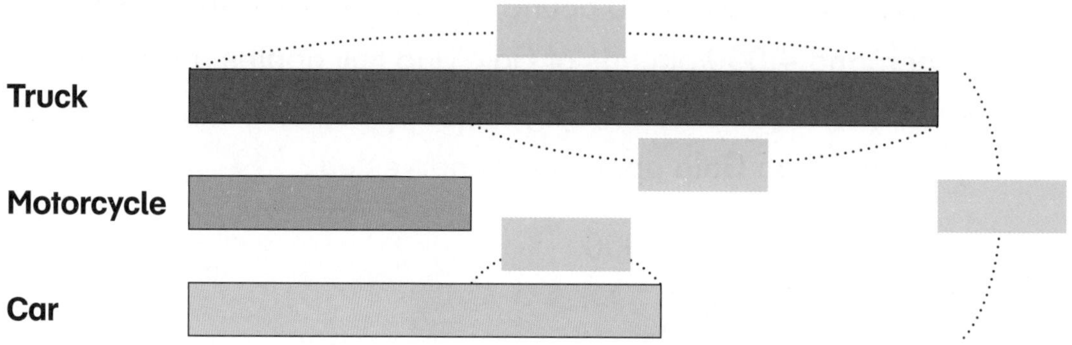

4 A rancher had 1,240 more cattle in the field than in the meadow. After he moved 560 cattle from the field to the meadow, there were 1,690 cattle in the meadow. How many cattle did he have in the field at first?

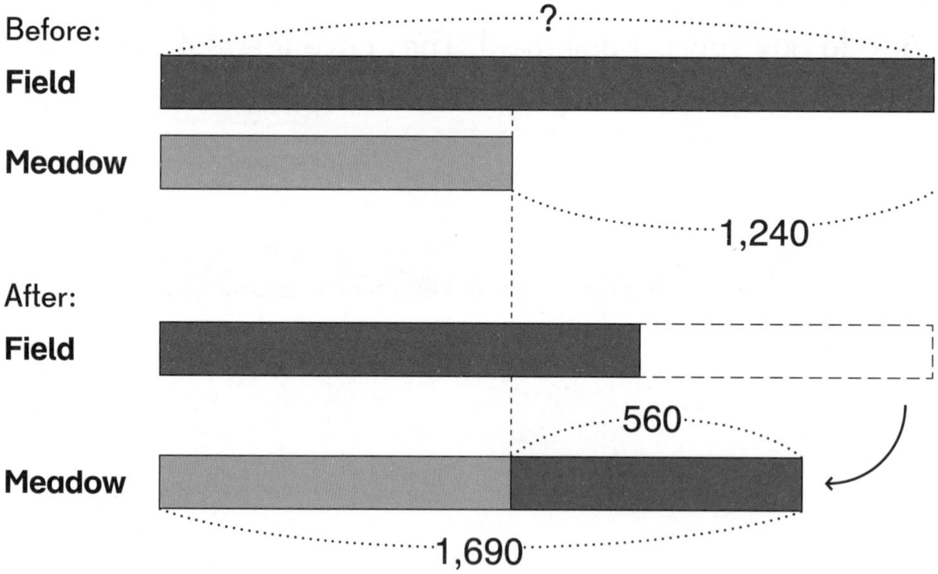

Exercise 5 • page 38

1 Find the missing digits.

(a)

	4	☐	,	2	9	☐
+		8	,	0	☐	7
	☐	6	,	☐	4	3

(b)

	8	☐	,	8	5	☐
−	3	6	,	0	☐	2
	☐	4	,	7	7	7

(c)

	☐	4	,	☐	2	0
−		5	,	0	3	☐
	8	☐	,	5	☐	3

(d)

		☐	6	,	1	8	6
		9	☐	,	7	☐	4
+			6	,	8	2	☐
	1	3	3	,	☐	4	0

2 Estimate the values. Then find the actual values.

(a) 23,746 + 785

(b) 8,057 + 42,906

(c) 57,250 – 44,987

(d) 75,034 – 788

(e) 60,005 – 4,462

(f) 85,002 + 37,999

(g) 45,900 + 17,200 + 19,780

(h) 16,270 + 28,906 + 2,755

3 Find the values.

(a) 30,000 – 270

(b) 5,600 – 65

(c) 3,332 + 199

(d) 8,021 – 499

(e) 5,328 – 79

(f) 5,200 + 8,400 + 156

4 (a) Eliza wants to walk at least 10,000 steps a day. So far, she has walked 5,687 steps today. How many more steps does she have to walk to reach her goal?

(b) In 3 days, she wants to walk at least 30,000 steps in all. On Monday, she walked 13,459 steps. On Tuesday, she walked 6,490 steps. On Wednesday, she walked 10,870 steps. Did she reach her goal?

5 68,277 people visited a museum on Saturday. 8,649 fewer people visited the museum on Sunday than on Saturday.

(a) About how many people visited the museum on both days?

(b) Exactly how many people visited the museum on both days?

6 There are 25,000 paintings in an art museum. 10,500 are oil paintings, 5,200 are watercolor paintings, and the rest are pastel paintings. How many more oil paintings than pastel paintings are there?

7 There were 34,000 residents in Upper Town. Lower Town had 950 fewer residents than Upper Town. The boundary between the two towns was moved and Upper Town now has 27,000 residents. How many residents does Lower Town have now?

Exercise 6 • page 42

Chapter 3

Multiples and Factors

There is a total of 24 pomegranates in each stack of boxes. How many pomegranates are in each box of the different stacks?

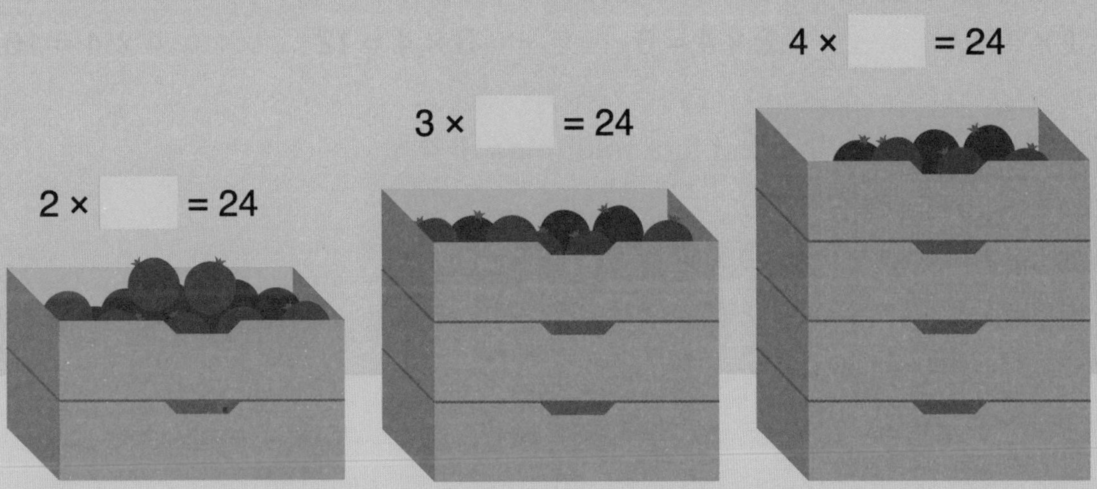

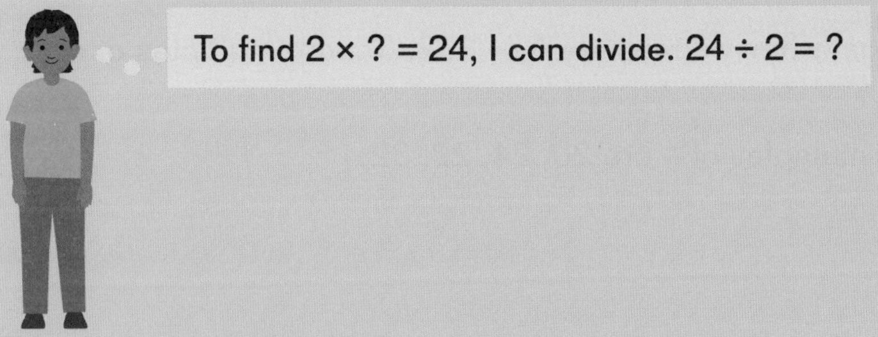

How many pomegranates would be in each box if the total number of pomegranates in each stack was 48?

How many pomegranates would be in each box if the total number of pomegranates in each stack was 36?

Lesson 1
Multiples

①

Think

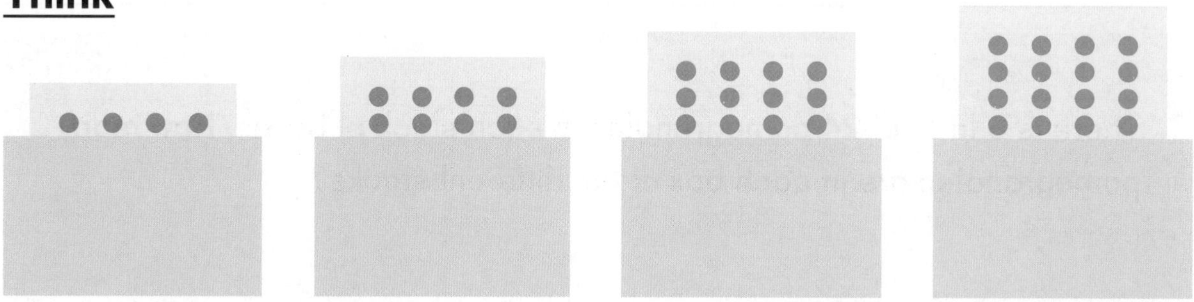

$1 \times 4 = 4$ $2 \times 4 = 8$ $3 \times 4 = 12$ $4 \times 4 = 16$

4, 8, 12, and 16 are the first four **multiples** of 4.

(a) List the next ten multiples of 4.

(b) Is 76 a multiple of 4?

Learn

The products we get when we multiply 4 by 1, 2, 3... are multiples of 4.

(a) The next ten multiples of 4 are 20, 24, 28, 32, ___, ___, ___, ___, ___, and ___.

(b)
```
    1 9
 4 ) 7 6
    4
   ----
    3 6
    3 6
   ----
      0
```

When a multiple of 4 is divided by 4, there is no remainder.

$4 \times$ ___ $= 76$ | 76 is the nineteenth multiple of 4.

Do

1 Complete the number patterns.

(a) 8, 16, 24, 32, ___, ___, ___, ___, ___, ___

(b) 6, 12, 18, 24, ___, ___, ___, ___, ___, ___

2 List the first ten multiples of 7.

3 (a) Is 91 a multiple of 7?

(b) Is 91 a multiple of 8?

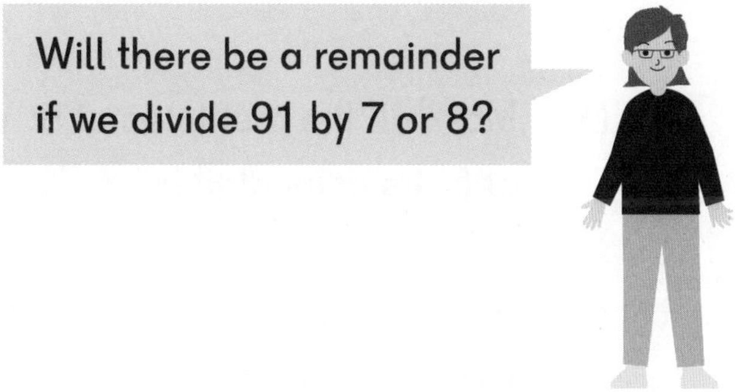

4 (a) Is 64 a multiple of 2?

(b) Is 64 a multiple of 3?

(c) Is 64 a multiple of 4?

(d) Is 64 a multiple of 5?

(e) Is 64 a multiple of 6?

5 (a) What is the fourth multiple of 9?

(b) What is the ninth multiple of 12?

6 Use a hundred chart.

1	✓2	✓3	4	✓5	6	7	8	9	10
11	12	13	14	15	16	17	18	19	20
21	22	23	24	25	26	27	28	29	30

(a) Mark all the multiples of 2. When a number is a multiple of 2, its ones digit is ___, ___, ___, ___, or ___.

A multiple of 2 is an even number.

(b) Mark all the multiples of 5. When a number is a multiple of 5, its ones digit is ___ or ___.

(c) Mark all the multiples of 3. Find the sum of the digits of each of the numbers that are multiples of 3. Is the sum a multiple of 3?

(d) List the first 12 multiples of 9. Find the sum of the digits of each. Are the sums of the digits multiples of 9?

I wonder if this works for other numbers besides 3 or 9...

7 9 | 18 | 30 | 35 | 78 | 80 | 117

Which of the above numbers are multiples of...

(a) 2? (b) 3? (c) 5? (d) 9?

Exercise 1 • page 47

Lesson 2
Common Multiples

Think

Pots come in boxes of 3. Seedlings come in trays of 4.
What is the least number of boxes of pots and trays of seedlings we can buy so that there is one seedling for every pot?

Learn

$1 \times 3 = 3$ $2 \times 3 = 6$ $3 \times 3 = 9$ $4 \times 3 = 12$

$1 \times 4 = 4$ $2 \times 4 = 8$ $3 \times 4 = 12$

3, 6, 9, and 12 are multiples of 3.

4, 8, and 12 are multiples of 4.

12 is a **common multiple** of 3 and 4.

We need to buy at least ___ boxes of pots and ___ trays of seedlings.

What are some other common multiples of 3 and 4?

Do

1 (a) Find the first two common multiples of 4 and 6.

Multiples of 4: 4, 8, 12, 16, 20, 24...

Multiples of 6: 6, 12, 18, 24, 30, 36...

___ and ___ are the first two common multiples of 4 and 6.

(b) What are some other common multiples of 4 and 6?

2 Find the first four common multiples of 2 and 7.

Instead of listing multiples of both numbers,
I could just list multiples of the greater number,
and check if they are multiples of 2 as well.

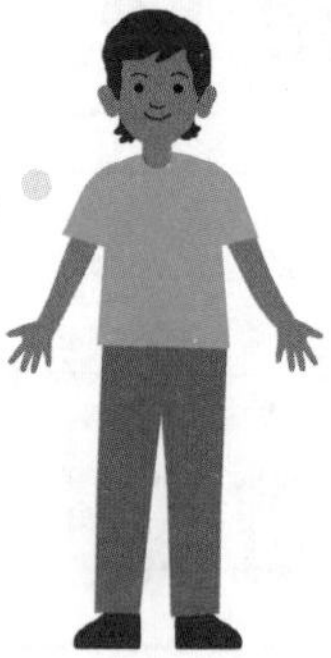

Multiples of 7: 7, 14, 21, 28, 35, 42, 49, 56...

The first four common multiples of 2 and 7 are ___, ___, ___, and ___.

3 Find a common multiple of 3, 5, and 10.

The multiples of 10 are 10, 20, 30, 40, 50...
30 is also a multiple of 3 and 5.

4 Use a hundred chart.

1	2	3	4	5	6	7	8	9	10
11	12	13	14	15	16	17	18	19	20

(a) Draw a square around each multiple of 2. Circle each multiple of 3. Draw a triangle around each multiple of 6. What do you notice?

Multiples of 6 are common multiples of ____ and ____.

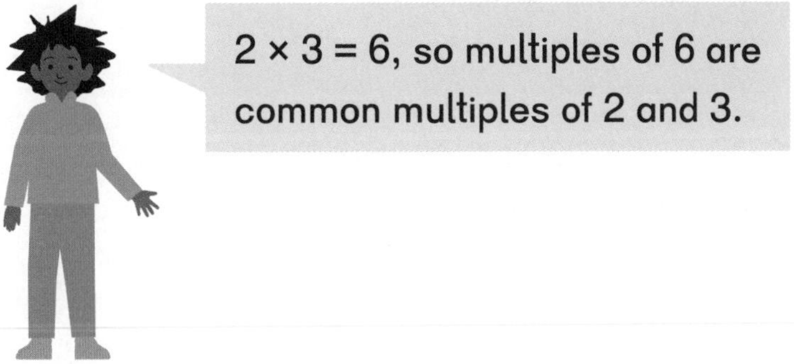

(b) Draw a diamond shape around each multiple of 4. Draw an X on each multiple of 8.

2 × 4 = 8, so multiples of 8 are common multiples of ____ and ____.

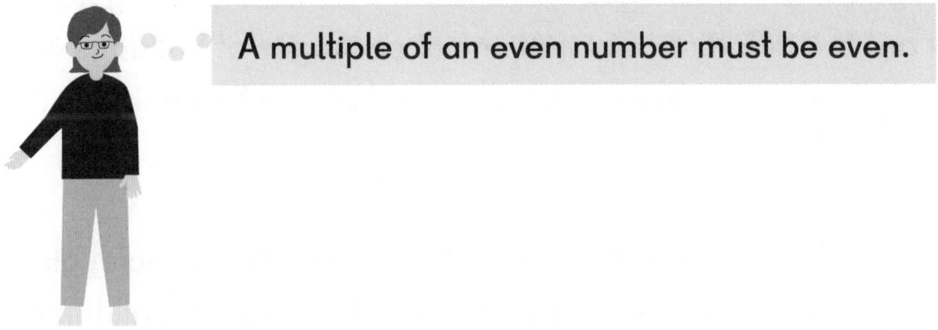

(c) Multiples of 15 are common multiples of 3 and ____.

5 Which of the following numbers are common multiples of 6 and 9?

9	18	36	45	54	108

6 Find three common multiples of 3 and 7.

7 Find the first two common multiples of 4, 6, and 8.

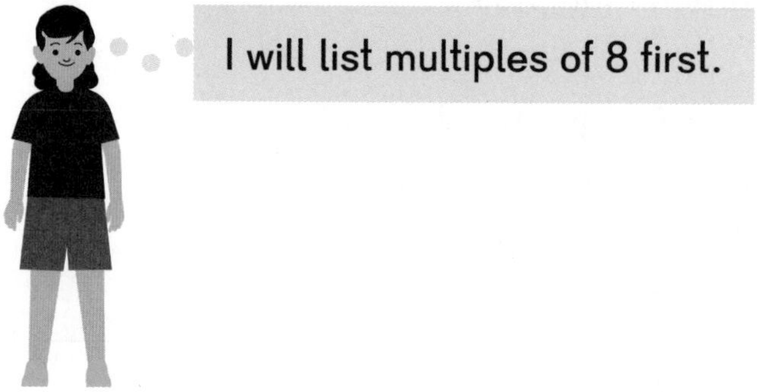

8

Hot dogs come in packages of 6 and buns come in packages of 8. What are two different combinations of packages of hot dogs and buns we could buy so that there is exactly one hot dog for each bun?

9 Mei waters her umbrella plant every 2 days, her African violet plant every 4 days, and her spider plant every 5 days. If she watered all three plants today, in how many days will she water them all on the same day again?

Exercise 2 • page 50

Think

How many different rectangles can you form using all 12 squares? How many squares are along each side of each rectangle?

Learn

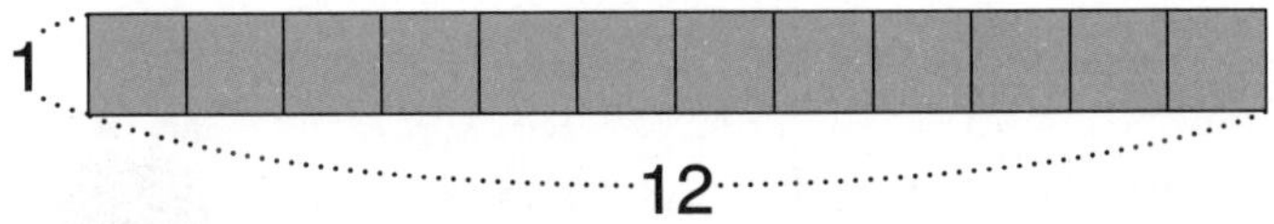

12 = **1** × **12**

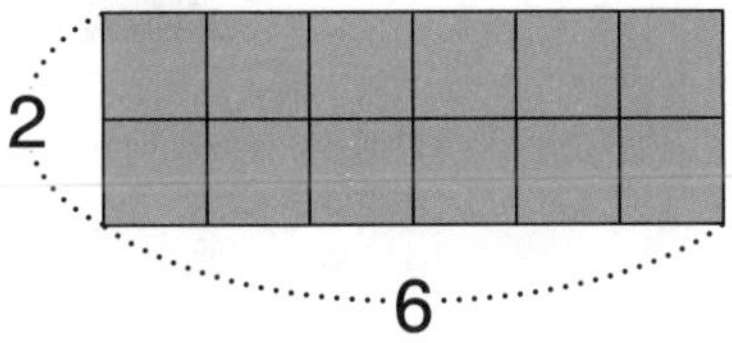

12 = **2** × **6**

There are only 3 different rectangles.
1 × 12 = 12 × 1

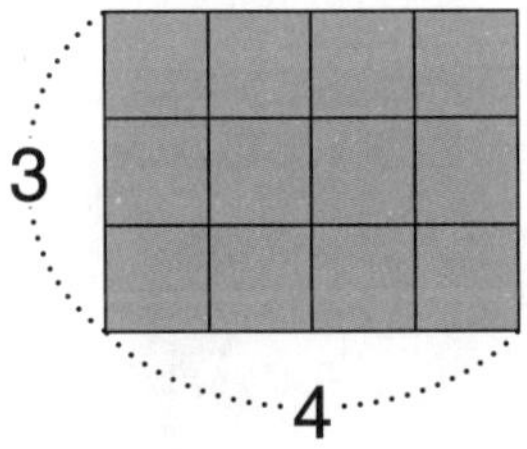

12 = **3** × **4**

1, 2, 3, 4, 6, and 12 are **factors** of 12.

12 is a multiple of all of its factors.

12 can be divided by 1, 2, 3, 4, 6, and 12 with no remainder. We say that 12 is **divisible** by 1, 2, 3, 4, 6, and 12.

Do

1 What are the factors of 8?

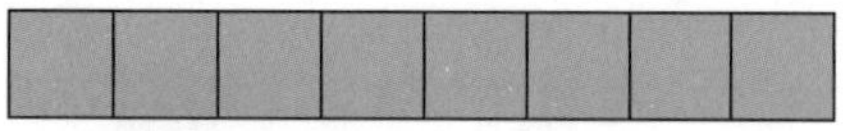

1 × 8 = 8

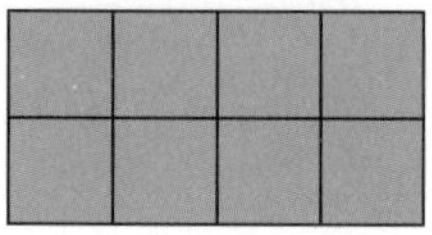

☐ × ☐ = 8

The factors of 8 are 1, ☐, ☐, and 8.

The factors of a number always include 1 and the number itself.

2 Find the factors of 18.

1 × ☐ = 18

2 × ☐ = 18

3 × ☐ = 18

Start with 1 and then try 2, 3, etc. Why do we not have to check 6 or any more numbers after 6?

The factors of 18 are 1, 2, 3, ☐, ☐, and ☐.

3 (a) Is 7 a factor of 14?

Is 14 divisible by 7? By 3?

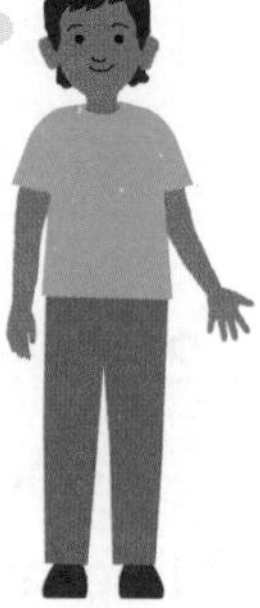

(b) Is 3 a factor of 14?

14 ÷ 3 will have a remainder.

4 Which of the following numbers have 6 as a factor?

6	16	36	46	54	60

5 Find the factors of 75.

1 × ___ = 75

3 × ___ = 75

5 × ___ = 75

75 is an odd number, so I do not have to check any even numbers.

The factors of 75 are 1, 3, ___, ___, ___, and ___.

6 List the factors of each number from least to greatest.

(a) 15 (b) 21 (c) 36 (d) 48

(e) 54 (f) 60 (g) 72 (h) 100

7 Find the missing factors.

(a) 6 × ___ = 72 (b) ___ × 7 = 105

(c) 100 = 4 × ___ (d) 80 = ___ × 5

Exercise 3 • page 53

Lesson 4
Prime Numbers and Composite Numbers

4

Think

(a) How many different rectangles can you form using all 5 squares? How many factors does 5 have?

(b) How many different rectangles can you form using all 6 squares? How many factors does 6 have?

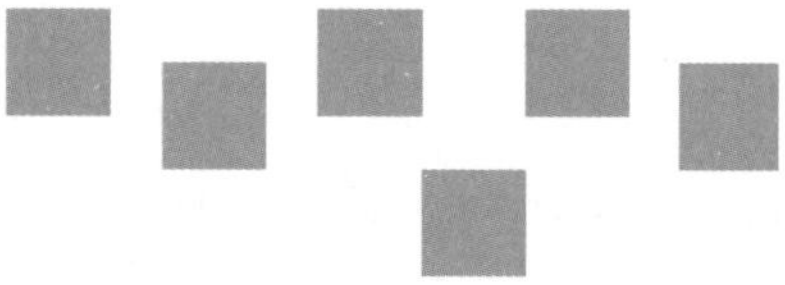

Learn

(a) 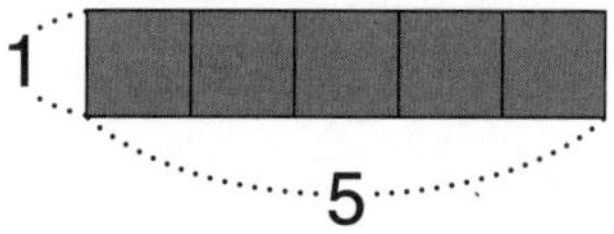

$5 = \mathbf{1} \times \mathbf{5}$

5 has ____ factors.

A number that has exactly 2 factors is called a **prime number**.

5 is a prime number. Its only factors are 1 and 5.

What are some other prime numbers?

(b) 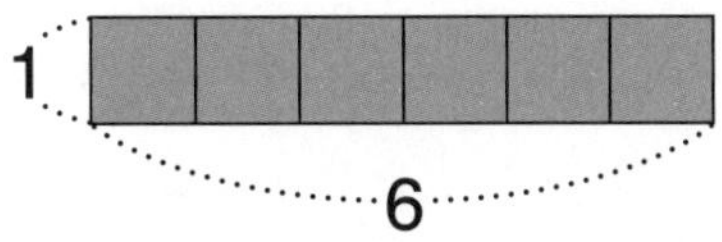

$6 = \mathbf{1} \times \mathbf{6}$

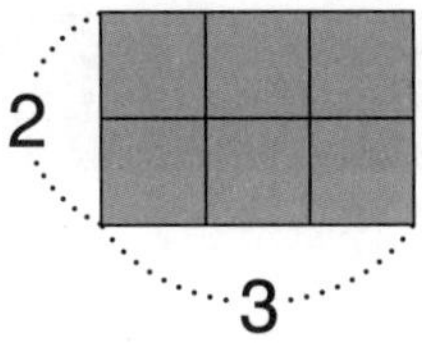

$6 = \mathbf{2} \times \mathbf{3}$

6 has ____ factors.

A number that has more than 2 factors is called a **composite number**.

6 is a composite number.
Its factors are 1, 2, 3, and 6.

What are some other composite numbers?

1 has only 1 factor, since 1 × 1 = 1.
1 is neither prime nor composite.

0 has an infinite number of factors
since 0 times any number is 0.
0 is neither prime nor composite.

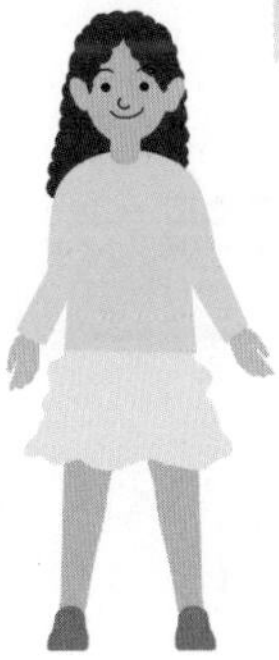

Do

1 Copy and complete the table.

Number	Factors	Prime	Composite
2	1, 2	✓	
3			
4	1, 2, 4		✓
7			
8			
9			
10			
11			
12			

2 (a) Is 39 prime or composite?

(b) Is 47 prime or composite?

3 Which of the following numbers are prime numbers?

15	13	21	53	565	1,312

4 Use a hundred chart.
Circle prime numbers and cross off composite numbers.

1	(2)	3	~~4~~	5	6	7	8	9	10
11	12	13	14	15	16	17	18	19	20
21	22	23	24	25	26	27	28	29	30

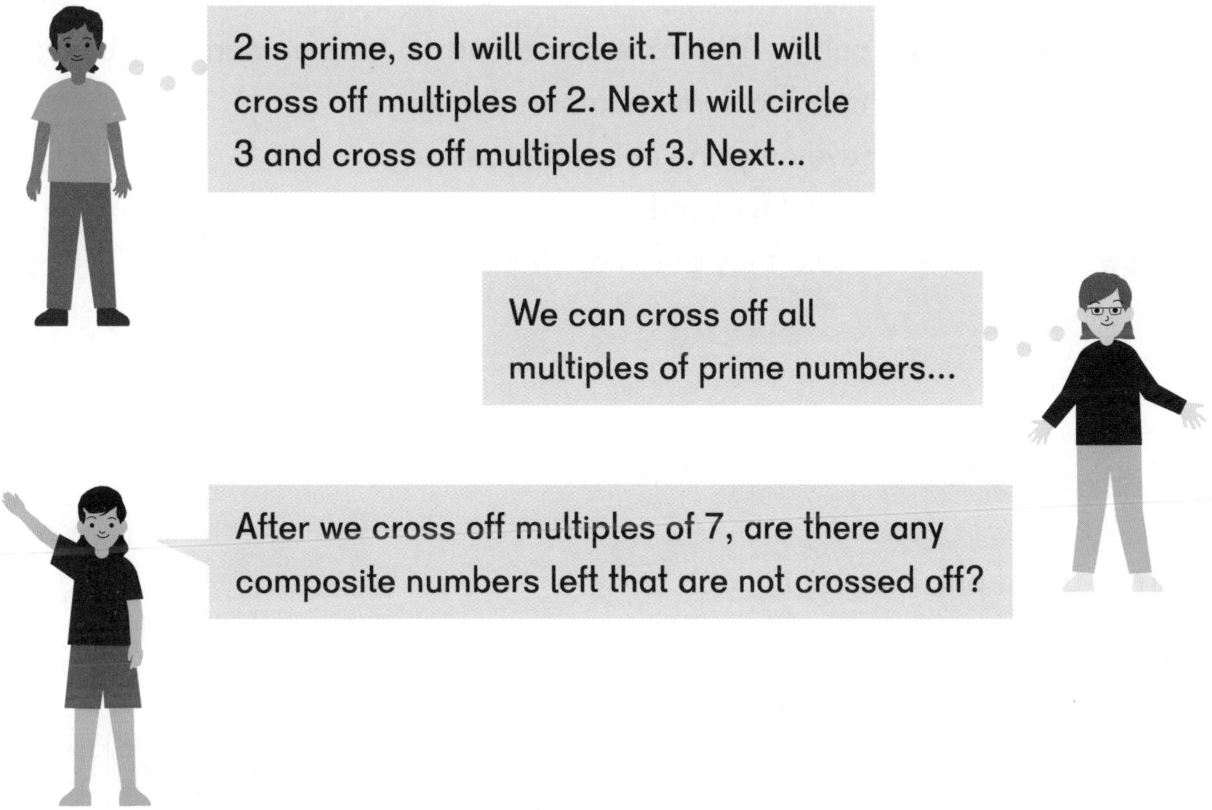

(a) How many prime numbers are there between 1 and 100?

(b) How many even prime numbers are there between 1 and 100?

(c) Why are prime numbers greater than 2 all odd numbers?

(d) What is the next prime number after 100?

Exercise 4 • page 57

Lesson 5
Common Factors

Think

Sofia and Alex are putting 12 pink erasers and 18 blue erasers into boxes.

- Each box must have the same number of erasers.
- Each box must have only one color of erasers.
- All the erasers should be used.

How many erasers could they put in each box?

Learn

1 × ☐ = 12 | 1 × ☐ = 18

They could put 1 eraser in each box.

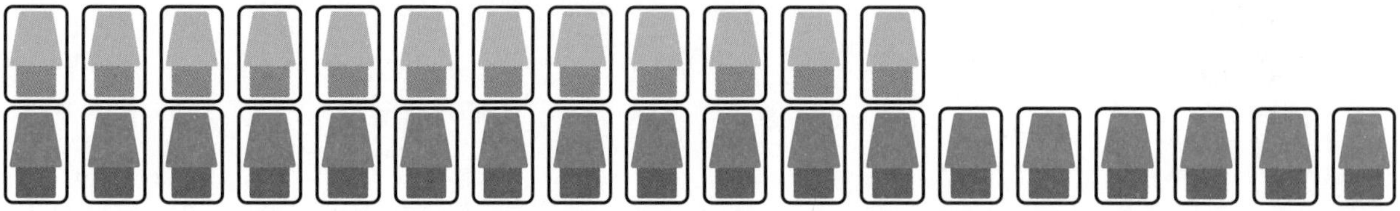

---

2 × ☐ = 12 | 2 × ☐ = 18

They could put 2 erasers in each box.

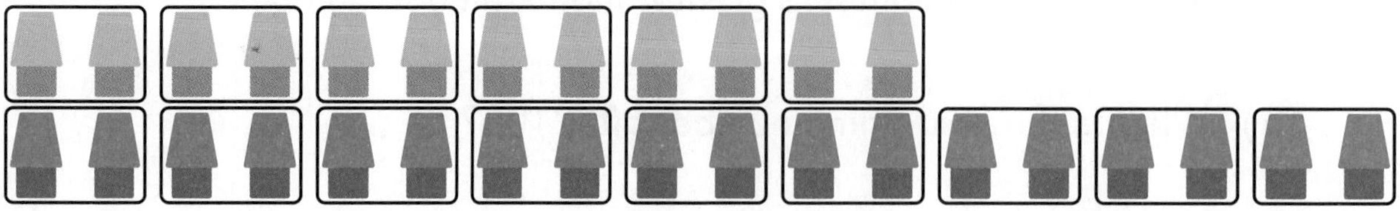

$3 \times \square = 12$ | $3 \times \square = 18$

They could put 3 erasers in each box.

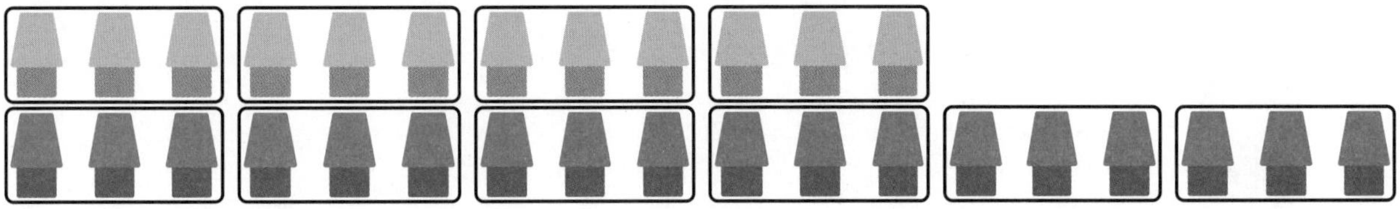

$6 \times \square = 12$ | $6 \times \square = 18$

They could put 6 erasers in each box.

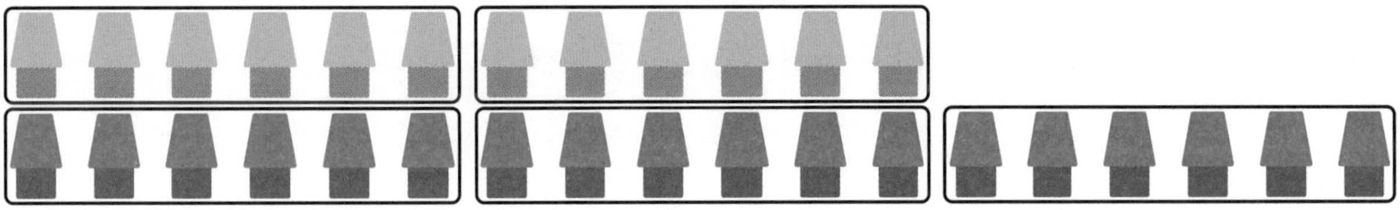

They could put 1, 2, 3, or 6 erasers in each box.

The factors of 12 are 1, 2, 3, 4, 6, and 12.
The factors of 18 are 1, 2, 3, 6, 9, and 18.

1, 2, 3, and 6 are **common factors** of 12 and 18.

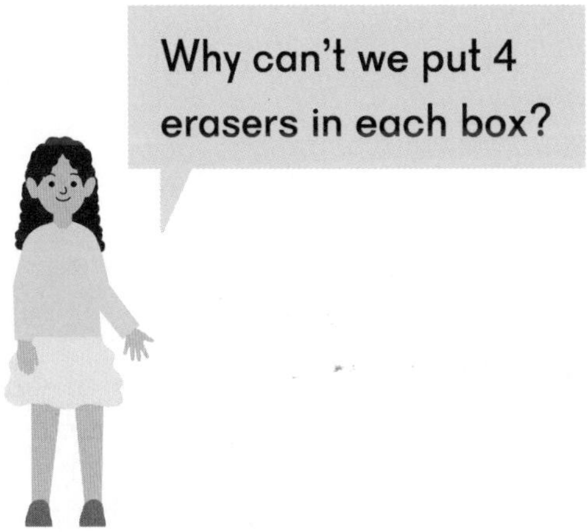

Do

1 Find the common factors of 6 and 8.

1 × ? = 6	1 × ? = 8
2 × ? = 6	2 × ? = 8
...	...

The factors of 6 are ___, ___, ___, and ___.

The factors of 8 are ___, ___, ___, and ___.

The common factors of 6 and 8 are ___ and ___.

2 Find the common factors of 24 and 36.

1 × ___ = 24	1 × ___ = 36
2 × ___ = 24	2 × ___ = 36
3 × ___ = 24	3 × ___ = 36
4 × ___ = 24	4 × ___ = 36
	6 × ___ = 36

3 Is 7 a common factor of 42 and 86?

Are both numbers divisible by 7?

4 (a) Is 4 a common factor of 48 and 92?

(b) Is 8 a common factor of 48 and 92?

5 (a) Which of the following numbers have 2 and 5 as common factors?

52	70	65	80

(b) Which of the following numbers have 3 and 9 as common factors?

54	42	75	90

6 Find the common factors of each pair of numbers.

(a) 6 and 9

(b) 10 and 20

(c) 18 and 30

(d) 36 and 60

7 Mei and Dion have 24 red roses and 32 yellow roses. They want to use all of them to make identical bouquets. Each bouquet has to have at least one rose of each color. What is the greatest number of bouquets they can make and how many roses of each color will be in each bouquet?

Exercise 5 • page 60

1. (a) List the first ten multiples of 7.

   (b) List the first twenty multiples of 3.

   (c) Which of the numbers found in (a) and (b) are common multiples of 3 and 7?

2. What are the first four common multiples of 2, 3, and 4?

3. Find all the factors of each number.

   (a) 20 (b) 28

   (c) 50 (d) 64

4. Which of the following numbers are multiples of 4?

64	78	92	100

5. Which of the following numbers are multiples of 7?

28	67	84	96

6 Which of the following numbers have 3 as a factor?

18	27	83	91	99	118

7 Which of the following numbers are composite?

18	27	83	91	99	118

8 List the nine prime numbers that are less than 25.

9 Find the common factors of each set of numbers.

(a) 21 and 42 (b) 48 and 60 (c) 25 and 100

10 Find the first two common multiples for each set of numbers.

(a) 1 and 7

(b) 3 and 9

(c) 3, 5, and 6

(d) 2, 5, and 10

11 (a) If a number has 9 as a factor, is 3 also a factor of that number?

(b) If a number is a common multiple of 4 and 5, is 2 a factor of that number?

12 Find the missing factors.

(a) $90 = 2 \times \square$

$90 = 2 \times 3 \times \square$

$90 = 2 \times 3 \times 3 \times \square$

(b) $81 = 3 \times \square$

$81 = 3 \times 3 \times \square$

$81 = 3 \times 3 \times 3 \times \square$

13 A bus for Route A leaves the station every 6 minutes. A bus for Route B leaves the same station every 9 minutes. Buses for both routes leave the station at 8:00 a.m. What is the next time that buses for both routes leave the station at the same time?

14

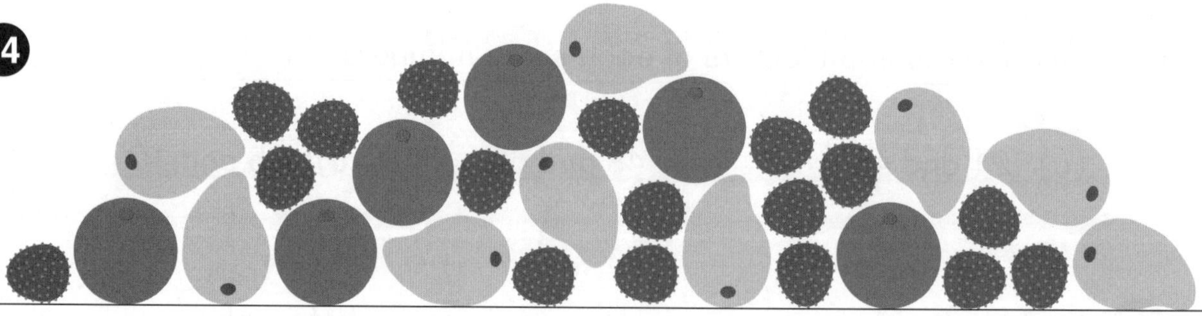

Clara is putting 9 mangoes, 18 lychees, and 6 oranges into baskets. Each basket must have the same combination of fruits. What is the greatest number of baskets she could have, and how many of each kind of fruit will be in each basket?

15 A number less than 70 is a multiple of 7. When it is divided by 6, there is a remainder of 1. When it is divided by 4, there is also a remainder of 1. What is the number?

Exercise 6 • page 63

Chapter 4

Multiplication

The students in the accounting club are helping the gym teacher buy basketball equipment by calculating the costs.

Item	Number Needed	Cost for 1
Backboard	4	$550
Backboard adjustment system	4	$1,200
Basketball	15	$34

I can use mental calculation to find the cost of the backboards.

550 × 4

500   50

I wonder how we could split $1,200 to easily find the cost of the backboard adjustment systems.

1,200 × 4

?   ?

10 basketballs will cost $340. 15 will cost...

Think

There are 2,300 nails in 1 box.
How many nails are in 5 boxes?

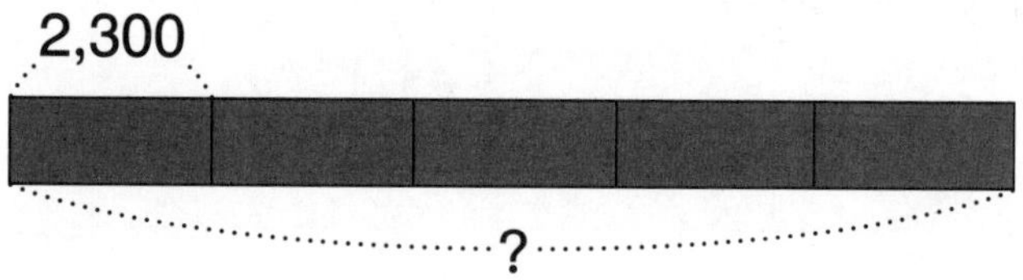

How can we use mental math to solve this problem?

Learn

2,300 × 5

Method 1

23 × 5 = 100 + 15 = 115
(23 split into 20 and 3)

23 × 5 = 115

23 hundreds × 5 = 115 hundreds
= 11,500

Method 2

2,300 × 5
(2,300 split into 2,000 and 300)

2,300 × 5 = 10,000 + 1,500
= 11,500

There are ______ nails in 5 boxes.

Do

1 Use mental calculation.

(a) 32 × 4 = ____

(b) 320 × 4 = ____

(c) 3,200 × 4 = ____

(d) 32,000 × 4 = ____

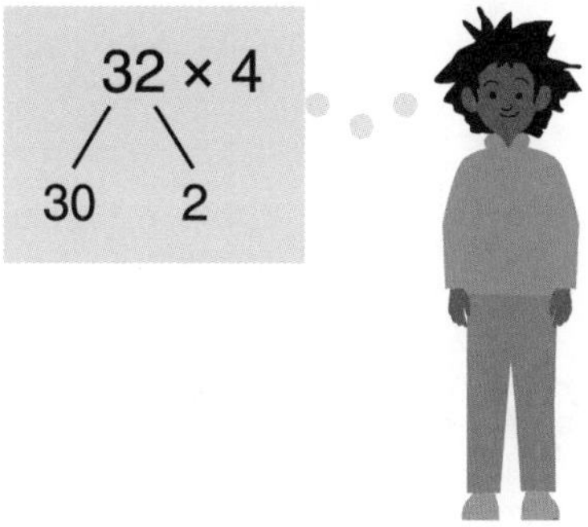

2 Use mental calculation.

(a) 28 × 3 = ____

(b) 280 × 3 = ____

(c) 2,800 × 3 = ____

(d) 28,000 × 3 = ____

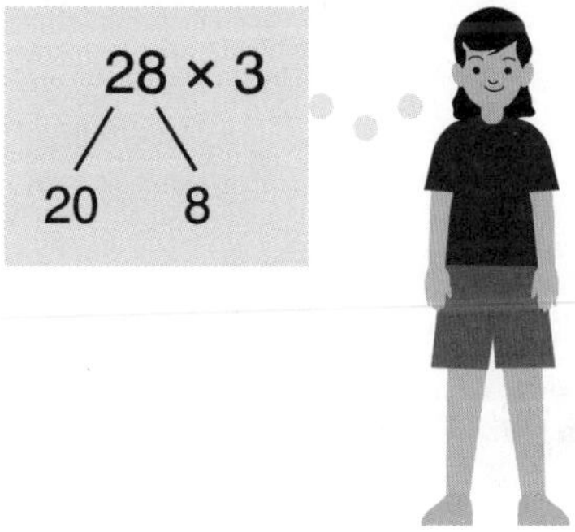

3 Multiply 2,700 by 4.

27 hundreds × 4 = ____ hundreds

= ____

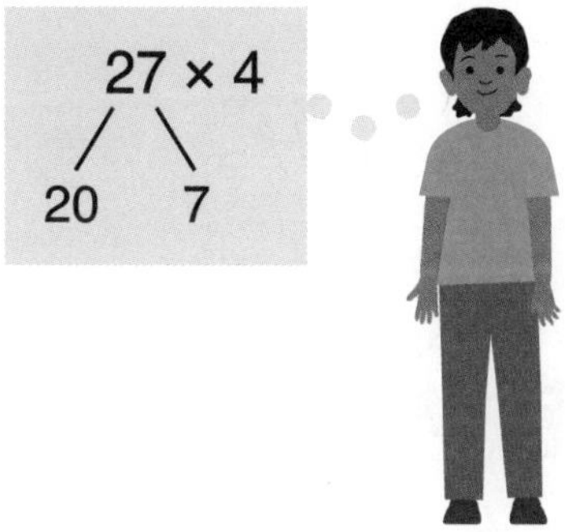

4 Find the product of 8 and 62,000.

62 × 8 → 60 and 2

62 thousands × 8 = ____ thousands

= ____

5 Multiply 8 by 99.

99 = 100 − 1

100 × 8 = 800

1 × 8 = 8

99 × 8 = 800 − 8

= ____

6 Find the product of 199 and 7.

199 = 200 − 1

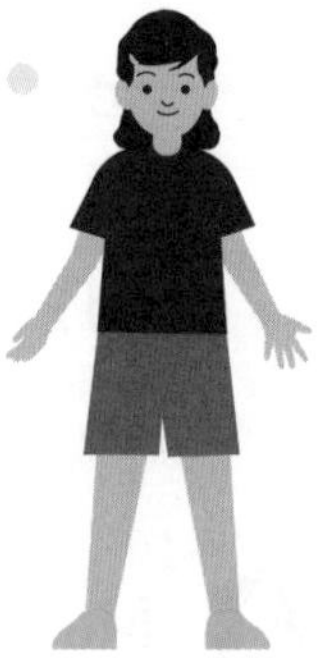

200 × 7 = ____

1 × 7 = ____

199 × 7 = ____

7 Multiply 399 by 6.

399 × 6 = 2,400 − 6 = ____

8 Use mental calculation to find the values.

(a) 42×4
(b) 38×2
(c) 120×4
(d) 3×270
(e) 260×6
(f) $2,500 \times 5$
(g) $1,900 \times 9$
(h) $16,000 \times 3$
(i) 99×9
(j) 5×199

9 There are 750 sheets of paper in a small box. A large box contains 3 times as many sheets of paper as a small box. How many sheets of paper are in a large box?

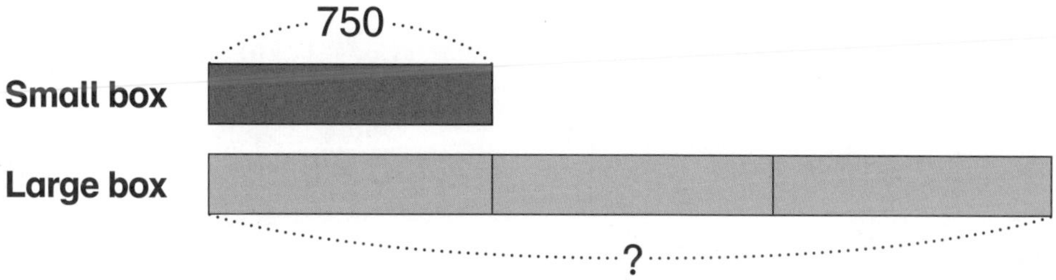

10 A gym charges \$99 a month for membership. At that price, how much does it cost to be a member for 6 months?

Exercise 1 • page 67

Lesson 2
Multiplying by a 1-Digit Number — Part 1

2

Think

A week at a resort costs $2,415 per person. How much will it cost for 3 people to stay at the resort for a week?

(a) Estimate the cost.

(b) Find the actual cost.

Learn

2,415 × 3

(a)

2,415 × 3
↓
2,000 × 3 = 6,000

2,415 × 3
↓
2,500 × 3 = 7,500

2,415 × 3 ≈ ______

Which estimate will be closer to the product?
Which estimate will be greater than the product?
Which estimate will be less than the product?

(b)

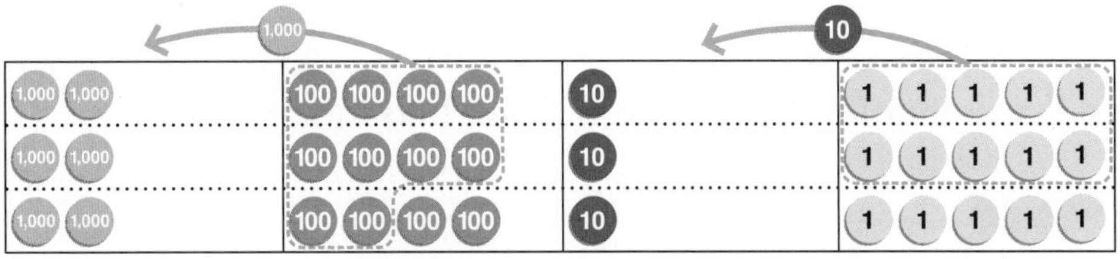

2,000 × 3 | 400 × 3 | 10 × 3 | 5 × 3

```
        1
  2, 4  1  5
×          3
-----------
           5
```

Multiply the ones by 3.
5 ones × 3 = 15 ones
= 1 ten 5 ones

```
        1
  2, 4  1  5
×          3
-----------
        4  5
```

Multiply the tens by 3.
Then add in the regroupped ten.
(1 ten × 3) + 1 ten = 4 tens

```
  1     1
  2, 4  1  5
×          3
-----------
     2  4  5
```

Multiply the hundreds by 3.
4 hundreds × 3 = 12 hundreds
= 1 thousand 2 hundreds

```
  1     1
  2, 4  1  5
×          3
-----------
  7, 2  4  5
```

Multiply the thousands by 3.
Then add in the regrouped thousand.
(2 thousands × 3) + 1 thousand = 7 thousands

The vacation will cost $______.

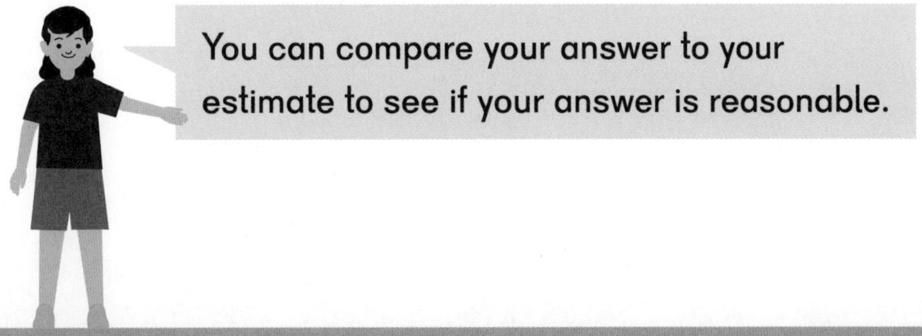

Do

1 Estimate the product of 8,712 and 4. Then find the product.

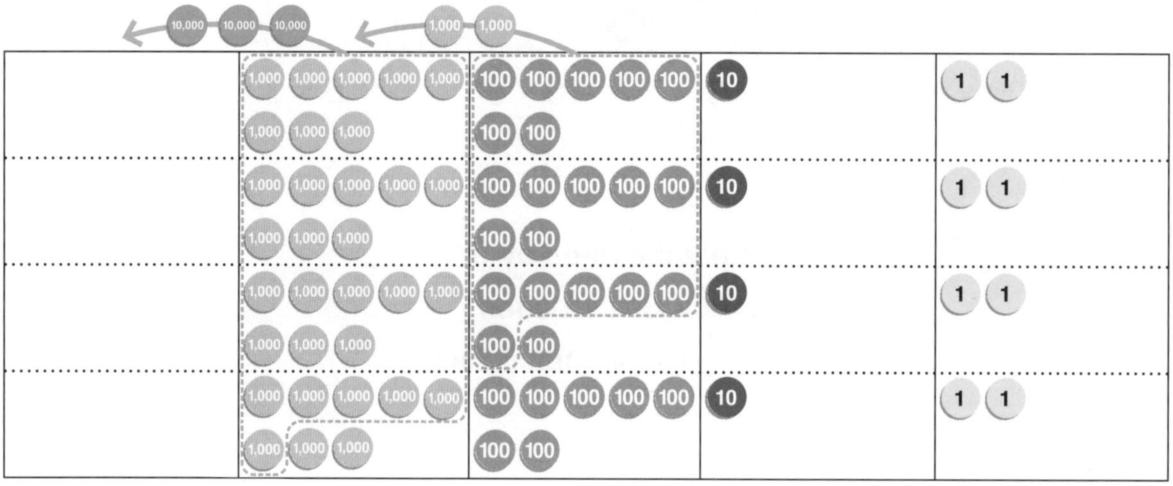

(a) 8,712 × 4

↓

______ × 4 = ______

(b)
$$\begin{array}{r} 8{,}712 \\ \times \quad 4 \\ \hline \end{array}$$

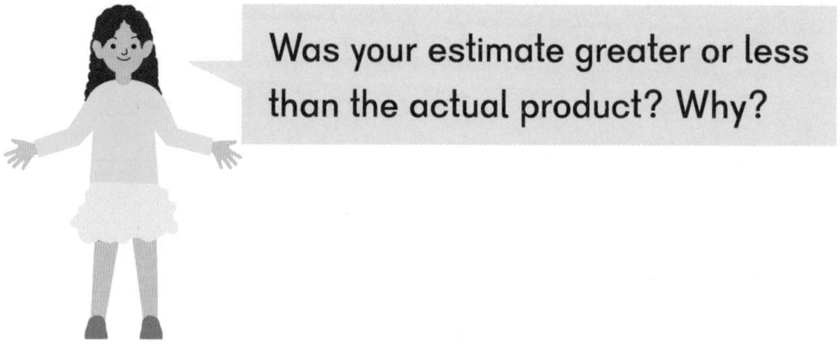

2 Estimate the product of 6 and 5,102. Then find the actual product.

(a) 5,102 × 6

↓

______ × 6 = ______

(b)
$$\begin{array}{r} 5{,}102 \\ \times \quad 6 \\ \hline \end{array}$$

3 Estimate the products. Then find the actual products.

(a) 3,290 × 3

(b) 4,316 × 2

(c) 1,803 × 4

(d) 1,563 × 3

(e) 1,603 × 6

(f) 3 × 9,332

(g) 8,007 × 9

(h) 7 × 6,114

(i) 4 × 4,512

(j) 8,310 × 8

4 An apartment costs $1,550 a month to rent. How much does it cost to rent it for 6 months?

5 A hotel wants to build an outdoor pool and an indoor pool. An outdoor pool costs $6,242. An indoor pool costs 3 times as much to build. How much will it cost to build both pools?

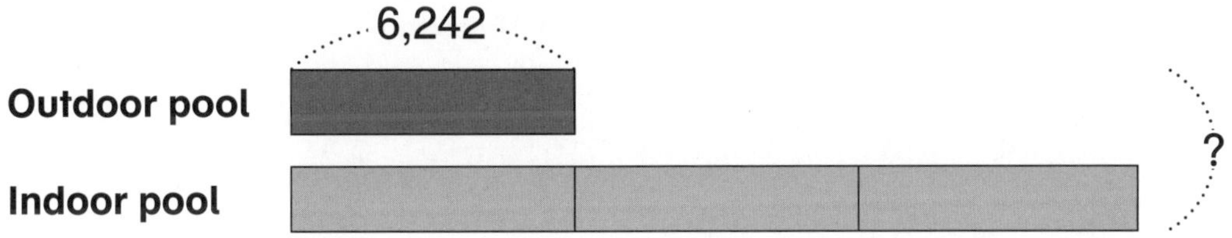

1 unit ⟶ 6,242
4 units ⟶ 4 × 6,242 = ______

It will cost $______ to build both pools.

Exercise 2 • page 69

Think

The bakers at a bakery made 3,423 muffins. They made 5 times as many rolls as muffins. How many rolls did they make?

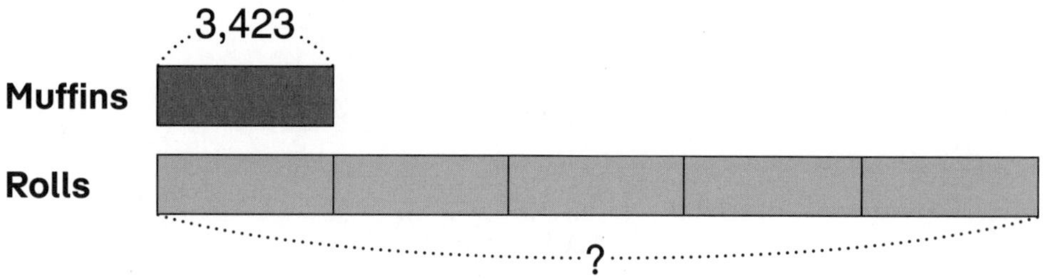

Learn

3,423 × 5

I used 3,000 × 5 to estimate the number of rolls. The answer will be more than my estimate.

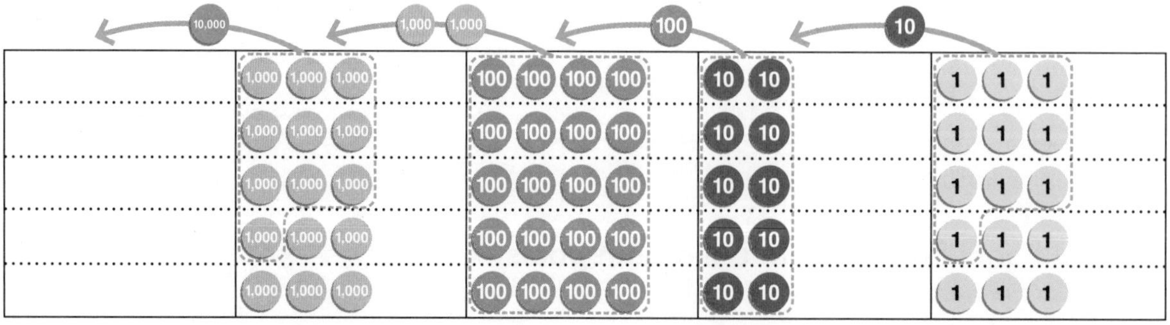

3,000 × 5 400 × 5 20 × 5 3 × 5

$$\begin{array}{rcccc} & & & \mathbf{1} & \\ & 3, & 4 & 2 & 3 \\ \times & & & & 5 \\ \hline & & & & \mathbf{5} \end{array}$$

Multiply the ones by 5.
3 ones × 5 = 15 ones
= 1 ten 5 ones

$$\begin{array}{rcccc} & & \mathbf{1} & 1 & \\ & 3, & 4 & 2 & 3 \\ \times & & & & 5 \\ \hline & & & \mathbf{1} & 5 \end{array}$$

Multiply the tens by 5.
Then add in the regrouped ten.
(2 tens × 5) + 1 ten = 11 tens
= 1 hundred 1 ten

$$\begin{array}{rcccc} & \mathbf{2} & 1 & 1 & \\ & 3, & 4 & 2 & 3 \\ \times & & & & 5 \\ \hline & & \mathbf{1} & 1 & 5 \end{array}$$

Multiply the hundreds by 5.
Then add the regrouped hundred.
(4 hundreds × 5) + 1 hundred
= 21 hundreds
= 2 thousands 1 hundred

$$\begin{array}{rcccc} & 2 & 1 & 1 & \\ & 3, & 4 & 2 & 3 \\ \times & & & & 5 \\ \hline \mathbf{1} & \mathbf{7}, & 1 & 1 & 5 \end{array}$$

Multiply the thousands by 5.
Then add in the regrouped thousands.
(3 thousands × 5) + 2 thousands
= 17 thousands

3,423 × 5 = 17,115

They made ______ rolls.

17,115 is close to my estimate of 15,000. The answer is reasonable.

Do

1 Estimate the product of 5,468 and 7. Then find the actual product.

(a) 5,468 × 7

↓

☐ × 7 = ☐

(b)

$$\begin{array}{r} 5{,}468 \\ \times \quad 7 \\ \hline \square \end{array}$$

2 Estimate the products. Then find the actual products.

(a) 4,958 × 2

(b) 6,269 × 4

(c) 5 × 7,635

(d) 9,057 × 8

(e) 1,285 × 6

(f) 9 × 7,219

(g) 9,999 × 9

(h) 16,879 × 7

3 A farm sold 3,489 duck eggs. It sold 4 times as many chicken eggs as duck eggs. How many more chicken eggs than duck eggs did it sell?

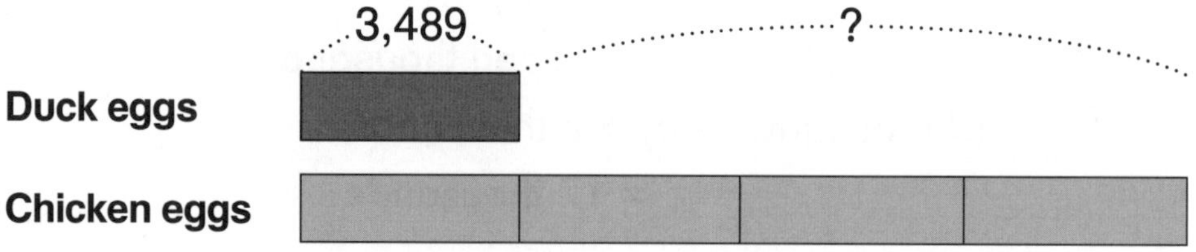

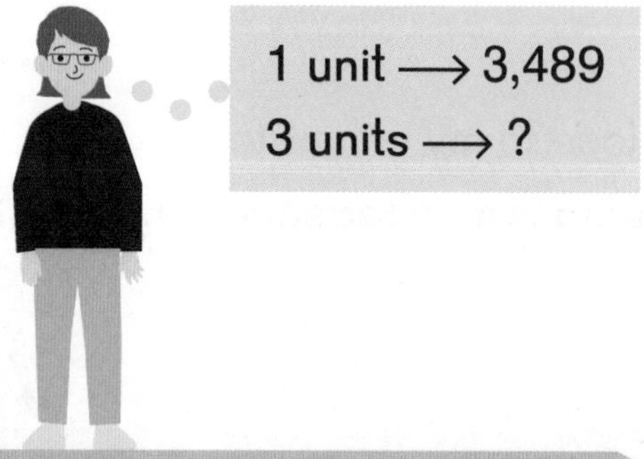

Exercise 3 • page 73

1 Multiply.

(a) 4 × 320

(b) 2,500 × 4

(c) 5 × 6,200

(d) 1,200 × 7

(e) 34,000 × 6

(f) 4 × 59

(g) 5 × 99

(h) 3 × 299

2 Estimate the products. Then find the actual products.

(a) 375 × 4

(b) 6 × 1,072

(c) 6 × 289

(d) 4,309 × 7

(e) 5,876 × 5

(f) 9 × 5,845

(g) 16,479 × 2

(h) 3 × 34,145

3

Ms. Green is buying 460 cups for a restaurant. Each cup costs $7. She estimated the cost by multiplying 500 by 7. When she calculated the actual cost as $3,920, she knew immediately that she made a mistake. How did she know? What error did she make?

4. Martin wants to save at least $2,000. If he saves $435 a month for 5 months, will he meet his goal?

5. There are 800 Ayrshire cows on a farm. There are twice as many Holstein cows as Ayrshire cows. There are 7 times as many Jersey cows as Ayrshire cows.

(a) How many cows are there altogether?

(b) How many more Jersey cows than Ayshire cows are there?

6. Mr. Gopal bought a rowboat and a motorboat. The rowboat cost $1,860. The motorboat cost 5 times as much as the rowboat.

(a) Estimate the total amount he paid for both boats altogether.

(b) Find the actual total amount he paid for both boats.

7 Ms. Chen saved \$445 a month for 6 months. She bought a motor scooter for \$1,899. How much money does she have left?

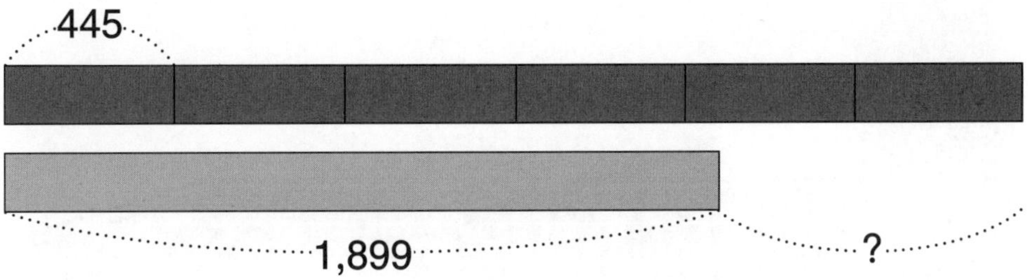

8 A farmer has twice as many cows as goats. After he sold 320 cows, he had 35 more goats than cows. How many cows and goats did he have in total at first?

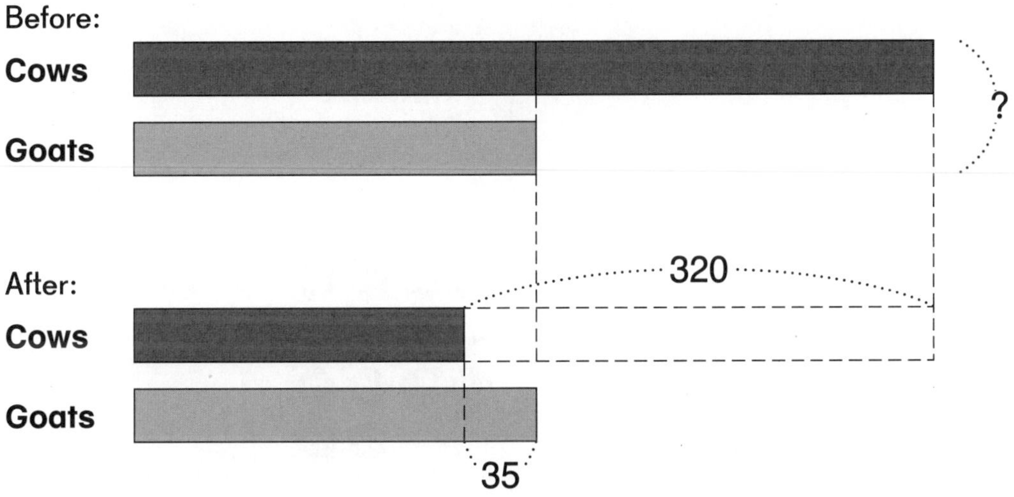

1 unit ⟶ 320 − 35
3 units ⟶ ?

Exercise 4 • page 77

Lesson 5
Multiplying by a Multiple of 10

5

Think

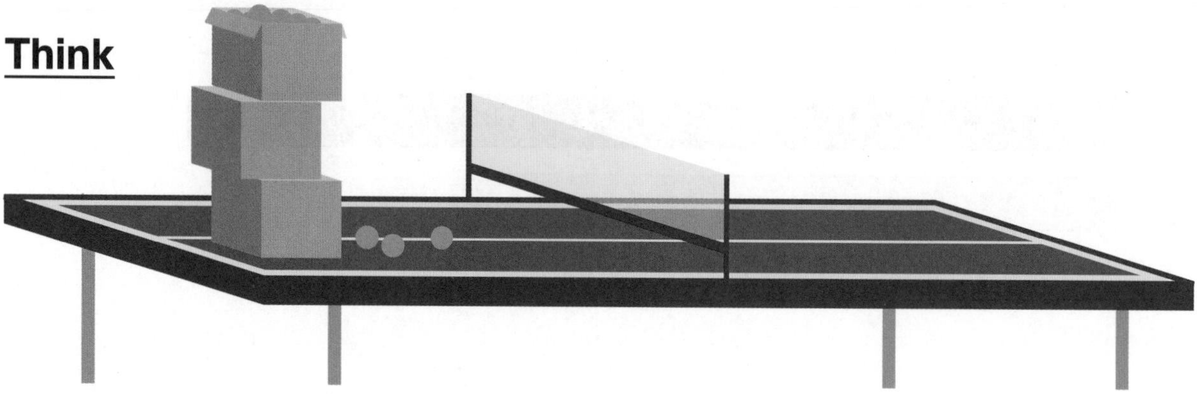

There are 34 ping pong balls in one box. How many ping pong balls are in 20 boxes?

Learn

34 × 20

Method 1

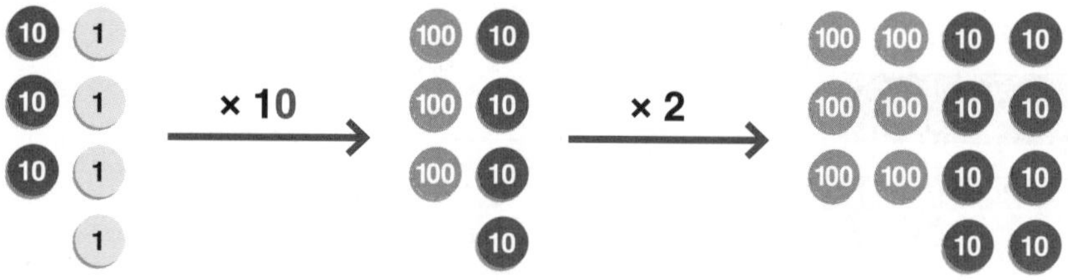

34 —× 10→ 340 —× 2→ 680

$$34 \times 20 = 34 \times 10 \times 2$$
$$= 340 \times 2$$

Method 2

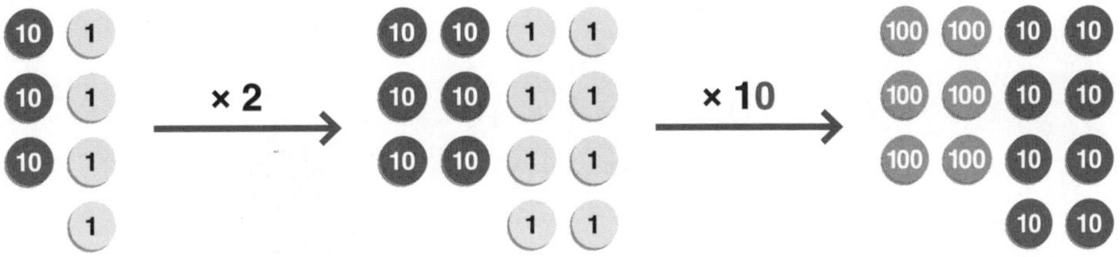

$$34 \xrightarrow{\times 2} 68 \xrightarrow{\times 10} 680$$

$34 \times 20 = 34 \times 2 \times 10$
$= 68 \times 10$

Method 3

34×2 tens $= 68$ tens
$= 680$

$34 \times 20 = 34 \times 10 \times 2$, so we can write a 0 in the ones place first, then multiply 34 by 2.

$$\begin{array}{r} 34 \\ \times\ 20 \\ \hline 0 \end{array} \longrightarrow \begin{array}{r} 34 \\ \times\ 20 \\ \hline 680 \end{array}$$

There are ______ ping pong balls in 20 boxes.

Do

1 Find the product of 60 and 70.

$60 \times 70 =$ ____

> $60 \times 70 = 60 \times 7 \times 10$
> $= 420 \times 10$

2 Find the product of 32 and 40.

$32 \times 40 = 32 \times$ ____ $\times 10$

$=$ ____ $\times 10$

$=$ ____

3 Find the product of 25 and 30.

25×3 tens $=$ ____ tens

$=$ ____

4 Find the values.

(a) 68×90

$$\begin{array}{r} 6\ 8 \\ \times \quad 9\ 0 \\ \hline \square\,\square\,\square\ 0 \end{array}$$

(b) 70×78

$$\begin{array}{r} 7\ 8 \\ \times \quad 7\ 0 \\ \hline \square\,\square\,\square\,\square \end{array}$$

5 Multiply 600 by 70.

600 × 70 = ____

600 × 70 = 600 × 7 × 10
= 4,200 × 10

6 Find the product of 150 and 40.

150 × 40 = 150 × ____ × 10

= ____ × 10

= ____

7 Multiply.

286 × 30

```
    2  8  6
×      3  0
-----------
   __ __ __ 0
```

We can write the regrouped digit above the number we will multiply next, to help remember to add them.

```
  2 1
  286
×  30
-----
```

8 Multiply.

(a) 90 × 80 (b) 20 × 56 (c) 75 × 60

(d) 58 × 30 (e) 50 × 400 (f) 70 × 800

(g) 410 × 80 (h) 620 × 30 (i) 60 × 572

Exercise 5 • page 80

Lesson 6
Multiplying by a 2-Digit Number — Part 1

6

Think

There are 24 onions in each box.
How many onions are in 12 boxes?

Learn

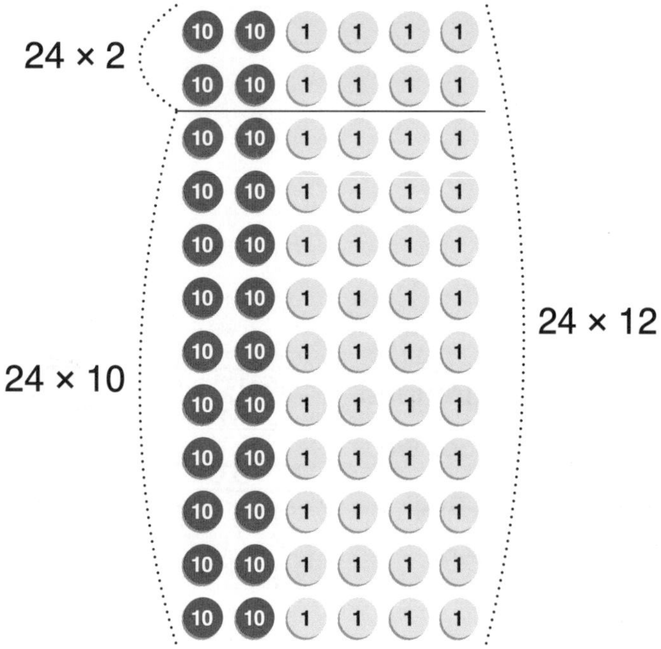

Multiply 24 by 2.

$$\begin{array}{rrr} & 2 & 4 \\ \times & 1 & 2 \\ \hline & \mathbf{4} & \mathbf{8} \end{array}$$

Multiply 24 by 10.

$$\begin{array}{rrr} & 2 & 4 \\ \times & 1 & 2 \\ \hline & 4 & 8 \\ \mathbf{2} & \mathbf{4} & 0 \\ \hline \end{array}$$

Add the products.

$$\begin{array}{rrrl} & 2 & 4 & \\ \times & 1 & 2 & \\ \hline & 4 & 8 & \longleftarrow 24 \times 2 \\ 2 & 4 & 0 & \longleftarrow 24 \times 10 \\ \hline \mathbf{2} & \mathbf{8} & \mathbf{8} & \end{array}$$

There are ______ onions in 12 boxes.

Do

1 Multiply 32 by 24.

```
      3  2
×     2  4
----------
   ☐  ☐  ☐   ← 32 × 4
   ☐  ☐  ☐   ← 32 × 20
----------
   ☐  ☐  ☐
```

To multiply 32 by 2 tens, we can first write 0 in the ones place, then find 32 × 2.

```
     32
×    24
-------
    128
    ☐ 0
    ↑
 32 × 2
```

2 Multiply 45 by 17.

```
      4  5
×     1  7
----------
   ☐  ☐  ☐   ← 45 × 7
   ☐  ☐  ☐   ← 45 × 10
----------
   ☐  ☐  ☐
```

We can write the regrouped digit above, to help remember to add it in later.

```
      3
     45
×    17
-------
    ☐ 5
```

3 Multiply 58 by 49.

```
         5  8
×        4  9
-------------
      ☐  ☐  ☐   ← 58 × 9
   ☐  ☐  ☐  ☐   ← 58 × 40
-------------
   ☐  ☐  ☐  ☐
```

We can write the regrouped digits on top.

```
      3
      7
     58
×    49
-------
    522
   ☐ 20
```

4 (a) Estimate the product of 37 and 48.

37 × 48
↓ ↓
40 × 50 = ☐

Will this estimate be greater than or less than the product?

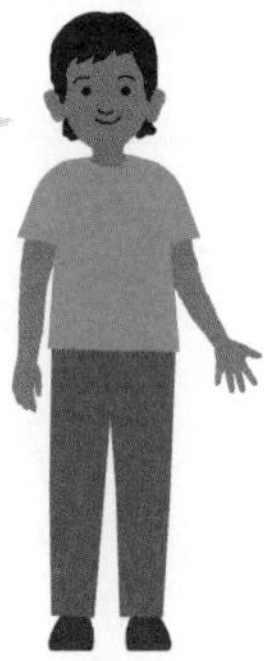

(b) Find the product of 37 and 48.

			3	7
×			4	8
		☐	☐	☐
	☐	☐	☐	☐
	☐	☐	☐	☐

Compare your answer to the estimate. Is your answer reasonable?

5 Estimate the products. Then find the actual products.

(a) 16 × 14 (b) 43 × 19 (c) 23 × 26

(d) 24 × 81 (e) 32 × 48 (f) 72 × 28

(g) 65 × 82 (h) 94 × 79 (i) 55 × 77

6

Dexter harvested 62 chanterelle mushrooms. He harvested 39 times as many morel mushrooms as chanterelles. How many morels did he harvest?

Exercise 6 • page 82

Multiplying by a 2-Digit Number — Part 2

Think

A mixer costs $212. A bakery is buying 13 mixers.
How much will it spend on mixers?

Learn

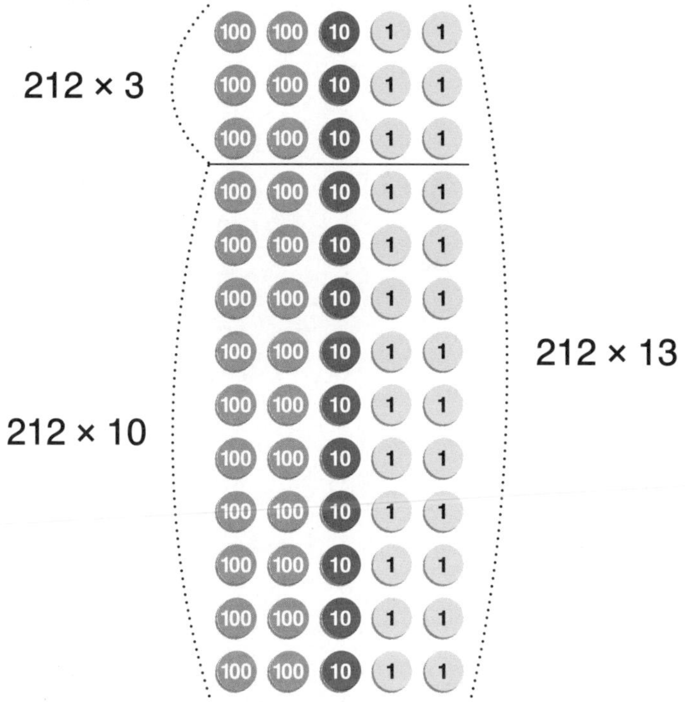

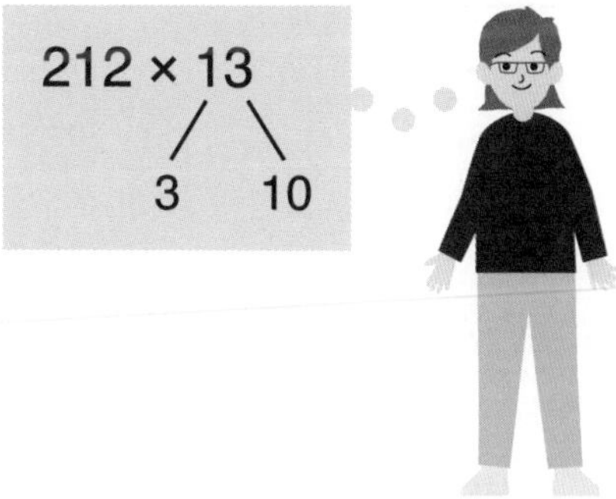

Multiply 212 by 3.

		2	1	2
×			1	3
		6	**3**	**6**

Multiply 212 by 10.

		2	1	2
×			1	3
		6	3	6
	2	**1**	**2**	**0**

Add the products.

		2	1	2	
×			1	3	
		6	3	6	⟵ 212 × 3
	2	1	2	0	⟵ 212 × 10
	2	**7,**	**5**	**6**	

It will spend $ ____ on mixers.

Do

1 Multiply 132 by 32.

```
     1 3 2
×      3 2
----------
    ☐ ☐ ☐   ← 132 × 2
  ☐ ☐ ☐ ☐   ← 132 × 30
----------
  ☐ ☐ ☐ ☐
```

To multiply by tens, we can first write a 0 in the ones place.

```
    132
×    32
-------
    264
   ☐☐0
```

132 × 3

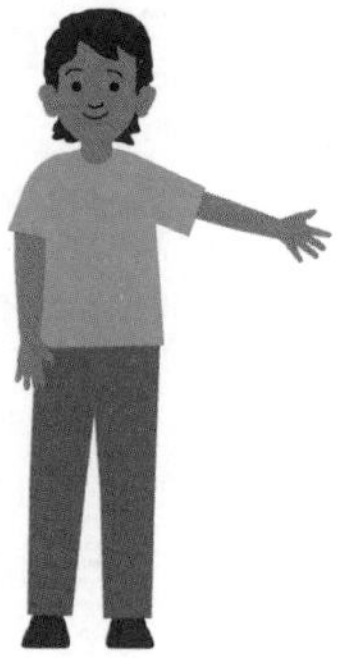

2 Multiply 603 by 25.

```
      6 0 3
×       2 5
-----------
    ☐ ☐ ☐ ☐   ← 603 × 5
  ☐ ☐ ☐ ☐ ☐   ← 603 × 20
-----------
  ☐ ☐ ☐ ☐ ☐
```

We can write the regrouped digits on top.

```
     1
    603
×    25
-------
   ☐☐☐5
```

3 Multiply 489 by 57.

```
      4 8 9
×       5 7
-----------
    ☐ ☐ ☐ ☐   ← 489 × 7
  ☐ ☐ ☐ ☐ ☐   ← 489 × 50
-----------
  ☐ ☐ ☐ ☐ ☐
```

We can write the regrouped digits on top.

```
    4 4
    6 6
    489
×    57
-------
   3423
  ☐450
```

4 (a) Estimate the product of 687 and 34.

687 × 34

↓ ↓

700 × 30 = ___

(b) Find the product of 687 and 34.

		6	8	7
×			3	4
	☐	☐	☐	☐
☐	☐	☐	☐	☐
☐	☐	☐	☐	☐

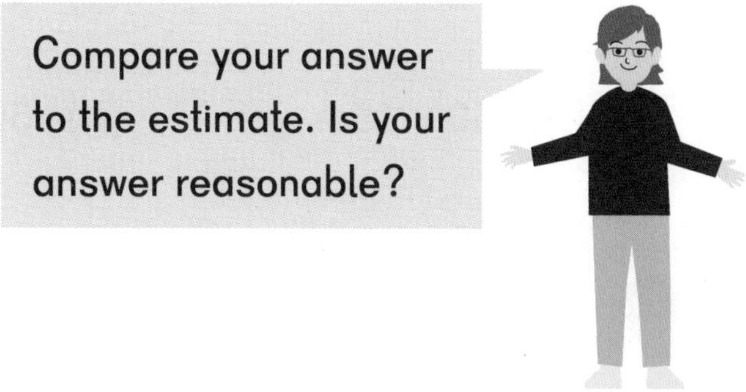

5 Estimate the products. Then find the actual products.

(a) 104 × 23

(b) 236 × 32

(c) 501 × 46

(d) 246 × 45

(e) 62 × 549

(f) 43 × 327

(g) 495 × 78

(h) 888 × 88

6 A skateboarding camp costs $155 a week per student. What is the cost for 28 students for one week?

Exercise 7 • page 86

1 Multiply.

(a) 83 × 3 (b) 90 × 90 (c) 10 × 560

(d) 3,200 × 4 (e) 299 × 5 (f) 54 × 20

(g) 50 × 15 (h) 50 × 800 (i) 5,000 × 70

2 Estimate the products. Then find the actual products.

(a) 18 × 45 (b) 43 × 77 (c) 72 × 63

(d) 87 × 34 (e) 99 × 99 (f) 206 × 81

(g) 713 × 62 (h) 75 × 409 (i) 864 × 98

3 A bag of flour weighs 28 lb. How much do 50 such bags of flour weigh?

4 A jeweler maker sold 48 necklaces for $895 each.

(a) Estimate to find out whether he received more than or less than $45,000 from selling the necklaces.

(b) How much money did he receive from selling the necklaces?

5 The students in the accounting club are helping the gym teacher buy basketball equipment by calculating the costs.

Item	Number Needed	Cost for 1
Backboard	4	\$550
Backboard adjustment system	4	\$1,200
Basketball	15	\$34

How much will it cost to buy all of the equipment?

6 A sailboat costs \$22,299 to buy and \$358 a month to dock at the marina. Estimate to find out if \$25,000 is enough to buy and dock the boat for the first year.

7 There are 1,682 ducks on a farm. There are twice as many rabbits as ducks. There are three times as many chickens as rabbits.

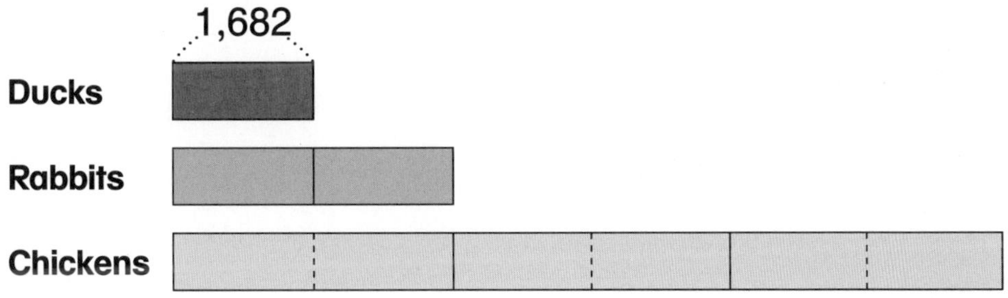

(a) How many ducks, rabbits, and chickens are there altogether?

(b) How many more chickens and ducks altogether are there than rabbits?

8

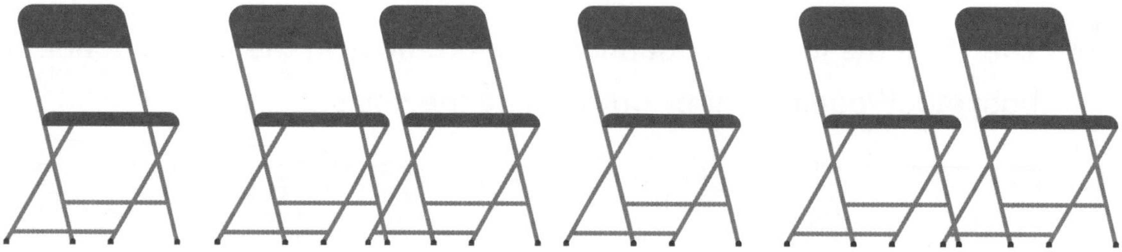

A folding chair costs $35. A school wants to buy enough chairs for 23 rows of 48 chairs. How much will the chairs cost altogether?

9 Last year, Jackelyn earned $780 a month. This year, she will have earned twice as much a month as last year. How much more will she earn at the end of this year than last year?

10 There are twice as many nails as screws in a bin. If 510 of the nails and 75 of the screws are used, there will be the same number of nails as screws. How many nails were in the bin to start with?

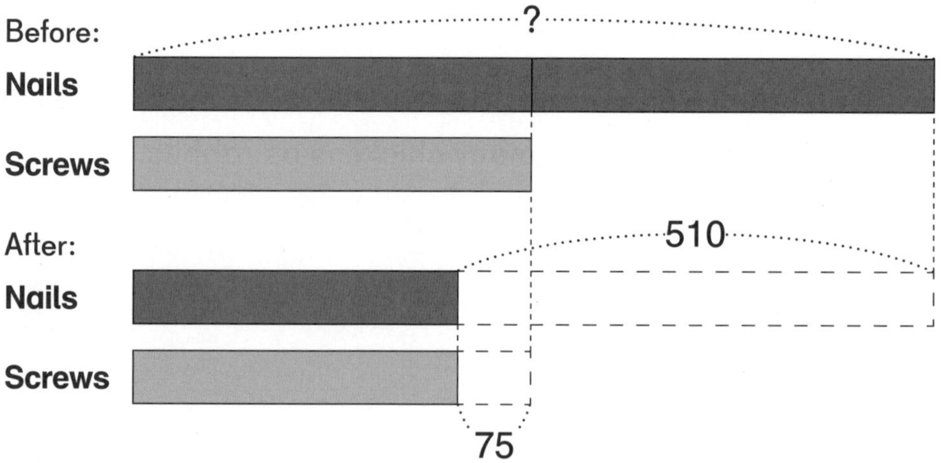

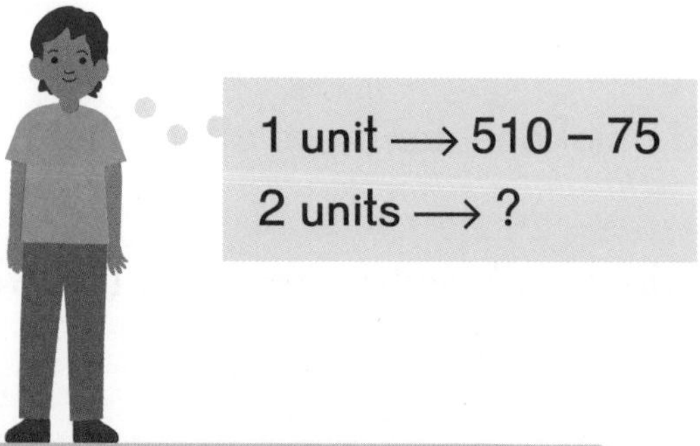

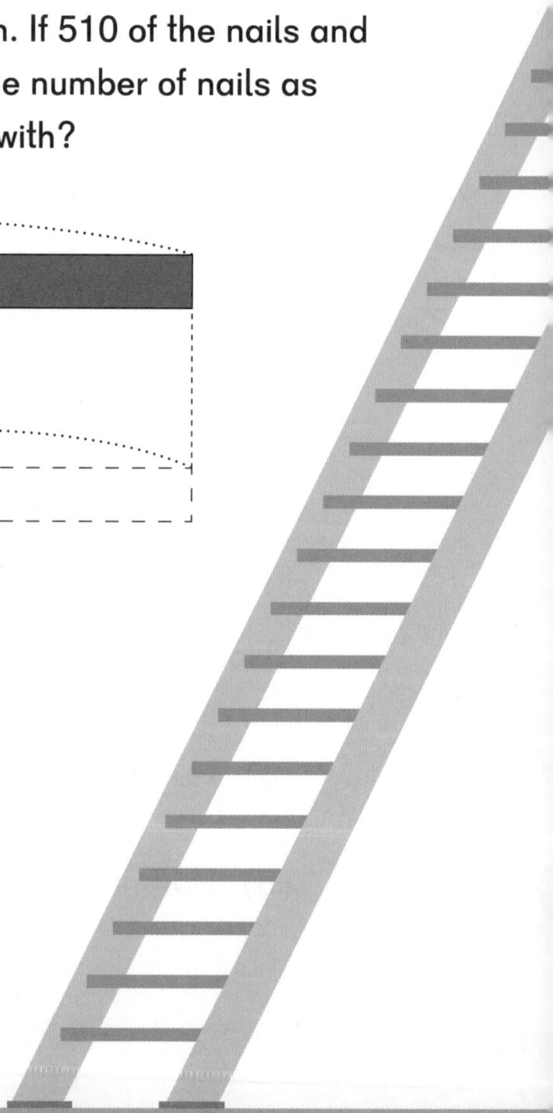

Exercise 8 • page 90

Chapter 5

Division

Lesson 1
Mental Math for Division

Think

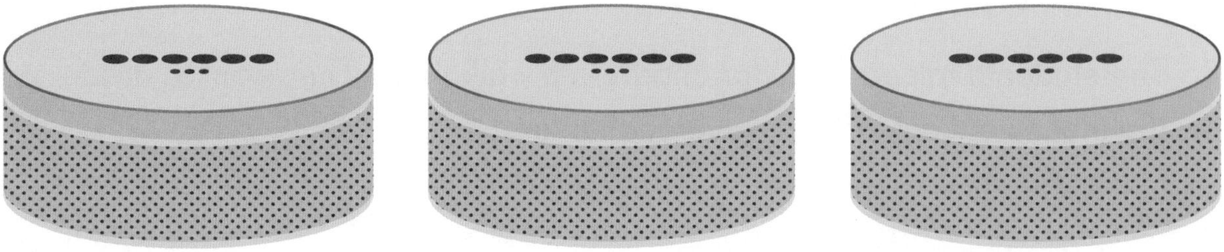

3 identical smart speakers cost $420.
How much does each smart speaker cost?

How can we use mental math to solve?

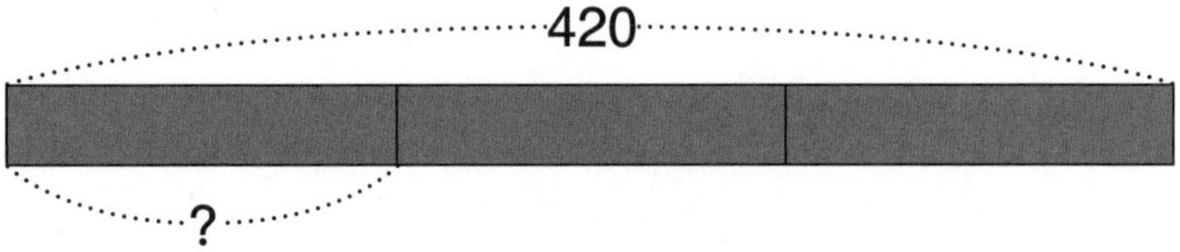

Learn

420 ÷ 3

30 tens ÷ 3 = 10 tens
12 tens ÷ 3 = 4 tens
42 tens ÷ 3 = 14 tens
42**0** ÷ 3 = 14**0**

42 ÷ 3
30   12

I can just divide 42 by 3, but the answer will be in tens.

Each smart speaker costs $ ______ .

What other ways could we split 420 so we can divide easily?

Do

1 Use mental calculation.

(a) 56 tens ÷ 8 = ____ tens

560 ÷ 8 = ____

(b) 56 hundreds ÷ 8 = ____ hundreds

5,600 ÷ 8 = ____

(c) 56 thousands ÷ 8 = ____ thousands

56,000 ÷ 8 = ____

2 Use mental calculation.

(a) 540 ÷ 6 = ____

(b) 5,400 ÷ 6 = ____

(c) 54,000 ÷ 6 = ____

3 Divide 800 by 5.

50 tens ÷ 5 = ____ tens = ____

30 tens ÷ 5 = ____ tens = ____

80 tens ÷ 5 = ____ tens = ____

4 Divide 96,000 by 6.

60,000 ÷ 6 = ____

36,000 ÷ 6 = ____

96,000 ÷ 6 = ____

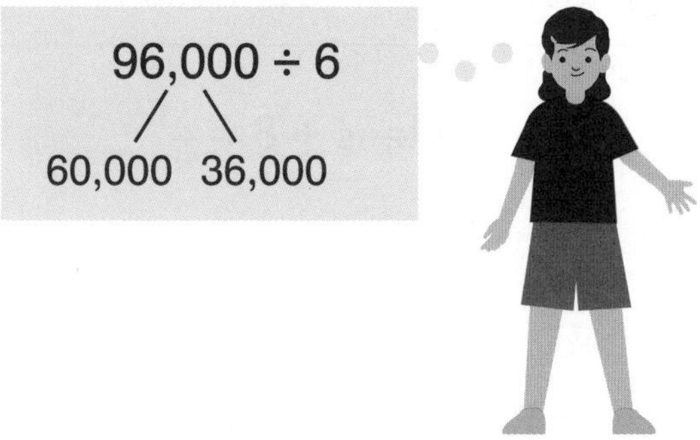

5 Use mental calculation to find the values.

(a) 480 ÷ 6 (b) 840 ÷ 7 (c) 540 ÷ 3 (d) 650 ÷ 5

(e) 6,300 ÷ 9 (f) 7,600 ÷ 4 (g) 8,400 ÷ 6 (h) 12,000 ÷ 8

6 A full-size fridge costs $570. It costs 3 times as much as a compact fridge. How much does the compact fridge cost?

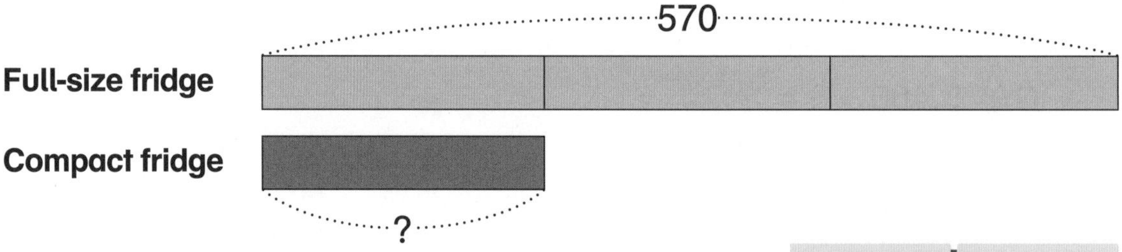

3 units ⟶ 570
1 unit ⟶ 570 ÷ 3 = ____

The compact fridge costs $____.

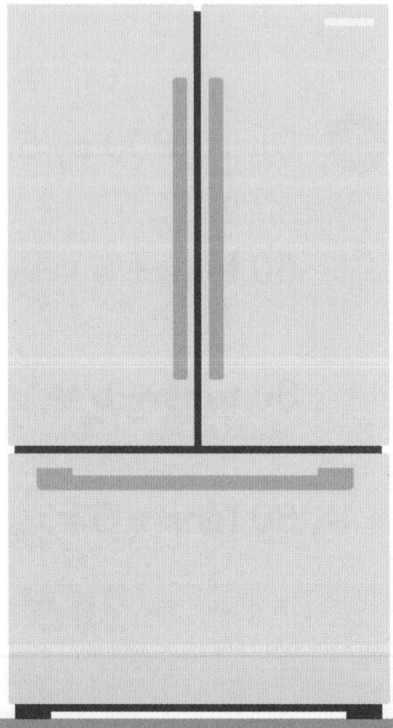

Exercise 1 • page 95

Think

Emma baked 143 cookies. She wants to put an equal amount of as many cookies as possible into 3 tins.

(a) Estimate the number of cookies that can go in each tin.

(b) Find the actual number of cookies that can go in each tin and the number of cookies that will be left over.

How do we estimate the answer to 143 ÷ 3?
100 ÷ 3 or 140 ÷ 3 are not easy to do mentally.

Learn

143 ÷ 3

12 and 15 are multiples of 3, so 120 and 150 are also multiples of 3. 143 is nearer to 150 than to 120.

(a) Estimate the quotient.

143 ÷ 3 → **120 ÷ 3**

143 ÷ 3 → **150 ÷ 3**

150 ÷ 3 = 50

143 ÷ 3 ≈ 50

Will the estimated quotient be greater than or less than the actual quotient?

(b) Divide 143 by 3.

Regroup the hundred and then divide the tens by 3.
14 tens ÷ 3 is ___ tens with ___ tens left over.

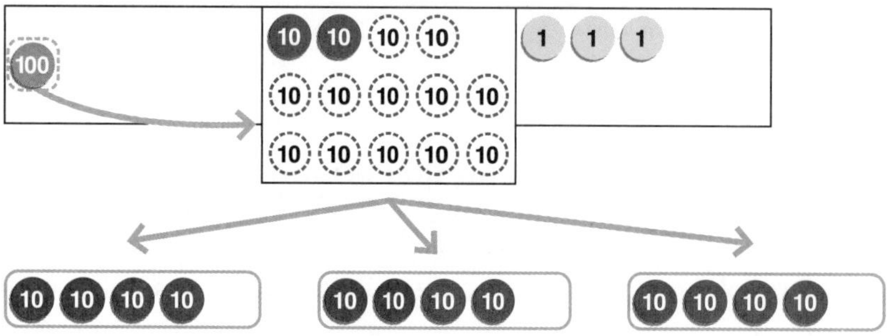

```
    4
3 ) 1 4 3
    1 2
      2
```

Regroup the remaining tens and then divide the ones by 3.
23 ones ÷ 3 is ___ ones with ___ ones left over.

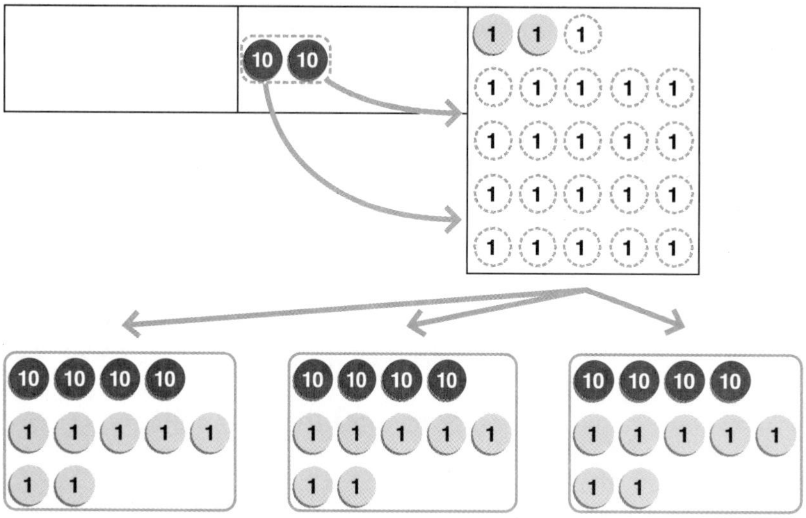

```
    4 7
3 ) 1 4 3
    1 2
      2 3
      2 1
        2
```

143 ÷ 3 is 47 with a remainder of 2.

Check: Does 47 × 3 + 2 = 143?

Each tin will get ___ cookies.

There will be ___ cookies left over.

We can use R to stand for **with a remainder of**.
143 ÷ 3 is 47 R 2.

Do

1 823 ÷ 3

(a) Estimate the value of 823 ÷ 3.

823 ÷ 3 → **6**00 ÷ 3

823 ÷ 3 → **9**00 ÷ 3

823 ÷ 3 ≈ ___

823 is closer to 900 than to 600. Will the estimate be greater than or less than the quotient?

(b) Divide 823 by 3.

```
    ___ ___ ___
3 ) 8   2   3      8 hundreds ÷ 3
    ___
    2   2          22 tens ÷ 3
    ___ ___
        1   3      13 ones ÷ 3
        ___ ___
            1
```

How do we know the quotient will be 3 digits instead of 2 digits?

823 ÷ 3 is ___ R 1.

Check: ___ × 3 + 1 = 823

Is your answer reasonable?

2 Estimate the value of 568 ÷ 9 and then find the value.

(a) 568 ÷ 9 → **540** ÷ 9, **630** ÷ 9

568 is nearer to 540 than 630.

568 ÷ 9 ≈ ____

(b)

```
     __ __
9 ) 5  6  8
   __ __
   ---------
      __ __
      __ __
   ---------
         __
```

568 ÷ 9 is ____ R ____

Check: ____ × 9 + 1 = 568

3 Estimate the value and then divide.

(a) 137 ÷ 5 (b) 875 ÷ 2 (c) 209 ÷ 3

(d) 685 ÷ 4 (e) 908 ÷ 7 (f) 819 ÷ 6

(g) 743 ÷ 8 (h) 688 ÷ 8 (i) 612 ÷ 7

Exercise 2 • page 97

Think

A company has 6,174 toys, which will be put in 4 boxes equally for shipment.

(a) About how many toys will go in each box?

(b) How many toys will go in each box? How many will be left over?

Learn

6,174 ÷ 4

(a) Estimate the value of 6,174 ÷ 4.

6,174 ÷ 4 → **4**,000 ÷ 4
6,174 ÷ 4 → **8**,000 ÷ 4

I know that 60 ÷ 4 = 15. I can get a closer estimate using **6,0**00 ÷ 4 = **1,5**00.

6,174 ÷ 4 ≈ ____

(b) Divide 6,174 by 4

Divide 6 thousands by 4.

6 thousands ÷ 4 is ____ thousand with ____ thousands left over.

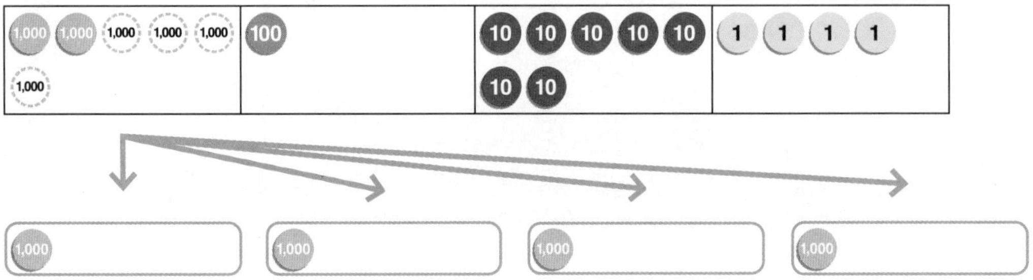

```
     1,
  4)6,174
    4
    -
    2
```

Regroup the remaining thousands, then divide 21 hundreds by 4.

21 hundreds ÷ 4 is ____ hundreds with ____ hundred left over.

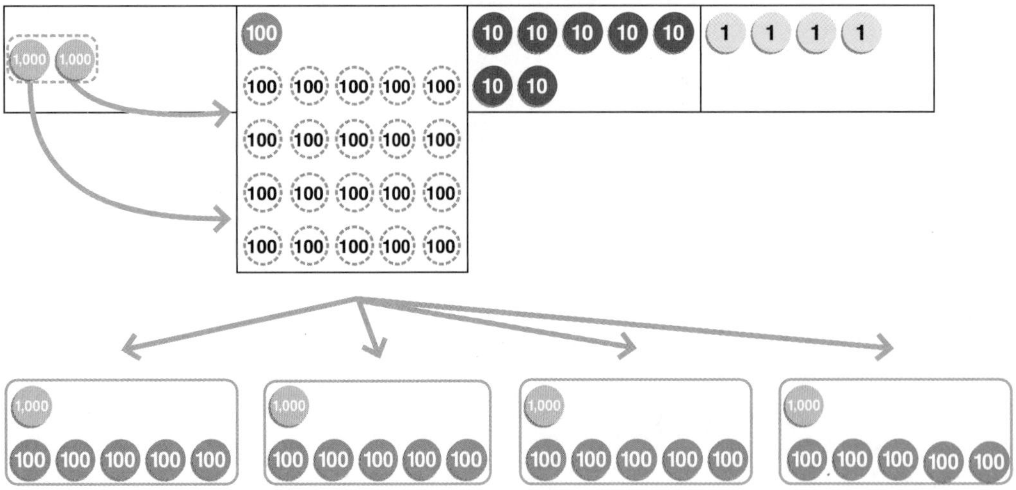

```
     1,5
  4)6,174
    4
    --
    21
    20
    --
     1
```

Regroup the remaining hundred, then divide 17 tens by 4.

17 tens ÷ 4 is ___ tens with ___ ten left over.

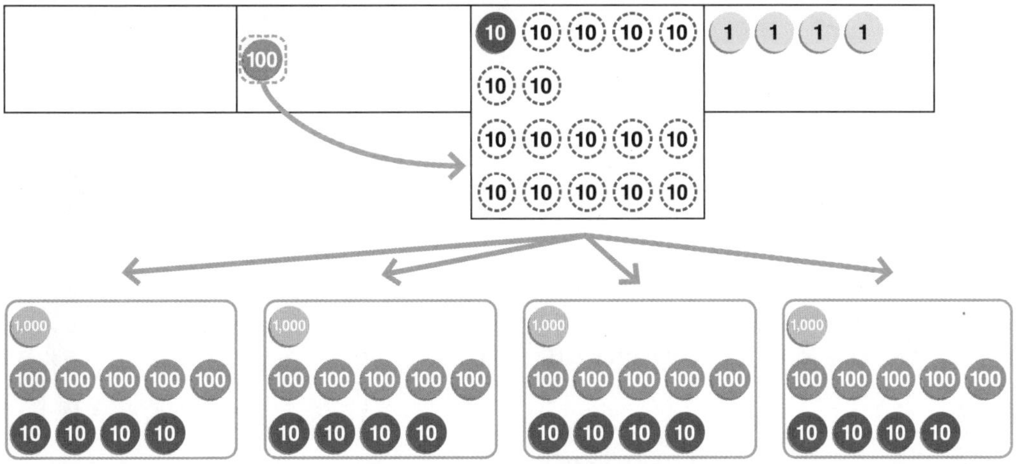

$$\begin{array}{r} 1{,}54 \\ 4\overline{)6{,}174} \\ 4 \\ \hline 21 \\ 20 \\ \hline 17 \\ 16 \\ \hline 1 \end{array}$$

Regroup the remaining ten, then divide 14 ones by 4.

14 ones ÷ 4 is ___ ones with ___ ones left over.

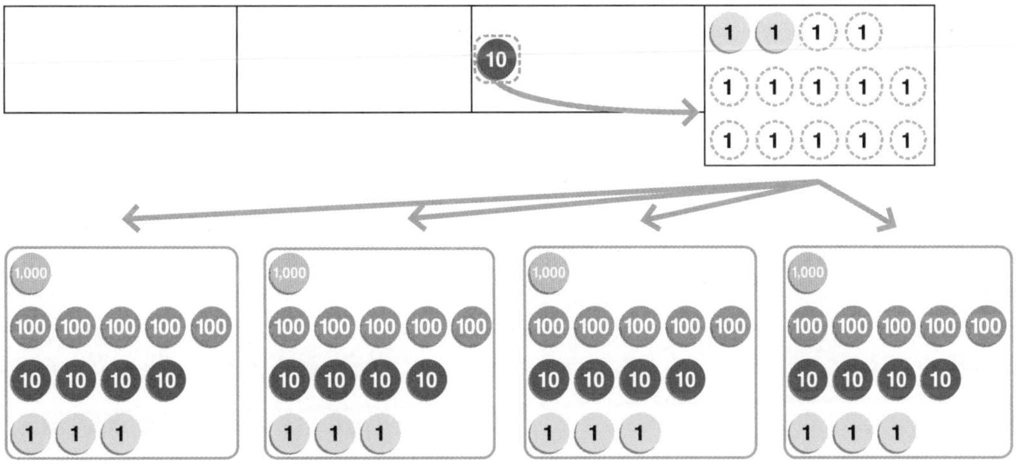

$$\begin{array}{r} 1{,}543 \\ 4\overline{)6{,}174} \\ 4 \\ \hline 21 \\ 20 \\ \hline 17 \\ 16 \\ \hline 14 \\ 12 \\ \hline 2 \end{array}$$

Each box will get ___ toys.

There will be ___ toys left over.

Check your answer. Does 1,543 × 4 + 2 = 6,174?

Do

1 Estimate the value and then divide 8,092 by 6.

(a) 8,092 ÷ 6 → **6**,000 ÷ 6 / **12**,000 ÷ 6

8,092 ÷ 6 ≈ ▢

(b)

```
     ▢ ▢ ▢ ▢
6 ) 8, 0 9 2     8 thousands ÷ 6
    ▢
    ---------
    2 0          20 hundreds ÷ 6
    ▢ ▢
    ---------
      2 9        29 tens ÷ 6
      ▢ ▢
    ---------
        5 2      52 ones ÷ 6
        ▢ ▢
    ---------
          ▢
```

2 Estimate the value and then divide 2,408 by 3.

(a) 2,408 ÷ 3 ≈ ▢

(b)

```
       ▢ ▢ ▢
3 ) 2, 4 0 8     24 hundreds ÷ 3
    ▢ ▢
    ---------
       0 0 8     8 ones ÷ 3
           ▢
    ---------
           ▢
```

3 Estimate the value and then divide 2,973 by 8.

(a) 2,973 ÷ 8 → **2,4**00 ÷ 8 / **3,2**00 ÷ 8

2,973 is nearer to 3,200 than 2,400.

2,973 ÷ 8 ≈ ______

(b) 2,973 ÷ 8 is ______ R ______.

4 Estimate the value and then divide 5,320 by 2.

(a) 5,320 ÷ 2 ≈ ______

5,000 ÷ 2 = ?

(b) 5,320 ÷ 2 = ______

5 Estimate the value and then divide.

(a) 8,160 ÷ 5

(b) 3,248 ÷ 8

(c) 2,827 ÷ 4

(d) 8,987 ÷ 7

(e) 6,878 ÷ 9

(f) 4,018 ÷ 2

4,018 ÷ 2 is easy to do mentally.
I don't even need to estimate.

Exercise 3 • page 101

1 Divide.

(a) $800 \div 4$ (b) $960 \div 3$ (c) $450 \div 5$

(d) $840 \div 7$ (e) $2{,}700 \div 3$ (f) $9{,}200 \div 2$

(g) $7{,}000 \div 5$ (h) $7{,}800 \div 6$ (i) $81{,}000 \div 3$

2 Estimate the value and then divide.

(a) $734 \div 5$ (b) $851 \div 4$ (c) $282 \div 6$

(d) $364 \div 8$ (e) $5{,}047 \div 3$ (f) $9{,}528 \div 8$

(g) $6{,}642 \div 7$ (h) $9{,}975 \div 2$ (i) $3{,}604 \div 9$

3 Karen wants to save $8,500 in 5 years. She wants to save the same amount each year. How much does she need to save each year?

4 A teacher has $580 to spend on compasses. Each compass costs $6.

(a) Estimate the number of compasses she can buy.

(b) Find the greatest number of compasses she can buy.

(c) How much money will she have left over if she buys that many?

5 Dion's goal is to raise $500 for the art club by selling hats for $6 each. What is the least number of hats he must sell to reach that goal?

6 Mei raised $408 for the art club by selling hats for $6 each. Estimate and then find the number of hats she sold.

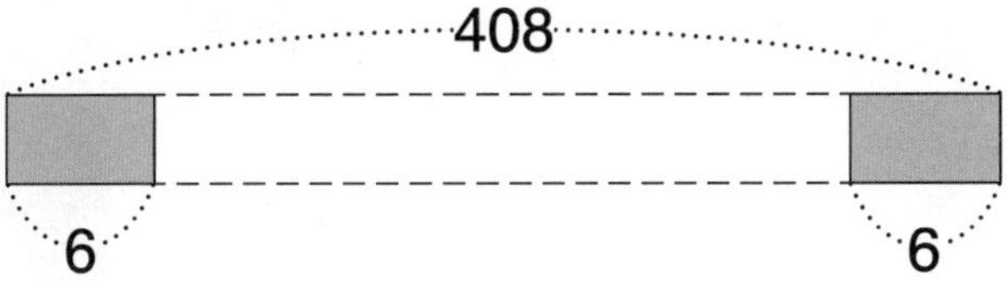

1 unit ⟶ 6
? units ⟶ 408

7 There are 4,115 people at a ball game. There are 4 times as many adults as there are children. Estimate and then find the number of children at the ball game.

8

There are 9,898 trees in a grove. There are twice as many grapefruit trees as lemon trees and twice as many orange trees as grapefruit trees. Estimate and then find the number of lemon trees.

Exercise 4 • page 105

Lesson 5
Word Problems

Think

Emma, Alex, and Sofia collected 3,045 pieces of trash in a beach clean-up project. Alex collected 230 more pieces of trash than Emma and 110 fewer pieces of trash than Sofia. How many pieces of trash did Alex collect?

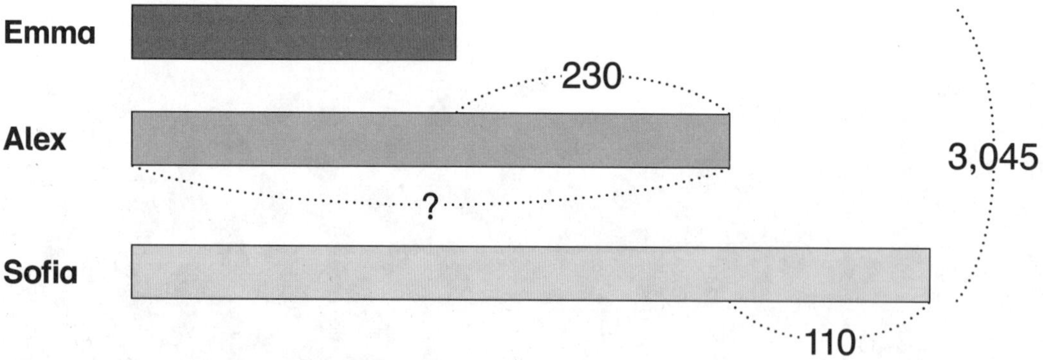

Which bar will I make 1 unit? How can I add or subtract to make equal units?

Learn

Method 1

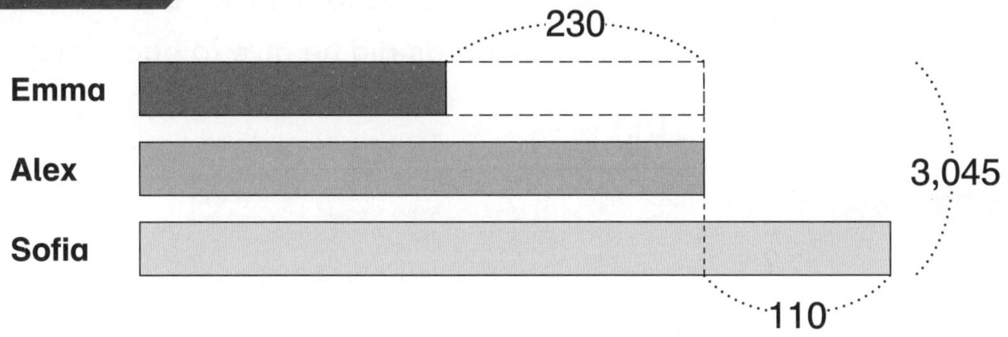

3 units $\longrightarrow$ 3,045 + 230 − 110 = 3,165

1 unit $\longrightarrow$ 3,165 ÷ 3 = ______

Method 2

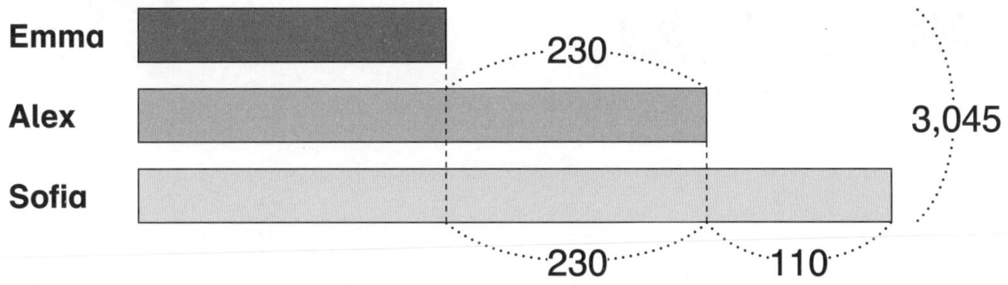

3 units $\longrightarrow$ 3,045 − 230 − 110 − 230 = 2,475

1 unit $\longrightarrow$ 2,475 ÷ 3 = 825

825 + 230 = ______

Alex collected ______ pieces of trash.

Whose bar was made 1 unit in each method?

Which method had fewer steps? Why?

Do

1 Dion had 1,180 trading cards. He kept 340 cards for himself and divided the rest equally among 5 friends. How many cards did he give to each friend?

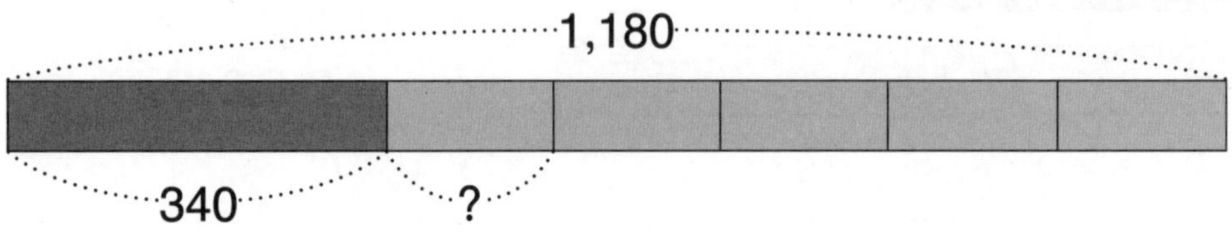

2 Mr. Lopez bought a table and 6 chairs. He spent $1,299. The table cost $284 more than one chair. How much did the table cost?

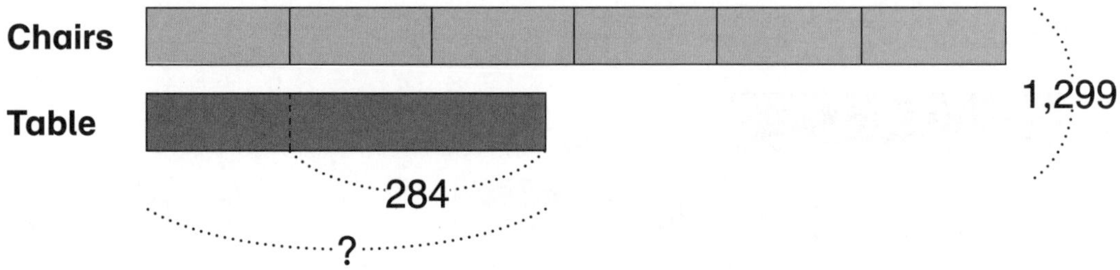

3 Mrs. Lopez bought 2 identical floor lamps and 3 identical table lamps for $505. Each table lamp costs $70 more than each floor lamp. How much did three table lamps cost altogether?

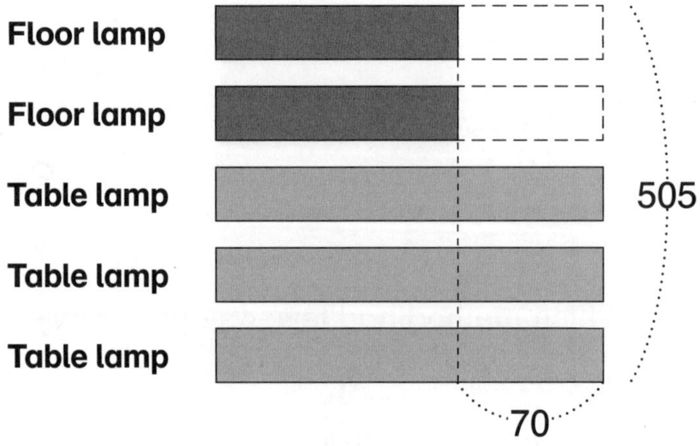

4 430 books are kept in 3 boxes. The second box has 25 fewer books than the first box and twice as many books as the third box. How many books are in the second box?

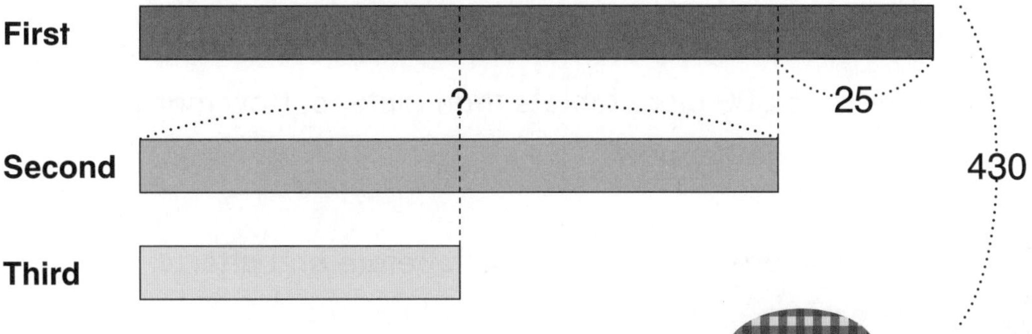

5 A vendor at the market is selling jam. She has 980 jars in total of huckleberry, blueberry, and peach jam. She has 75 fewer jars of blueberry jam than huckleberry jam. She has three times as many jars of peach jam than blueberry jam. How many jars of peach jam does she have?

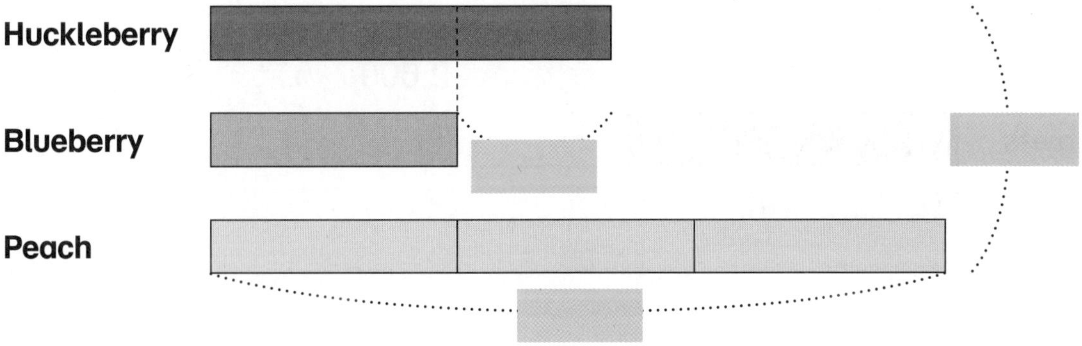

6 The sum of two numbers is 3,750. The second number is 180 less than twice the first number. What are the two numbers?

Exercise 5 • page 109

Challenging Word Problems

Think

A store had 3 times as many tablets as laptops in stock. After 2,600 tablets were sold, there were 500 more tablets than laptops. How many tablets and laptops are there altogether now?

We can draw a model for both before and after. The number of laptops does not change.

Learn

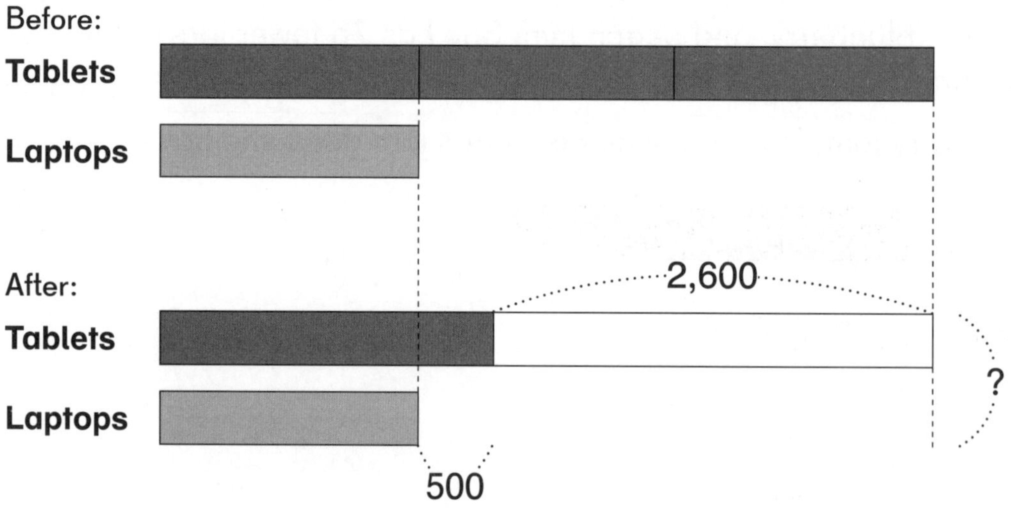

2 units ⟶ 2,600 + 500 = 3,100

3,100 + 500 = ______

There are ______ tablets and laptops now.

We could also find the value of 1 unit first.

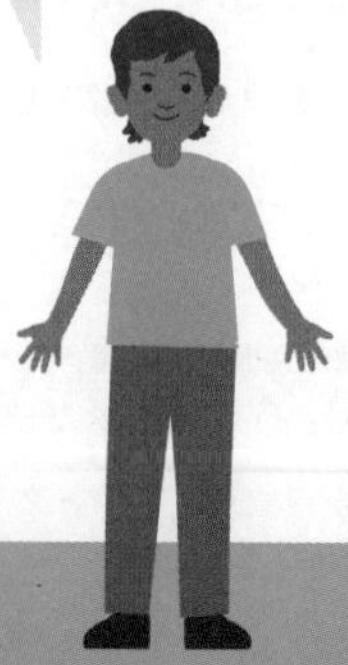

Do

1

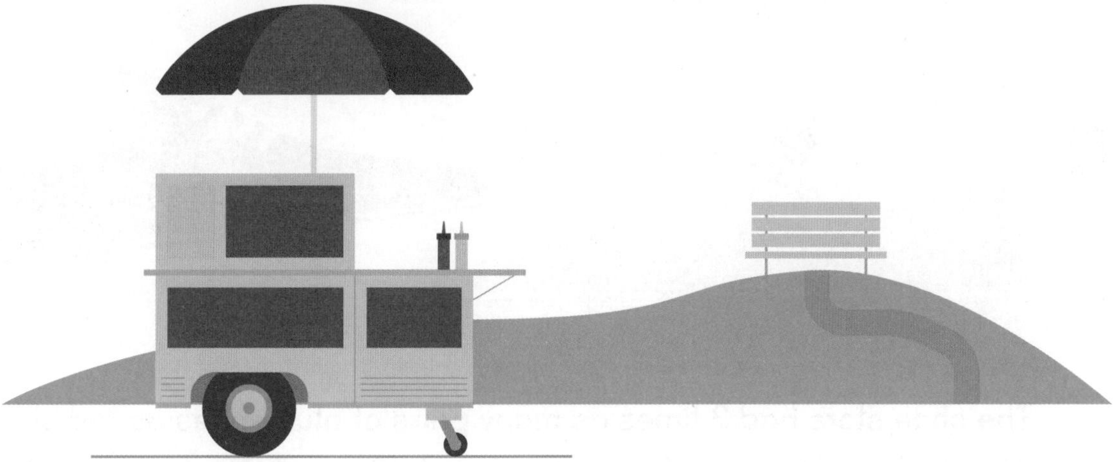

A vendor had 769 turkey and vegan hot dogs. After she sold 355 turkey hot dogs, she had 5 times as many vegan hot dogs as turkey hot dogs. How many vegan hot dogs does she have?

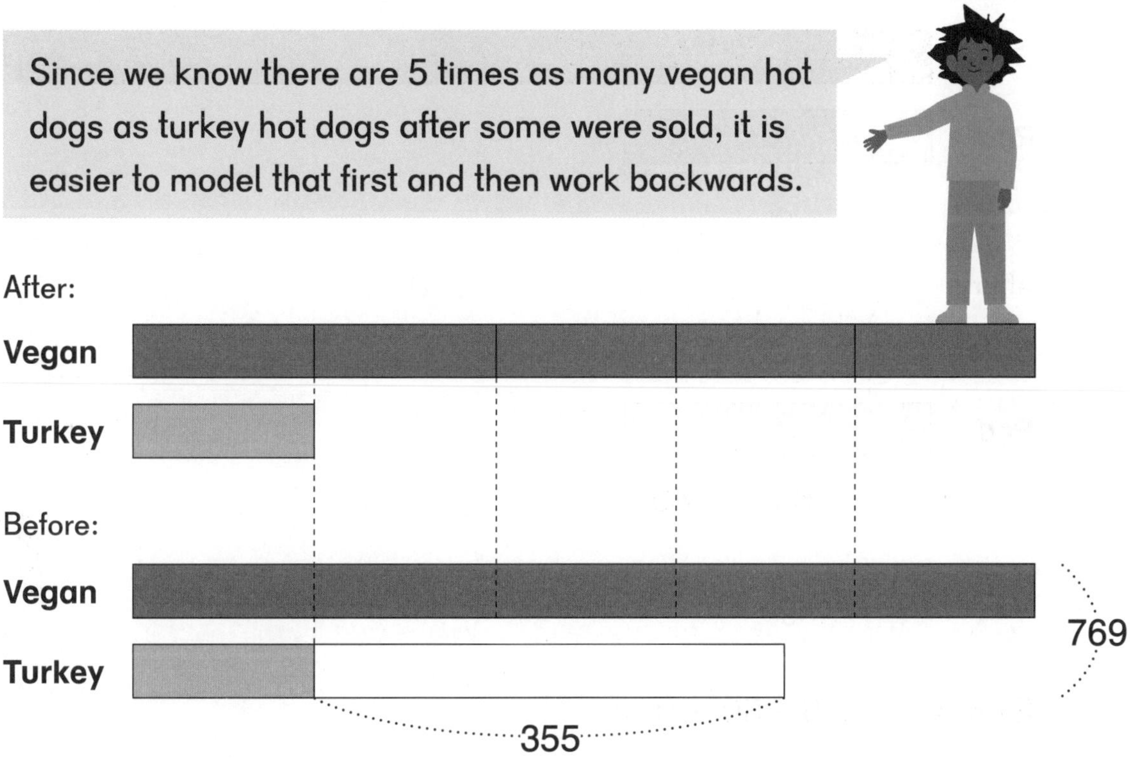

6 units ⟶ 769 − 355 = 414

1 unit ⟶ 414 ÷ 6 = ______

5 units ⟶ 5 × ______ = ______

She has ______ vegan hot dogs.

2

The shoe store had 3 times as many pairs of blue shoes as red shoes. After it sold 360 pairs of blue shoes and 40 pairs of red shoes, it had 60 more pairs of red shoes than blue shoes. How many pairs of blue shoes does the store have left?

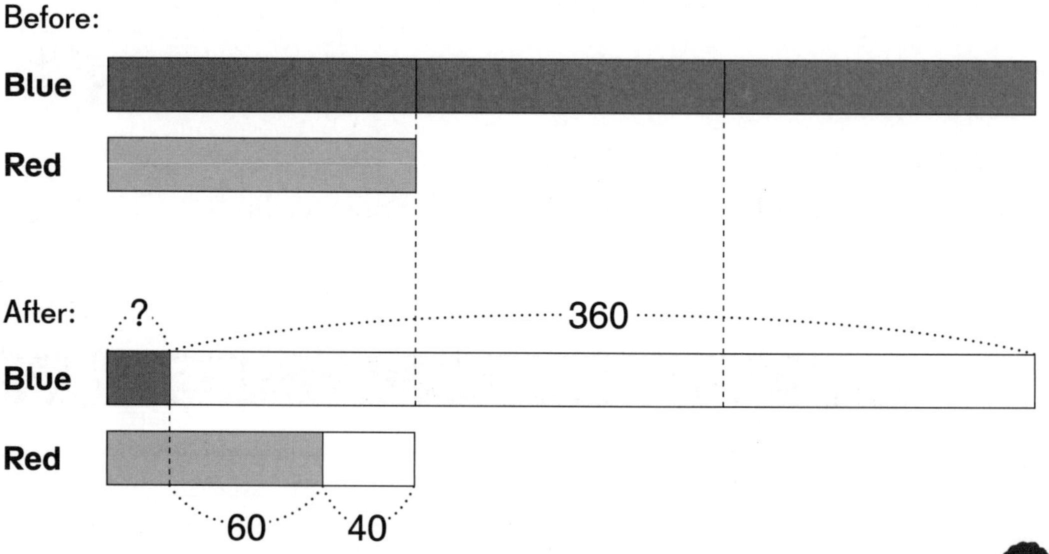

We have enough information to know the value of 2 units.

2 units ⟶ 360 – 60 – 40 = ____

1 unit ⟶ ____ ÷ 2 = ____

Now that we know the value of 1 unit, we can find the answer. What calculation will you use to find the number of pairs of blue shoes?

The store has ____ pairs of blue shoes left.

3 There were 4 times as many people living in North Town as people living in South Town. 360 people moved out of North Town. There are now 1,800 more people living in North Town than living in South Town. How many people are living in South Town?

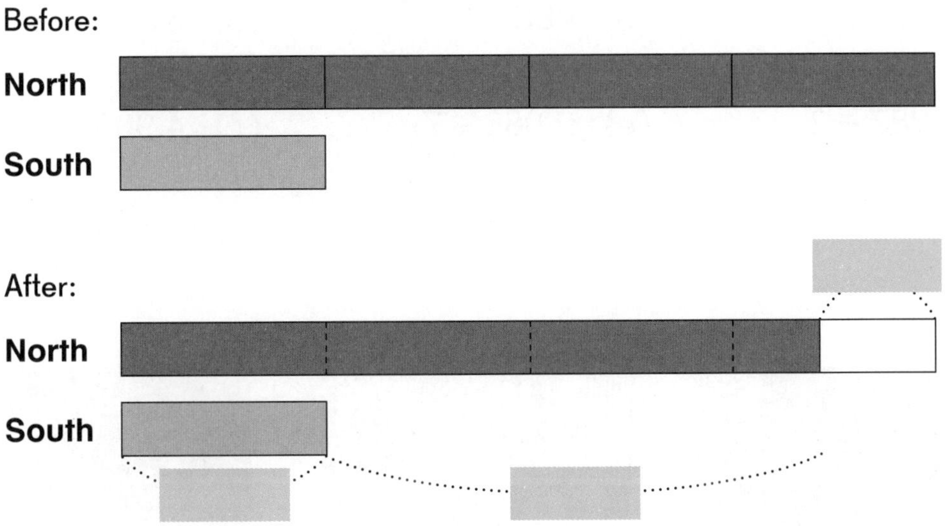

4

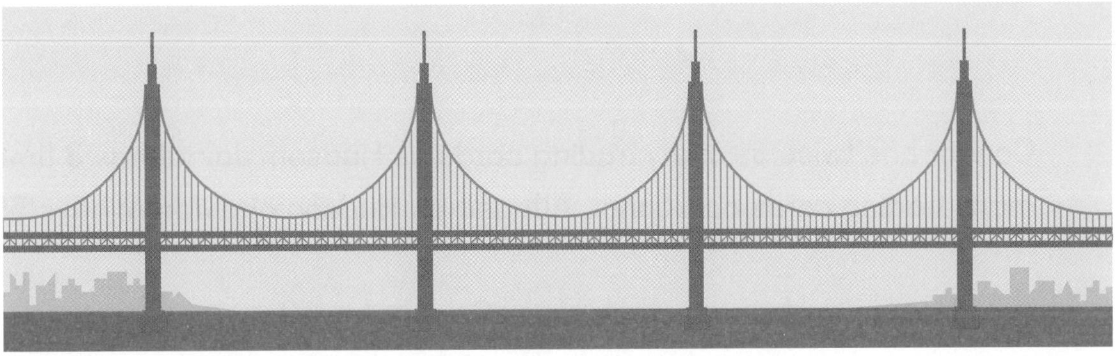

There were 4 times as many people living in East Town as people living in West Town. 360 more people moved into East Town. There are now 1,800 more people living in East Town than living in West Town. How many people are living in West Town?

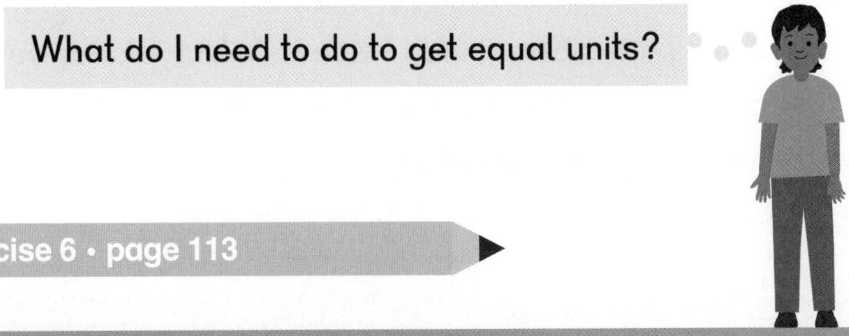

Exercise 6 • page 113

Lesson 7
Practice B

P 7

1 Estimate the value and then divide.

(a) $602 \div 3$ (b) $785 \div 9$ (c) $518 \div 5$

(d) $6{,}287 \div 2$ (e) $2{,}086 \div 7$ (f) $4{,}905 \div 8$

(g) $5{,}970 \div 4$ (h) $8{,}004 \div 6$ (i) $9{,}986 \div 8$

2

Connor has twice as many trading cards as Hudson. Jamal has 3 times as many trading cards as Connor. Altogether, Hudson and Jamal have 595 cards.

(a) How many trading cards does Connor have?

(b) How many more trading cards does Jamal have than Connor?

(c) How many trading cards do all three boys have altogether?

3 Julia raised \$580 selling hats. She raised twice as much money selling fruit baskets. She gave the money equally to 5 different charities. How much money did she give to each charity?

4 A community center had $5,000 to spend on computers. It bought 2 desktop computers for $980 each and 5 laptops for $588 each. How much money did the community center have left over?

5 The community center spent $550 on audio visual equipment. It bought 2 projector screens and 2 projector stands. Each projector stand cost $25 more than each projector screen. How much did each projector stand cost?

6 Ada has 3 times as many trading cards as Dana. Clara has 72 more trading cards than Ada. Holly has 59 fewer trading cards than Ada. Altogether, they have 633 trading cards. How many trading cards does Holly have?

7 

A supermarket has 5 times as many gray shopping carts as green shopping carts. After it got 85 more green shopping carts, it had 355 shopping carts in all. How many gray shopping carts does it have?

8 Tiara had twice as much money as Violet. Violet had twice as much money as Nina. Altogether, they had $840. Then Tiara spent $130. How much money does Tiara have left?

Exercise 7 • page 118

1

156,207	234,920	628,080	95,789

(a) Round each number to the nearest ten thousand.

(b) Round each number to the nearest hundred thousand.

(c) Write each number in expanded form.

2 Complete the number patterns.

(a)

57,875	58,875			61,875	

(b)

102,350		82,350	72,350		52,350

(c)

365,006	375,006	385,006			

3 List the eleventh through fifteenth multiples of 8.

4 Which of the following numbers have 7 as a factor?

14	36	47	77	84	91	133

5. What sign, > or <, goes in each ◯?

   (a) 6,100 × 9 ◯ 6,200 – 800

   (b) 90,000 ÷ 6 ◯ 16,000 – 1

6. Find the common factors of 12 and 20.

7. Find the first three common multiples of 2, 3, and 5.

8. Which of the following numbers are prime?

4	16	23	37	62	73	89	91

9. Estimate the values, then find the actual values.

   (a) 48,584 + 24,907

   (b) 92,785 + 42,906

   (c) 90,207 + 18,319

   (d) 80,000 – 52,505

   (e) 38 × 27

   (f) 69 × 36

   (g) 459 × 34

   (h) 89 × 249

   (i) 698 ÷ 3

   (j) 4,105 ÷ 9

   (k) 6,080 ÷ 7

   (l) 5,005 ÷ 8

10 3 pieces of yarn are 24 inches, 32 inches, and 40 inches long. To make pom-poms, they all need to be cut into pieces of equal length. What lengths could they all be cut into to have no leftover yarn?

11 At a store opening, some customers are given tickets to trade in for prizes. Every sixth customer will get a yellow ticket, every tenth customer will get a blue ticket, and every fifteenth customer will get a green ticket. What number customer will be the first to get all three colors of tickets?

12

Madison made $340 a week for 24 weeks as a swim instructor. She saved $2,000, spent $3,360 on her college tuition, and spent the rest of the money on 2 couches that cost the same amount. How much did each couch cost?

13 700 children went on a field trip. 27 buses transported 24 students each. The rest of the students were transported equally in 4 minibuses. How many children went in each minibus?

14 Sofia has 3 times as many European coins as Asian coins and 45 more African coins than Asian coins. After she gets 55 more Asian coins, she has 260 of the three types of coins altogether. How many of each kind of coin does she have?

Exercise 8 • page 121

Chapter 6

Fractions

Which of the following shapes show $\frac{6}{8}$ of the shape colored?

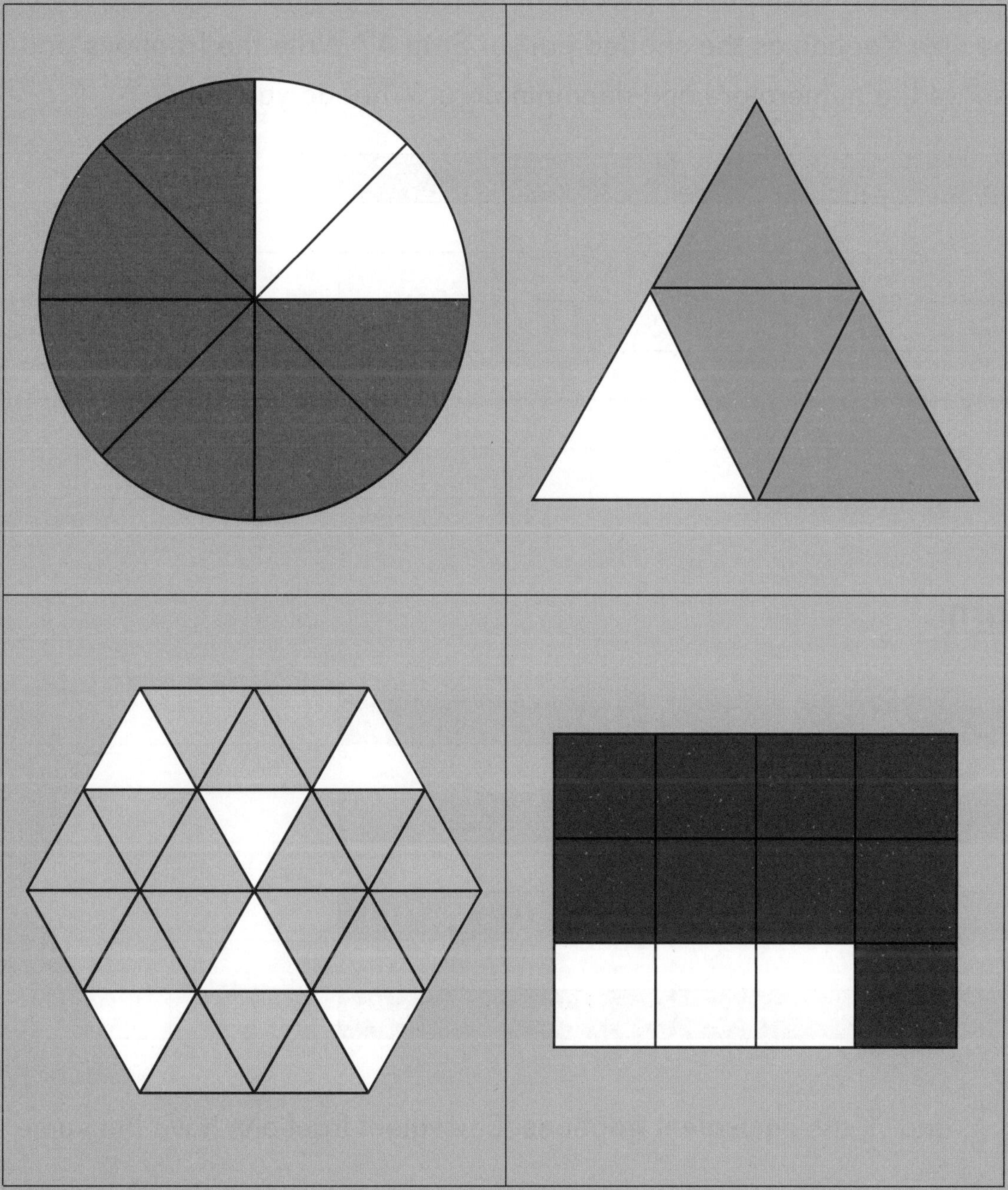

Think

$\frac{2}{3}$ of Strip A is shaded.

How many parts need to be shaded on each of the other strips to show the same size fraction as the shaded part of Strip A? Write the fractions and compare the numerators and denominators. What do you notice?

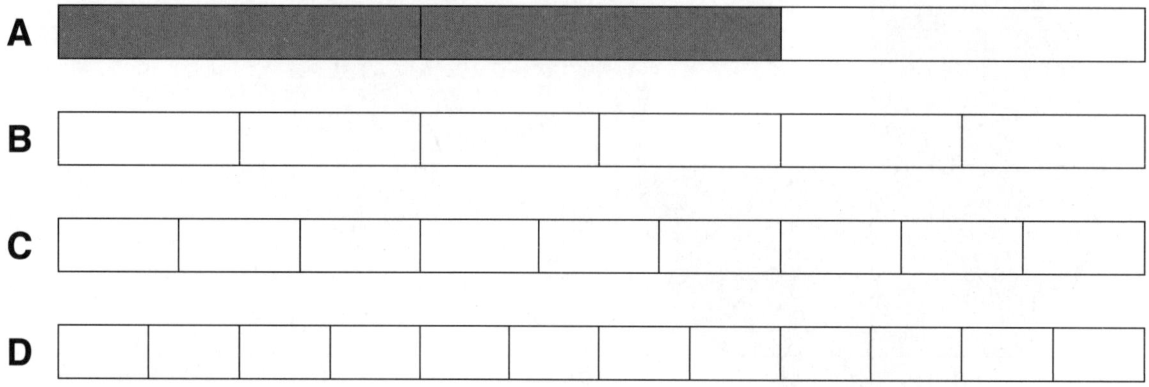

Learn

$\frac{2}{3}$, $\frac{4}{6}$, $\frac{6}{9}$, and $\frac{8}{12}$ are **equivalent fractions**. Equivalent fractions have the same value.

$$\text{Strip A } \frac{2}{3} \xrightarrow{\times 2} \frac{4}{6} \text{ Strip B}$$

Strip A $\frac{2}{3}$ = $\frac{4}{6}$ Strip B (× 2 on numerator, × 2 on denominator)

If we double the number of parts in the whole, the number of shaded parts also doubles, but the size of each part is smaller.

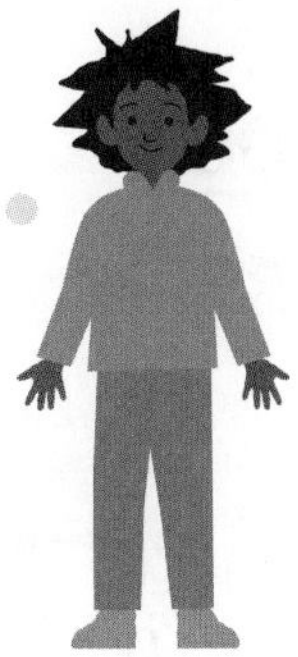

We can find equivalent fractions by multiplying or dividing the numerator and denominator by the same number.

$$\frac{2}{3} = \frac{4}{6} = \frac{6}{9} = \frac{8}{12}$$

(× 2, × 3, × 4 on numerator and denominator)

We can prove that $\frac{8}{12} = \frac{6}{9}$ by showing that they are both equal to $\frac{2}{3}$.

$$\frac{8}{12} = \frac{6}{9} = \frac{4}{6} = \frac{2}{3}$$

(÷ 2, ÷ 4 on numerator and denominator)

When we divide both the numerator and denominator by a common factor, we are **simplifying** the fraction.

The **simplest form** of $\frac{8}{12}$ is $\frac{2}{3}$ because 1 is the only common factor of both the numerator and denominator of $\frac{2}{3}$.

Do

1 Find equivalent fractions using these number lines.

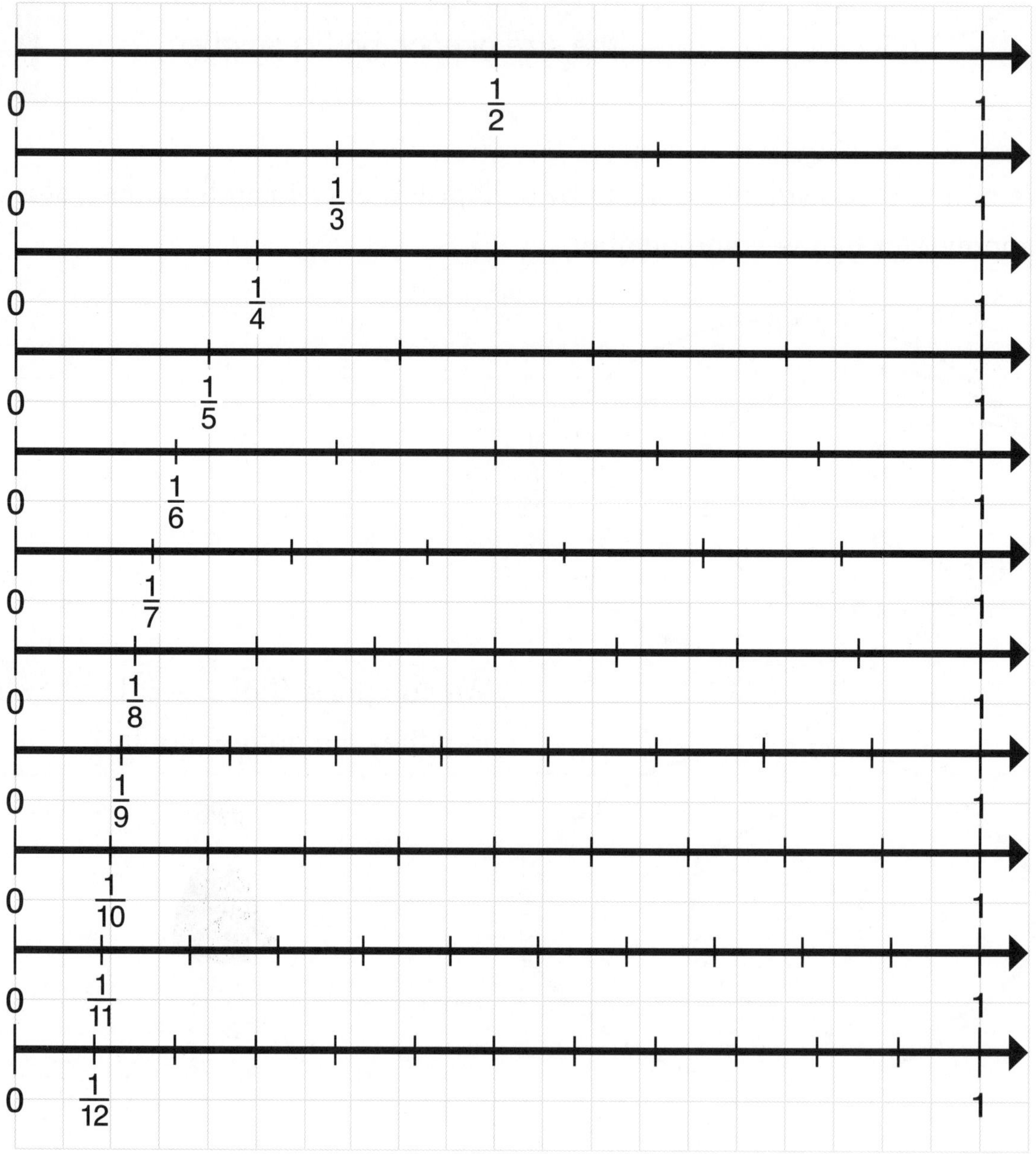

2 Find equivalent fractions for $\frac{2}{8}$.

(a) $\frac{2}{8} \overset{\times 2}{=} \frac{\square}{\square}$ (× 2 above and below)

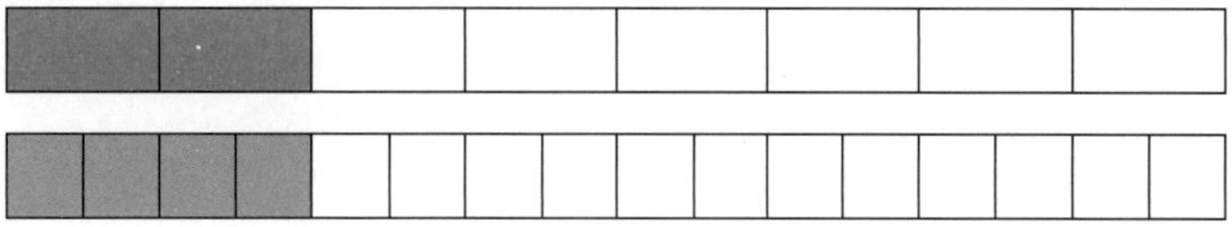

(b) $\frac{2}{8} \overset{\div 2}{=} \frac{\square}{\square}$ (÷ 2 above and below)

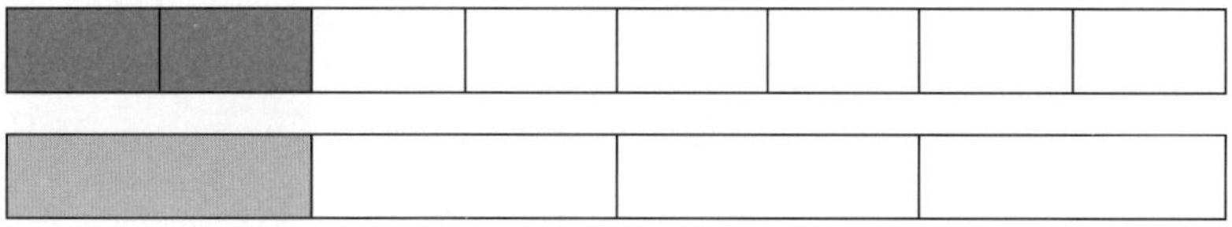

(c) Find three other fractions equivalent to $\frac{2}{8}$.

(d) The simplest form of $\frac{2}{8}$ is $\frac{\square}{\square}$.

3 Find the equivalent fractions.

(a) $\frac{3}{4} = \frac{\square}{16}$ (× $\square$ above and below)

(b) $\frac{12}{18} = \frac{\square}{3}$ (÷ $\square$ above and below)

(c) $\frac{3}{5} = \frac{15}{\square}$ (× $\square$ above and below)

(d) $\frac{9}{36} = \frac{1}{\square}$ (÷ $\square$ above and below)

4 For each fraction, write three equivalent fractions.

(a) $\frac{1}{5}$ (b) $\frac{15}{30}$

5 Find the simplest form of $\frac{12}{16}$.

(a) $\frac{12}{16} \xrightarrow{\div 2} \frac{\square}{\square} \xrightarrow{\div 2} \frac{\square}{\square}$

$\frac{12}{16} = \frac{\square}{\square}$ (numerator and denominator each $\div 2$, then $\div 2$)

(b) $\frac{12}{16} = \frac{\square}{\square}$ (numerator and denominator each $\div 4$)

Divide the numerator and denominator by a common factor of 12 and 16.

12 ⟶ 1, **2**, 3, **4**, 6, 12

16 ⟶ 1, **2**, **4**, 8, 16

6 Express each fraction in simplest form.

(a) $\frac{4}{10}$ (b) $\frac{6}{8}$ (c) $\frac{9}{12}$

(d) $\frac{15}{20}$ (e) $\frac{15}{21}$ (f) $\frac{32}{48}$

(g) $\frac{28}{35}$ (h) $\frac{25}{50}$ (i) $\frac{75}{100}$

7 Sydney cut a cake into 15 pieces of the same size. She and 4 friends each ate 1 piece. What fraction of the cake was eaten?

Express answers in simplest form.

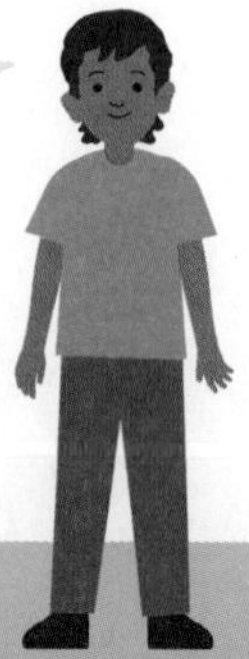

Exercise 1 • page 127

Think

Dion ran $\frac{2}{3}$ of a mile and Emma ran $\frac{4}{5}$ of a mile. Who ran farther?

Learn

Method 1

Find equivalent fractions with a common denominator.

Find a common multiple of the denominators.
5 ⟶ 5, 10, **15**
3 ⟶ 3, 6, 9, 12, **15**

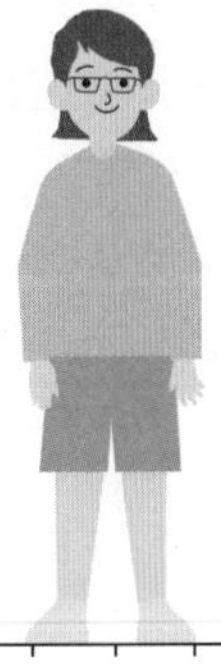

Dion $\frac{2}{3} = \frac{2 \times 5}{3 \times 5} = \frac{10}{15}$

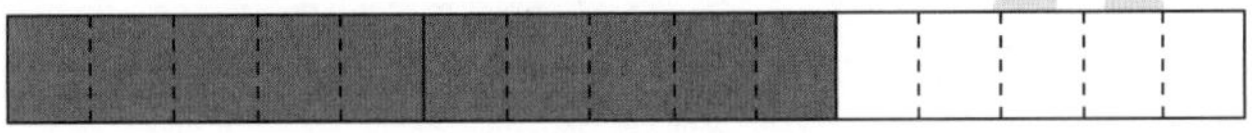

Emma $\frac{4}{5} = \frac{4 \times 3}{5 \times 3} = \frac{12}{15}$

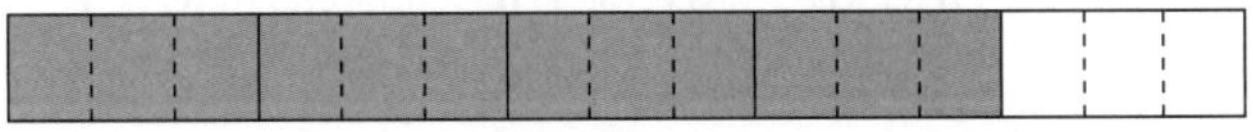

If the denominators are the same, the size of the parts is the same. The fraction with the greater numerator is the greater fraction.

$\frac{12}{15}$ is greater than $\frac{10}{15}$, so Emma ran farther.

Method 2

Find equivalent fractions with a common numerator.

4 is a common multiple of both numerators.

Dion $\frac{2}{3} \overset{\times 2}{=} \frac{4}{6}$ (numerator × 2, denominator × 2)

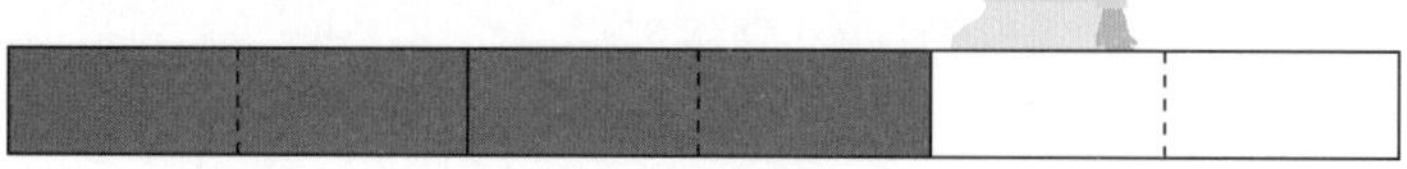

Emma $\frac{4}{5}$

Since the numerators are the same, the fraction with the lesser denominator is the greater fraction.
$\frac{1}{5} > \frac{1}{6}$, so $\frac{4}{5} > \frac{4}{6}$.

$\frac{4}{5}$ is greater than $\frac{4}{6}$, so Emma ran farther than Dion.

Method 3

Compare both fractions to a third number.

Since the numerator is one less than the denominator for each, it is easy to compare the fractions to 1.

Dion $\frac{2}{3}$ and $\frac{1}{3}$ make 1.

Emma $\frac{4}{5}$ and $\frac{1}{5}$ make 1.

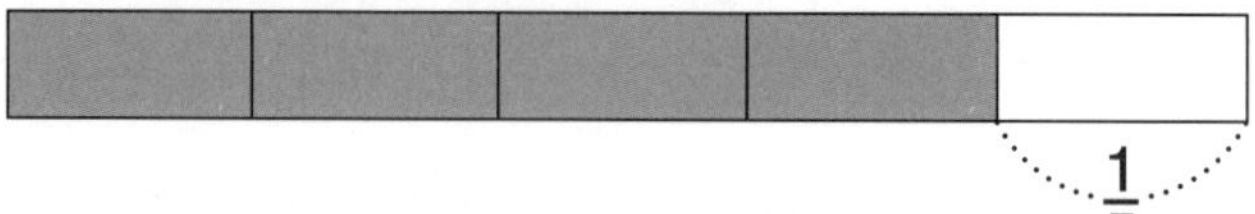

Since $\frac{1}{5}$ is less than $\frac{1}{3}$, $\frac{4}{5}$ is closer to 1 than $\frac{2}{3}$ is, so Emma ran farther than Dion.

Do

1 What sign, > or <, goes in the ◯?

(a) $\frac{5}{9} \bigcirc \frac{7}{9}$

The denominators are the same.

(b) $\frac{3}{5} \bigcirc \frac{3}{8}$

$\frac{1}{8} < \frac{1}{5}$ so...

(c) $\frac{3}{4} \bigcirc \frac{6}{11}$

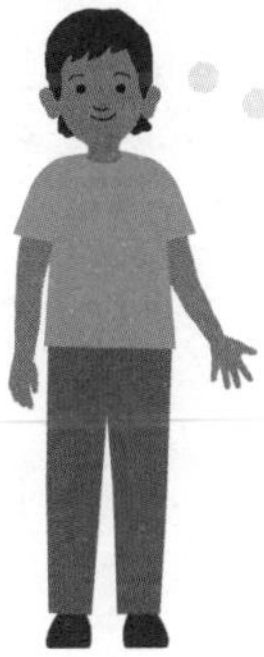

$\frac{3}{4} = \frac{6}{8}$

(d) $\frac{3}{5} \bigcirc \frac{7}{10}$

$\frac{3}{5} = \frac{6}{10}$

2 Which is greater, $\frac{3}{4}$ or $\frac{7}{10}$?

10 ⟶ 10, **20**
4 ⟶ 4, 8, 12, 16, **20**
I will find equivalent fractions with the denominator 20.

40 is also a common multiple of 4 and 10, so I will find equivalent fractions with a denominator of 40.

3 Which is less, $\frac{3}{8}$ or $\frac{4}{5}$?

$\frac{1}{2} = \frac{4}{8}$, so I can compare both fractions to $\frac{1}{2}$.

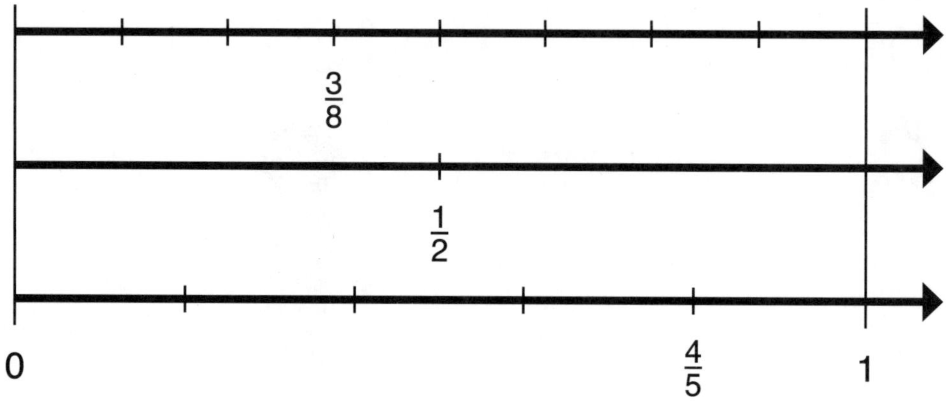

4 What sign, > or <, goes in each ◯?

(a) $\frac{3}{8}$ ◯ $\frac{5}{6}$ (b) $\frac{2}{6}$ ◯ $\frac{2}{3}$ (c) $\frac{5}{8}$ ◯ $\frac{1}{2}$

(d) $\frac{7}{8}$ ◯ $\frac{3}{4}$ (e) $\frac{1}{2}$ ◯ $\frac{3}{7}$ (f) $\frac{2}{3}$ ◯ $\frac{1}{5}$

(g) $\frac{9}{10}$ ◯ $\frac{2}{3}$ (h) $\frac{6}{7}$ ◯ $\frac{8}{9}$ (i) $\frac{1}{3}$ ◯ $\frac{3}{8}$

5 Put the fractions in order from least to greatest.

(a) $\frac{2}{5}, \frac{2}{3}, \frac{2}{7}$ (b) $\frac{2}{3}, \frac{5}{6}, \frac{4}{9}$

(c) $\frac{3}{5}, \frac{7}{10}, \frac{3}{8}, \frac{5}{6}$ (d) $\frac{2}{7}, \frac{9}{10}, \frac{1}{2}, \frac{5}{8}$

6 $\frac{3}{10}$ of a bag of flour was used to make a vanilla cake. $\frac{4}{7}$ of the same bag was used to make a chocolate cake. Which cake took more flour?

Exercise 2 • page 130

Improper Fractions and Mixed Numbers

Think

How can we express the length of this rope in meters?

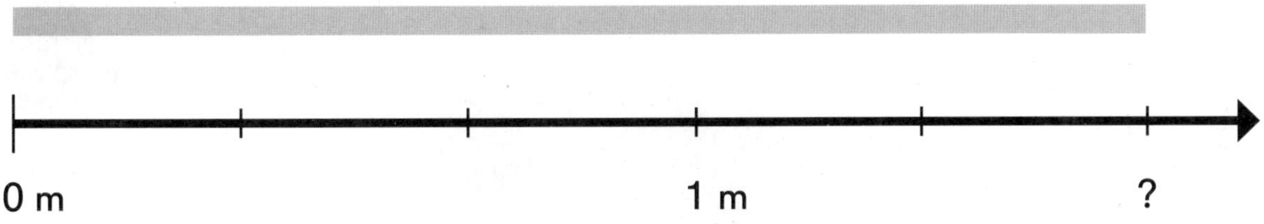

Learn

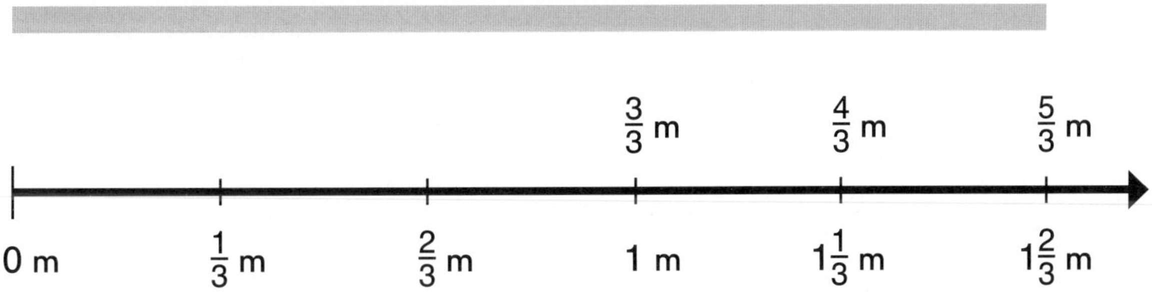

The rope is $\frac{\square}{3}$ m long.

The rope is $1\frac{\square}{3}$ m long.

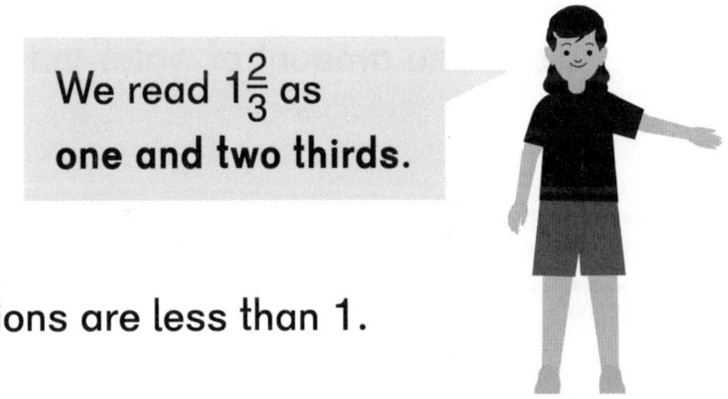

$\frac{1}{3}$ and $\frac{2}{3}$ are **proper fractions**. Proper fractions are less than 1.

$\frac{3}{3}$, $\frac{4}{3}$, and $\frac{5}{3}$ are **improper fractions**. An improper fraction is equal to or greater than 1.

$1\frac{1}{3}$ and $1\frac{2}{3}$ are **mixed numbers**. A mixed number is the sum of a whole number and a fraction.

Do

1 (a) $1 = \frac{\square}{4}$

(b) $2 = \frac{\square}{4}$

(c) $3 = \frac{\square}{4}$

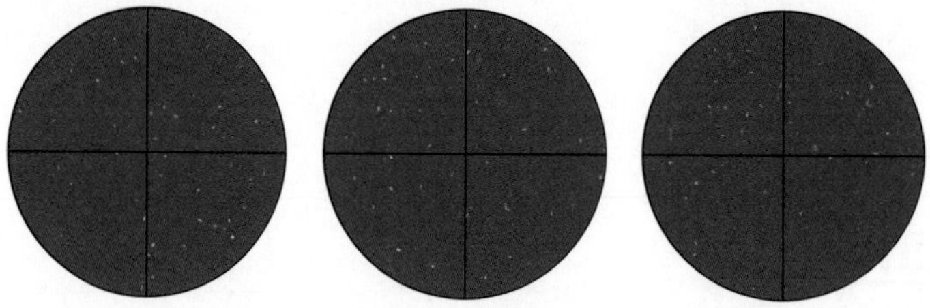

How many fourths are in 1 whole?

2 $\frac{3}{2} = \square$ halves

$\frac{3}{2} = \frac{\square}{2} + \frac{1}{2}$

$\frac{3}{2} = 1 + \frac{\square}{2}$

$\frac{3}{2} = 1\frac{\square}{2}$

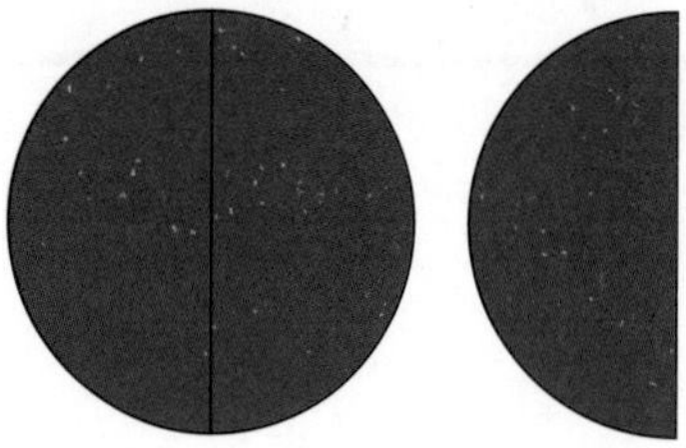

3 Express each of the following measurements as an improper fraction and as a mixed number.

(a) The amount of water in liters.

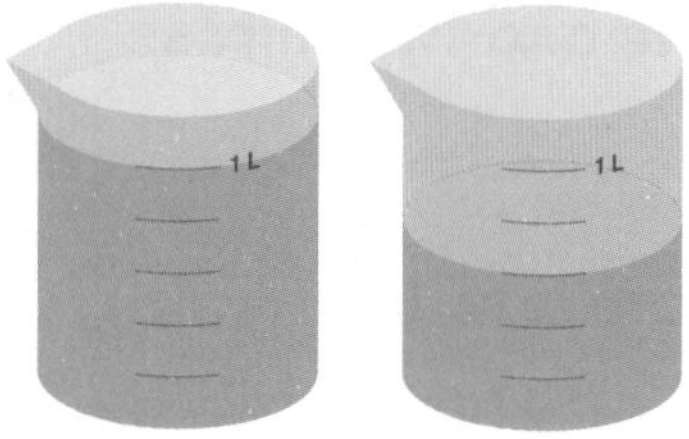

(b) The weight of the pumpkin in kilograms.

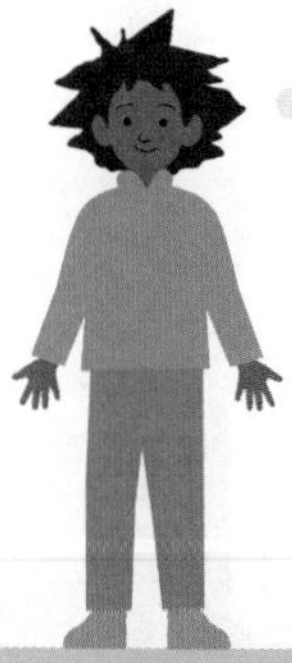

$2\frac{4}{10} = 2\frac{?}{5}$

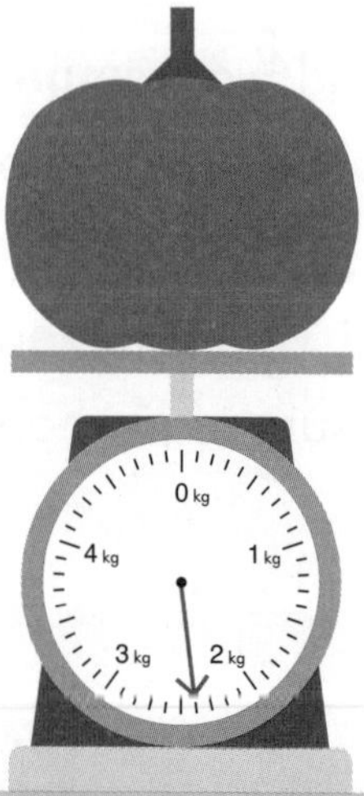

(c) The length of the nail in inches.

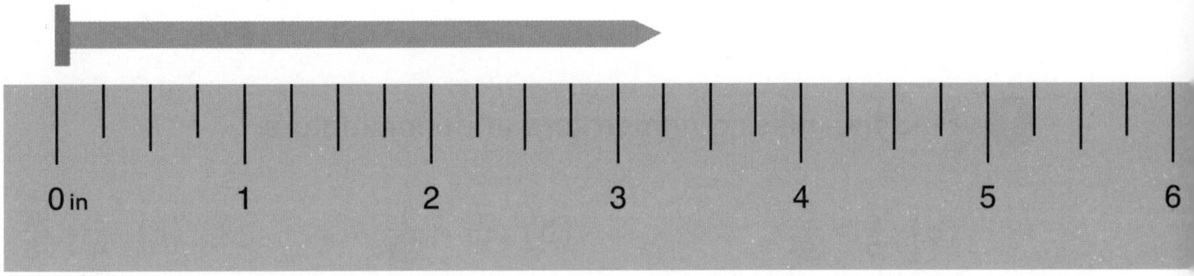

4 What numbers are indicated by each letter? Express numbers greater than 1 as both an improper fraction and a mixed number. Use simplest form.

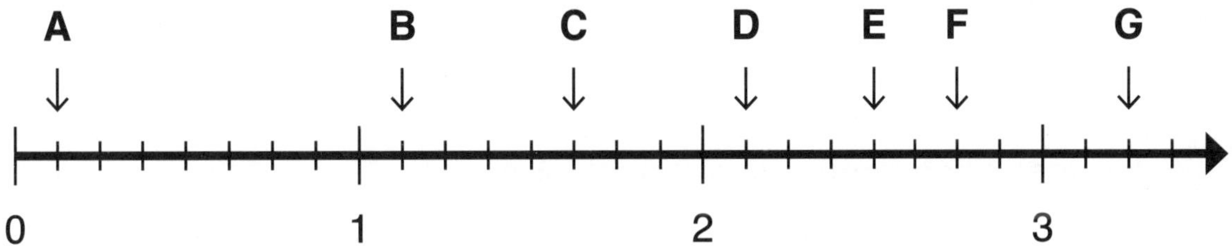

5 Express each value as a mixed number in simplest form.

(a) $2 + \frac{2}{8}$

(b) $2 - \frac{1}{8}$

(c) $2 + \frac{5}{8}$

(d) $3 - \frac{5}{8}$

(e) $\frac{2}{5} + 1$

(f) $2 - \frac{1}{4}$

(g) $9 + \frac{5}{12}$

(h) $5 - \frac{4}{6}$

(i) $\frac{7}{10} + 4$

6 Daniela ran 2 km. Hunter ran $\frac{3}{5}$ km farther than Daniela. Jada ran $\frac{2}{5}$ km farther than Hunter.

(a) How far did Hunter run?

(b) How far did Jada run?

Exercise 3 • page 133

Lesson 4
Practice A

P 4

1 Find the missing numerators or denominators.

(a) $\frac{2}{5} = \frac{6}{\square}$ (b) $\frac{7}{14} = \frac{1}{\square}$ (c) $\frac{1}{4} = \frac{\square}{8} = \frac{3}{\square}$

(d) $\frac{8}{12} = \frac{\square}{3}$ (e) $\frac{3}{3} = \frac{\square}{10}$ (f) $\frac{6}{18} = \frac{1}{\square} = \frac{\square}{12}$

2 Find three other fractions equivalent to $\frac{9}{12}$.

3 Express each fraction in simplest form.

(a) $\frac{4}{8}$ (b) $\frac{6}{9}$ (c) $\frac{8}{12}$

(d) $\frac{10}{15}$ (e) $\frac{10}{25}$ (f) $\frac{36}{60}$

4 What sign, >, <, or =, goes in each ◯?

(a) $\frac{5}{9}$ ◯ $\frac{7}{9}$ (b) $\frac{3}{8}$ ◯ $\frac{3}{7}$ (c) $\frac{5}{6}$ ◯ $\frac{10}{12}$

(d) $\frac{1}{2}$ ◯ $\frac{5}{9}$ (e) $\frac{3}{7}$ ◯ $\frac{1}{2}$ (f) $\frac{8}{9}$ ◯ $\frac{7}{8}$

(g) $\frac{7}{10}$ ◯ $\frac{2}{7}$ (h) $\frac{5}{7}$ ◯ $\frac{4}{9}$ (i) $\frac{2}{3}$ ◯ $\frac{3}{8}$

5 Put the fractions in order from least to greatest.

(a) $\frac{12}{11}, \frac{7}{11}, \frac{10}{11}, \frac{2}{11}, \frac{8}{11}$

(b) $\frac{3}{8}, \frac{3}{10}, \frac{3}{4}, \frac{3}{11}, \frac{3}{7}$

(c) $\frac{4}{5}, \frac{9}{10}, \frac{7}{8}, \frac{5}{6}, \frac{3}{4}, \frac{8}{9}$

(d) $\frac{2}{7}, \frac{7}{12}, \frac{1}{2}, \frac{5}{8}, \frac{5}{6}, \frac{7}{9}$

6 What numbers are indicated by each letter? Express numbers greater than 1 as both an improper fraction and a mixed number or whole number.

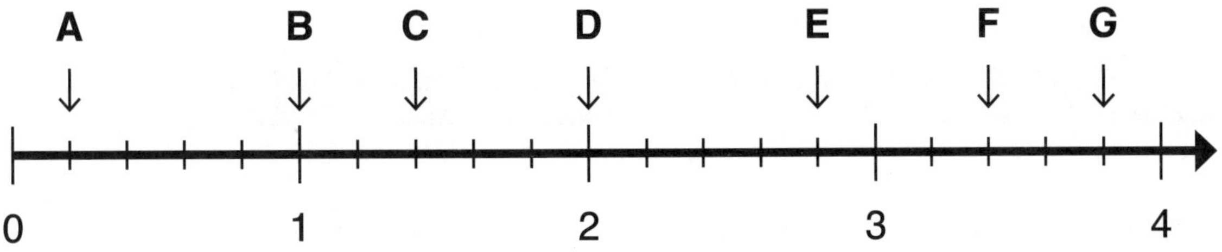

7 Express each value as a mixed number in simplest form.

(a) $1 + \frac{3}{7}$

(b) $3 + \frac{1}{5}$

(c) $\frac{6}{8} + 2$

(d) $3 - \frac{6}{9}$

(e) $2 + \frac{5}{8}$

(f) $5 - \frac{3}{12}$

8 A jug has $\frac{2}{3}$ L of milk. A bottle has $\frac{4}{7}$ L of milk. Which container has more milk?

9 A bag of flour weighs 5 lb. $\frac{5}{7}$ lb of flour was used to make bread. How many pounds of flour are still in the bag? Give your answer as a mixed number.

Exercise 4 • page 136

Lesson 5

Expressing an Improper Fraction as a Mixed Number

5

Think

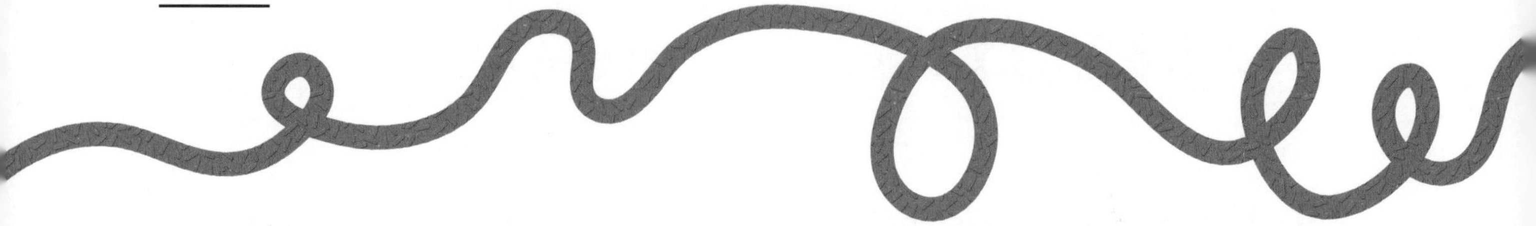

Mei made a yarn rope that is $\frac{8}{5}$ m long.

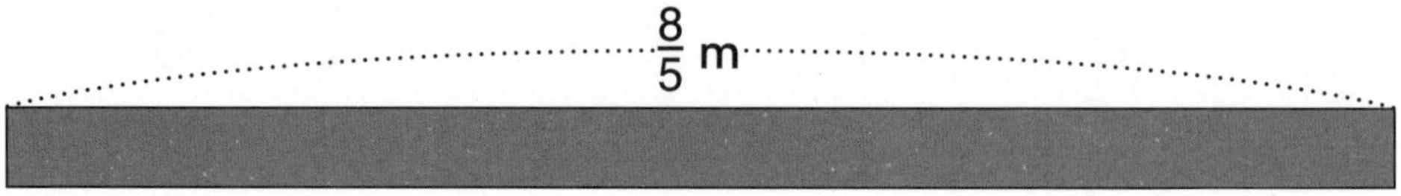

Express the length of her yarn rope as a mixed number.

Learn

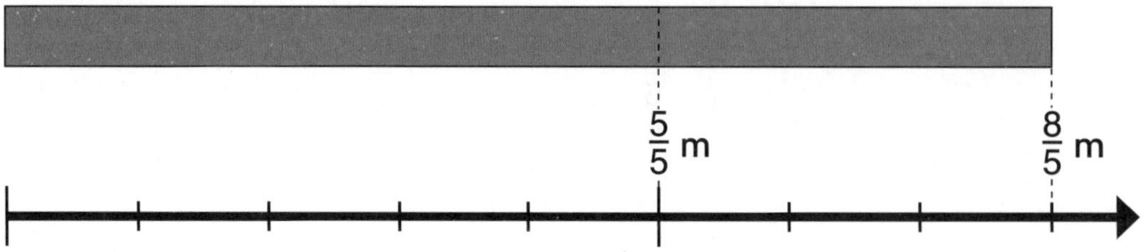

$\frac{8}{5} = \frac{5}{5} + \frac{3}{5}$

$= 1 + \frac{3}{5}$

$= 1\frac{3}{5}$

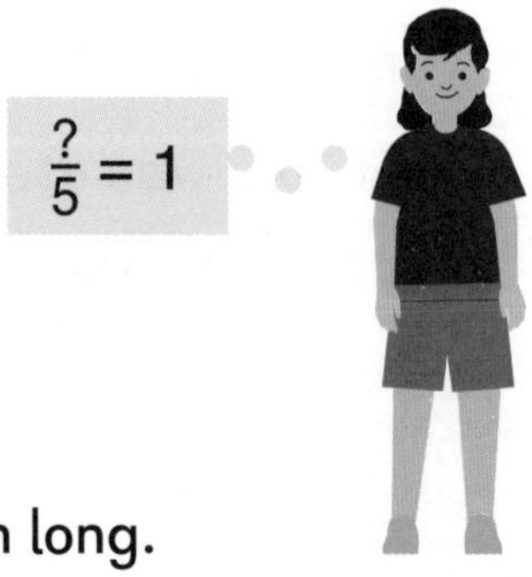

Mei's yarn rope is $\square\frac{\square}{\square}$ m long.

Do

1 (a)

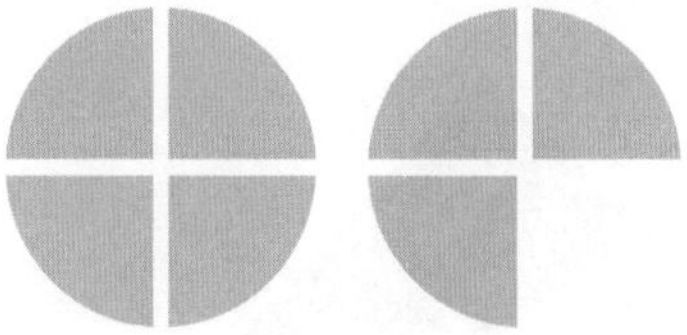

$\frac{7}{4} = \frac{4}{4} + \frac{\square}{4}$

$= 1 + \frac{\square}{4}$

$= 1\frac{\square}{4}$

(b)

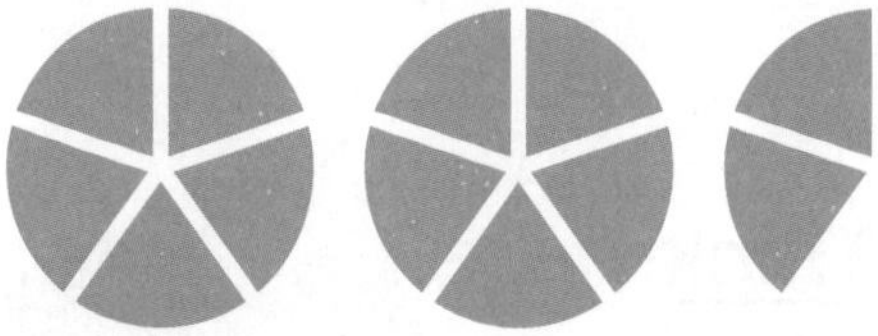

$\frac{12}{5} = \frac{\square}{5} + \frac{2}{5}$

$= \square + \frac{2}{5}$

$= \square\frac{\square}{5}$

2

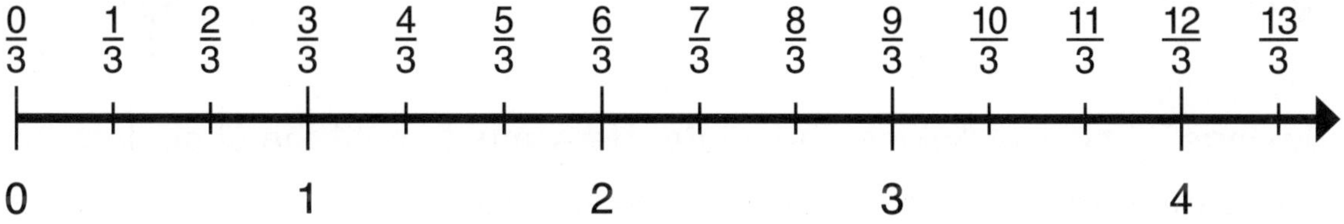

(a) $\frac{5}{3} = \square\frac{\square}{3}$ (b) $\frac{6}{3} = \square$ (c) $\frac{8}{3} = \square\frac{\square}{3}$

(d) $\frac{10}{3} = \square\frac{\square}{3}$ (e) $\frac{12}{3} = \square$ (f) $\frac{13}{3} = \square\frac{\square}{3}$

3 Express each improper fraction as a mixed number or whole number.

(a) $\frac{9}{2}$ (b) $\frac{10}{3}$ (c) $\frac{12}{4}$

(d) $\frac{18}{5}$ (e) $\frac{19}{6}$ (f) $\frac{45}{9}$

4 Wyatt walked $\frac{7}{5}$ km on Monday and $1\frac{3}{5}$ km on Tuesday. On which day did he walk farther?

Exercise 5 • page 139

Expressing a Mixed Number as an Improper Fraction

Think

Alex has $2\frac{3}{4}$ bars of baking chocolate. He wants to split the chocolate bar into pieces that are each $\frac{1}{4}$ of a bar for a baking project.

(a) How many $\frac{1}{4}$-bar pieces will he have?

(b) Express $2\frac{3}{4}$ as an improper fraction.

Learn

$$2\frac{3}{4} = 2 + \frac{3}{4}$$

$$= \frac{8}{4} + \frac{3}{4}$$

$$= \frac{11}{4}$$

(a) He will have ☐ $\frac{1}{4}$-bar pieces.

(b) $2\frac{3}{4} = \frac{\square}{4}$

Do

1 (a) $4\frac{1}{3} = 4 + \frac{1}{3}$

$= \frac{\square}{3} + \frac{1}{3}$

$= \frac{\square}{3}$

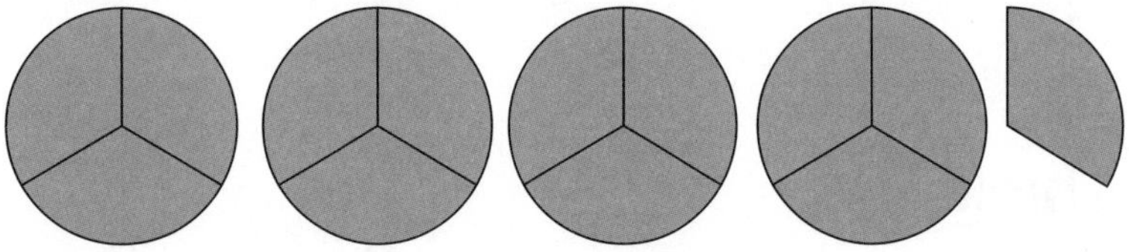

(b) $3\frac{4}{9} = 3 + \frac{4}{9}$

$= \frac{\square}{9} + \frac{4}{9}$

$= \frac{\square}{9}$

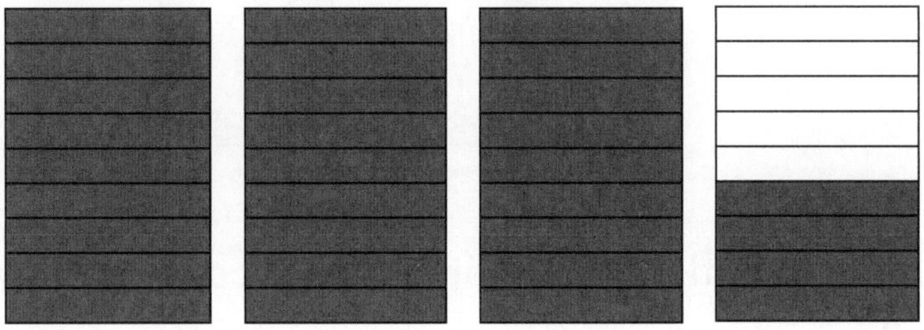

2

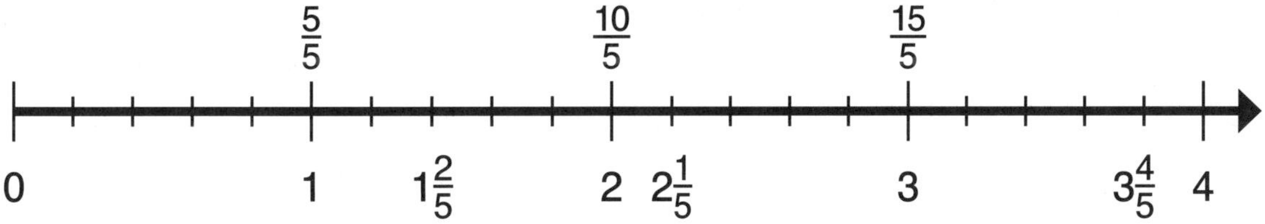

(a) $1\frac{2}{5} = \frac{\square}{5}$ (b) $2\frac{1}{5} = \frac{\square}{5}$ (c) $3\frac{4}{5} = \frac{\square}{5}$

3 Express each of the following as an improper fraction.

(a) $1\frac{1}{2}$ (b) $3\frac{1}{4}$ (c) $5\frac{3}{7}$

(d) $3\frac{5}{6}$ (e) $4\frac{7}{10}$ (f) $2\frac{1}{12}$

4 Put the numbers in order from least to greatest.

(a) $\frac{4}{3}, 2\frac{1}{2}, \frac{3}{4}$ (b) $3\frac{1}{5}, \frac{12}{4}, \frac{9}{2}$ (c) $\frac{10}{5}, 1\frac{3}{5}, \frac{15}{6}$

Exercise 6 • page 142

Think

Emma is putting equal amounts of cake on 3 platters for a party. Each cake is the same size.

(a) If she starts with 2 cakes, what fraction of a cake will be on each platter?

(b) If she starts with 5 cakes, how much cake will be on each platter?

Learn

(a) $2 \div 3$

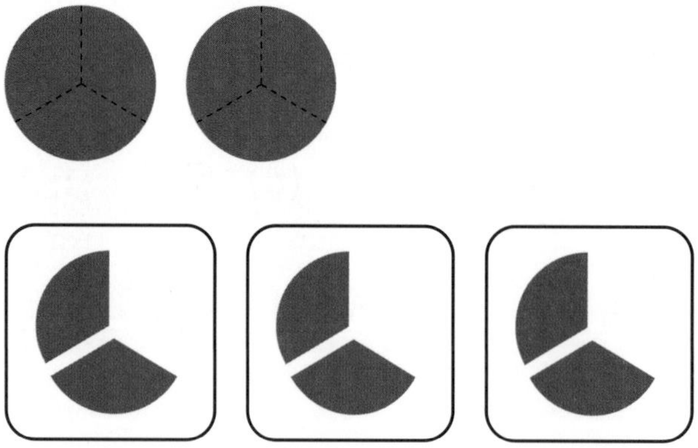

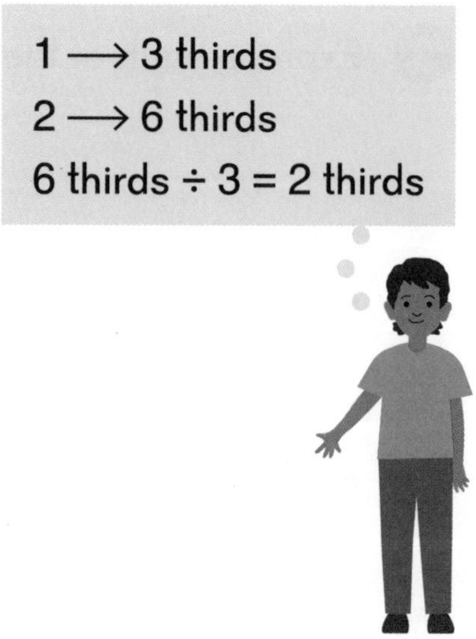

$2 \div 3 = \frac{2}{3}$

Each platter will have $\frac{\square}{\square}$ of a cake.

(b) 5 ÷ 3

5 ⟶ 15 thirds
15 thirds ÷ 3 = 5 thirds

Method 1

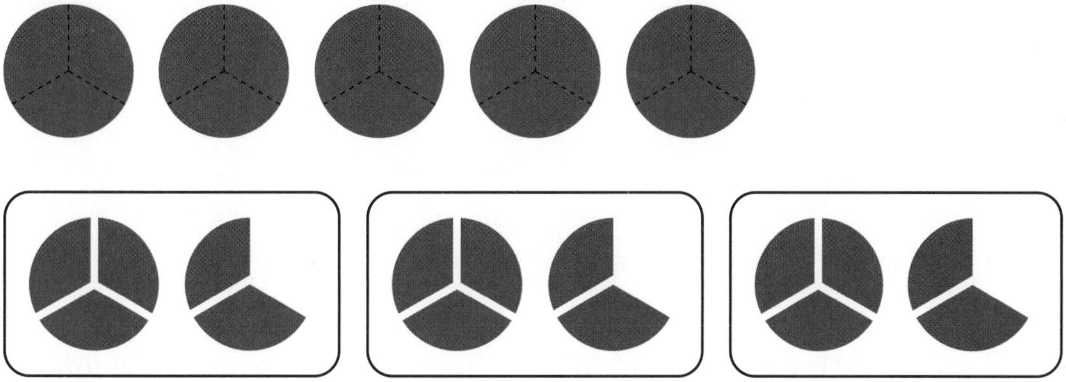

Method 2

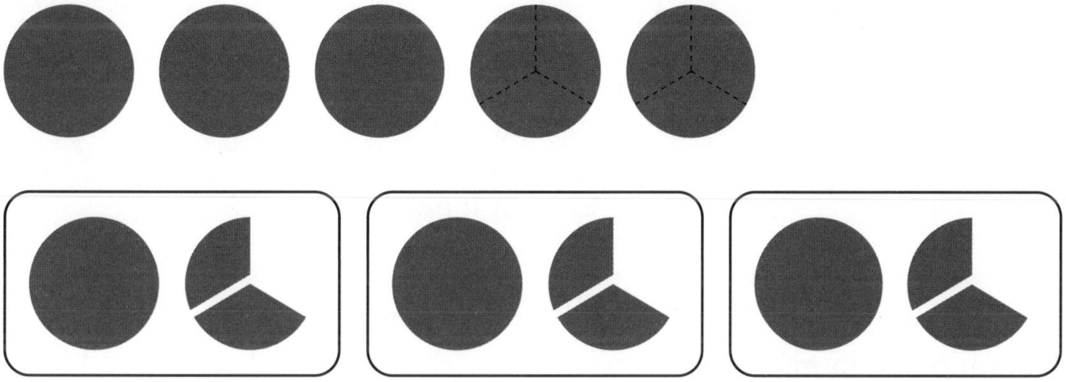

$$\begin{array}{r} 1 \\ 3\overline{)5} \\ \underline{3} \\ 2 \end{array}$$

5 ÷ 3 is 1 R 2. There will be 1 whole cake on each platter. Then we can divide the remaining 2 cakes among 3 platters. Each platter gets another $\frac{2}{3}$ cake.

$5 \div 3 = \frac{5}{3} = 1\frac{2}{3}$

Each platter will have ☐ $\frac{☐}{☐}$ cakes.

Do

1 (a) A 1-meter long ribbon is cut into 4 equal-length pieces. How long is each piece in meters?

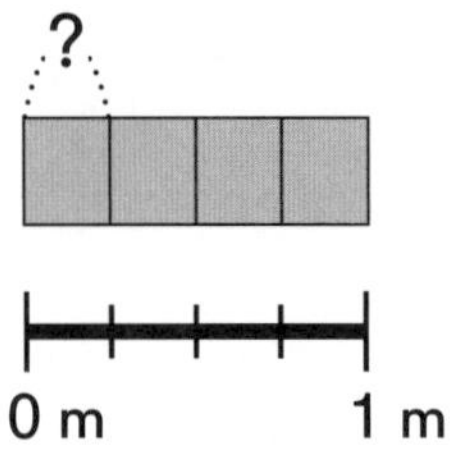

$1 \div 4 = \frac{\square}{\square}$ | Each piece is $\frac{\square}{\square}$ m long.

(b) A 3-meter long ribbon is cut into 4 equal-length pieces. How long is each piece in meters?

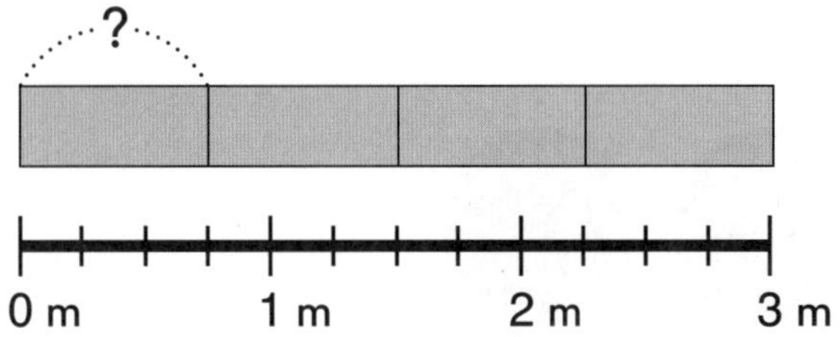

$3 \div 4 = \frac{\square}{\square}$ | Each piece is $\frac{\square}{\square}$ m long.

(c) A 6-meter long ribbon is cut into 4 equal-length pieces. How long is each piece in meters?

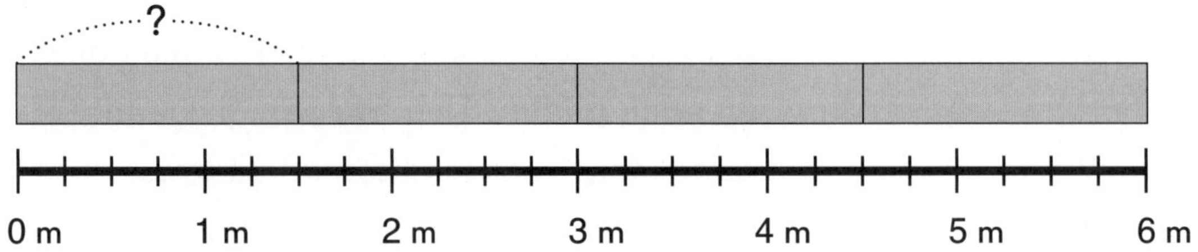

$6 \div 4 = \frac{6}{4} = 1\frac{\square}{4} = 1\frac{\square}{2}$

Each piece is $\square\frac{\square}{\square}$ m long.

$$\begin{array}{r} 1 \\ 4\overline{)6} \\ \underline{4} \\ 2 \end{array}$$

$2 \div 4 = \frac{2}{4} = \frac{1}{2}$

2 (a) Sofia divided 3 L of water equally into 4 bottles. How much water is in each bottle?

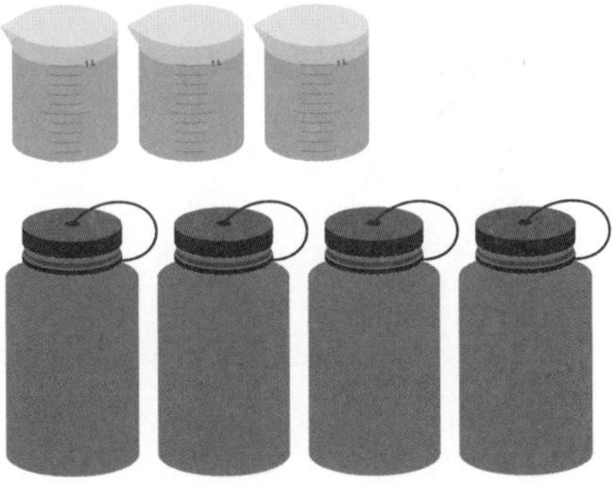

Each bottle will get less than a liter.

(b) Dion divided 4 L of water equally into 3 bottles. How much water is in each bottle?

We can put 1 L in each bottle and then divide the last liter equally.

3 Express 15 ÷ 2 as an improper fraction and then as a mixed number.

$15 \div 2 = \frac{15}{2} = \square\frac{\square}{2}$

$\frac{15}{2} = \frac{14}{2} + \frac{1}{2}$

$= 7 + \frac{1}{2}$

$$\begin{array}{r} 7 \\ 2\overline{)15} \\ \underline{14} \\ 1 \end{array}$$

$1 \div 2 = \frac{1}{2}$

4 (a) Express $21 \div 8$ as a mixed number.

$21 \div 8 = 2\frac{\square}{8}$

```
     2
8 ) 2 1
    1 6
    ---
      5
```

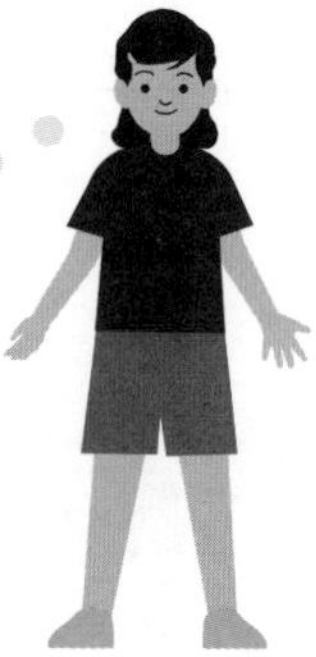

(b) Express $2\frac{5}{8}$ as an improper fraction.

$2\frac{5}{8}$ = 2 × 8 eighths + 5 eighths

5 Express $3\frac{4}{5}$ as an improper fraction.

$3 + \frac{4}{5}$

3 × 5 fifths + 4 fifths

6 Express each value as a proper fraction or mixed number in simplest form.

(a) $1 \div 8$ (b) $7 \div 9$ (c) $5 \div 4$

(d) $10 \div 8$ (e) $24 \div 7$ (f) $15 \div 6$

Exercise 7 • page 145

1. Express each improper fraction either as a mixed number in simplest form or as a whole number.

(a) $\frac{13}{2}$ (b) $\frac{11}{3}$ (c) $\frac{12}{5}$

(d) $\frac{18}{7}$ (e) $\frac{18}{3}$ (f) $\frac{30}{9}$

2. Express each mixed number as an improper fraction.

(a) $1\frac{7}{8}$ (b) $3\frac{4}{5}$ (c) $5\frac{1}{9}$

(d) $3\frac{3}{4}$ (e) $3\frac{3}{10}$ (f) $2\frac{3}{16}$

3. Express each of the following as either a proper fraction or an improper fraction in simplest form.

(a) $9 \div 15$ (b) $3 \div 9$ (c) $4 \div 12$

(d) $15 \div 9$ (e) $26 \div 6$ (f) $30 \div 8$

4. Express each of the following as a mixed number in simplest form.

(a) $18 \div 7$ (b) $9 \div 2$ (c) $8 \div 3$

(d) $15 \div 9$ (e) $26 \div 6$ (f) $30 \div 8$

5 What sign, >, <, or =, goes in each ◯?

(a) $1\frac{3}{8}$ ◯ $\frac{3}{8}$ (b) $1\frac{1}{3}$ ◯ $1\frac{1}{4}$ (c) $2\frac{5}{6}$ ◯ $2\frac{10}{12}$

(d) $3\frac{1}{2}$ ◯ $3\frac{5}{9}$ (e) $\frac{9}{8}$ ◯ $\frac{8}{9}$ (f) $\frac{6}{5}$ ◯ $\frac{7}{6}$

(g) $1\frac{1}{2}$ ◯ $\frac{5}{2}$ (h) $\frac{7}{5}$ ◯ $1\frac{4}{5}$ (i) $\frac{15}{2}$ ◯ $\frac{16}{3}$

6 Put the numbers in order from least to greatest.

(a) $\frac{9}{3}$, 2, $\frac{5}{2}$, $\frac{7}{9}$ (b) $3\frac{1}{3}$, $\frac{21}{6}$, $\frac{9}{3}$, $\frac{18}{9}$ (c) 4, $\frac{15}{5}$, $\frac{3}{5}$, $\frac{25}{10}$

7 (a) Austin ran the same distance 4 times during practice. In all, he ran 3 miles. How many miles did he run each of the 4 times?

(b) Franco ran the same distance 5 times during practice. In all, he ran 4 miles. How many miles did he run each of the 5 times?

(c) Who ran farther during practice, Austin or Franco?

8 A 20-meter long rope is cut into 8 parts of equal length. How long is each part in meters?

9 A store manager has 15 lb of coffee beans. He sells 10 lb and puts the remaining beans equally in 10 bags. How many pounds of coffee beans are in each bag?

Exercise 8 • page 148

Chapter 7

Adding and Subtracting Fractions

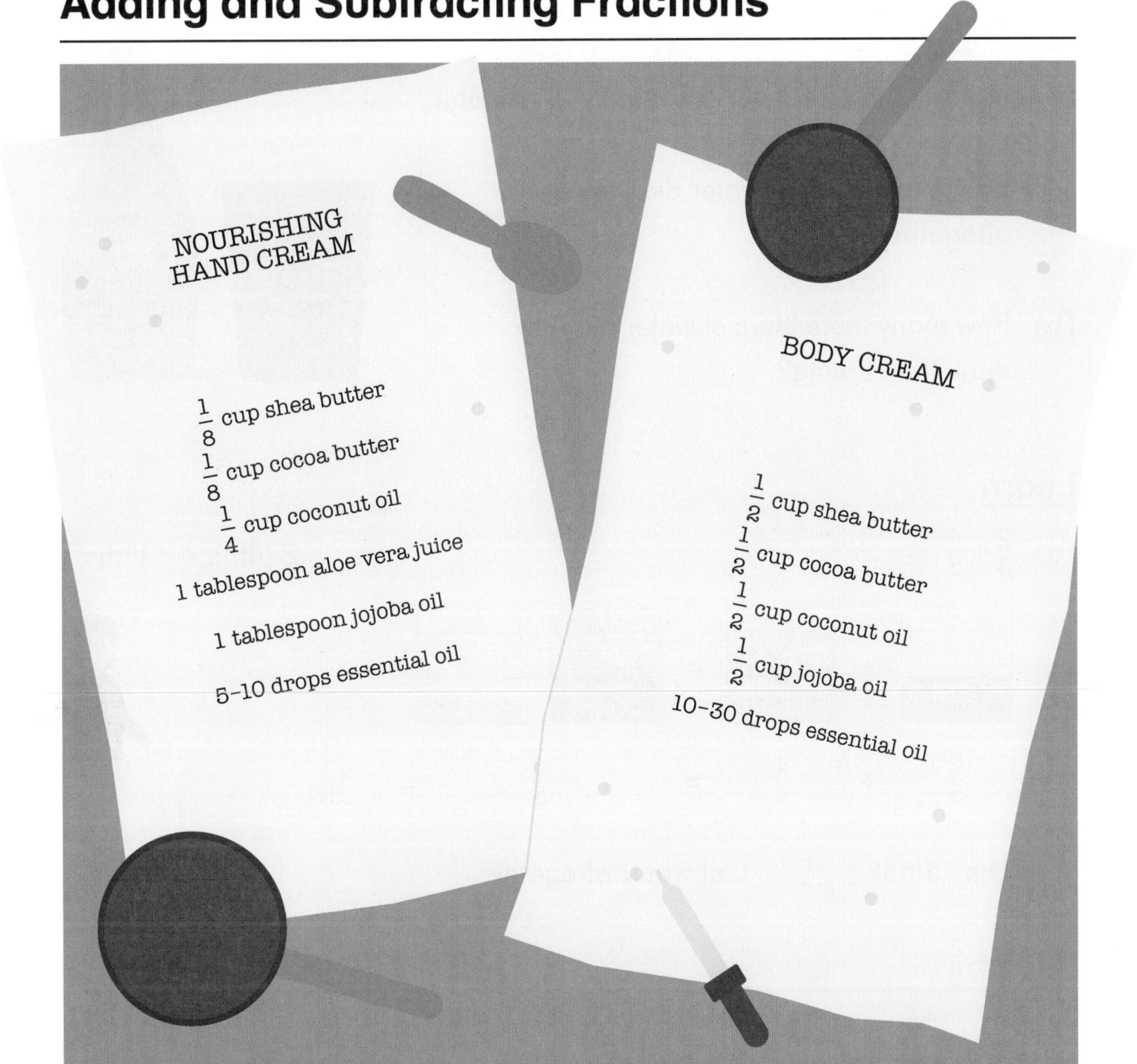

Emma wants to make both of these creams. How much shea butter, cocoa butter, and coconut oil does she need altogether?

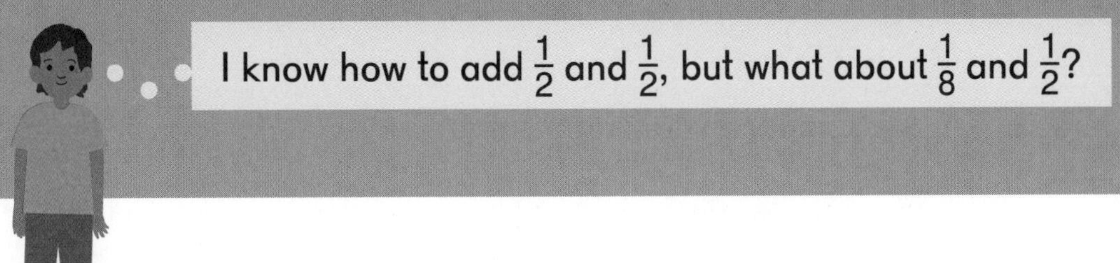

Lesson 1
Adding and Subtracting Fractions — Part 1

1

Think

Emma drank $\frac{2}{5}$ L of water. Alex drank $\frac{4}{5}$ L of water.

(a) How many liters of water did they drink altogether?

(b) How many more liters of water did Alex drink than Emma?

Learn

(a) $\frac{2}{5} + \frac{4}{5}$

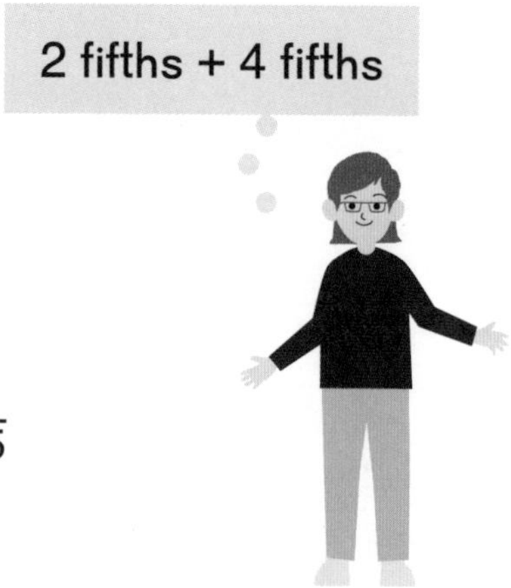

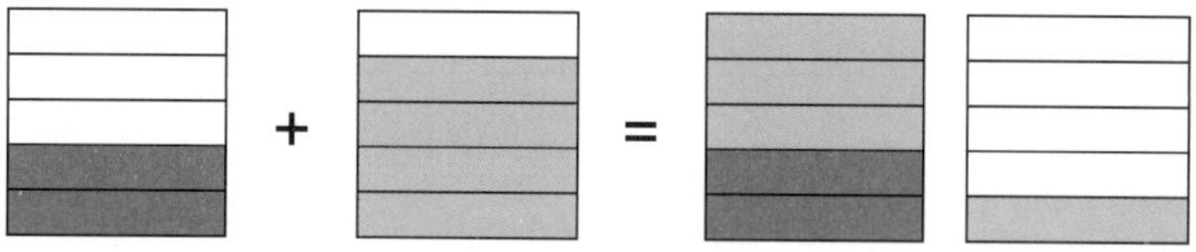

$$\frac{2}{5} + \frac{4}{5} = \frac{6}{5} = 1\frac{1}{5}$$

They drank _______ L of water altogether.

(b) $\frac{4}{5} - \frac{2}{5}$

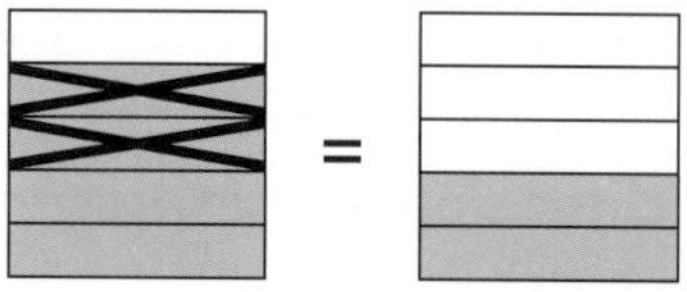

$$\frac{4}{5} - \frac{2}{5} = \frac{2}{5}$$

Alex drank _______ L more water than Emma.

Do

1 Add $\frac{1}{6}$ and $\frac{3}{6}$.

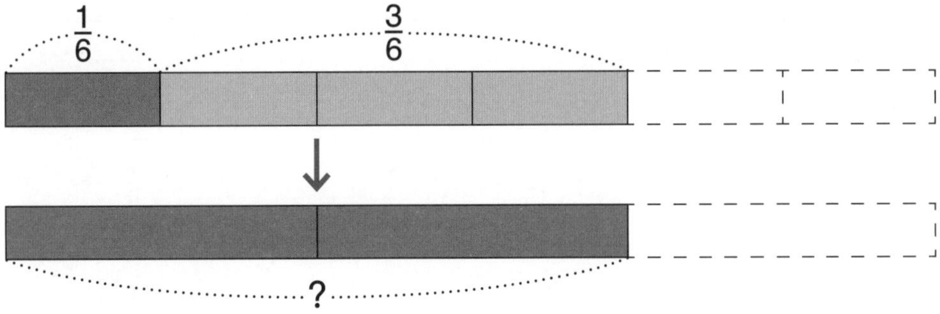

$\frac{1}{6} + \frac{3}{6} = \frac{\square}{6} = \frac{\square}{\square}$

2 Subtract $\frac{1}{4}$ from $\frac{3}{4}$.

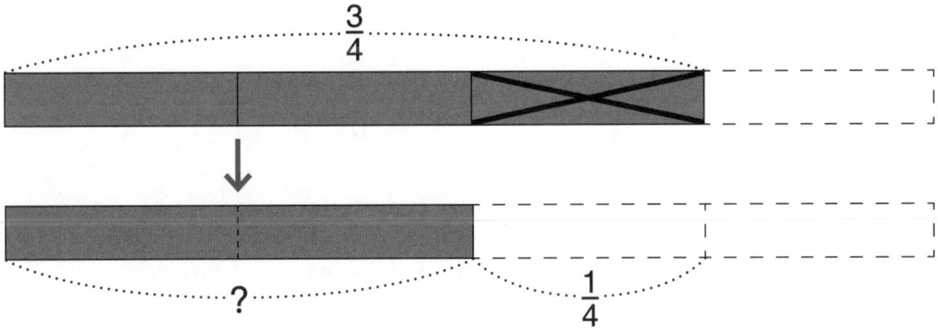

$\frac{3}{4} - \frac{1}{4} = \frac{\square}{4} = \frac{\square}{\square}$

3 Add $\frac{5}{8}$ and $\frac{5}{8}$.

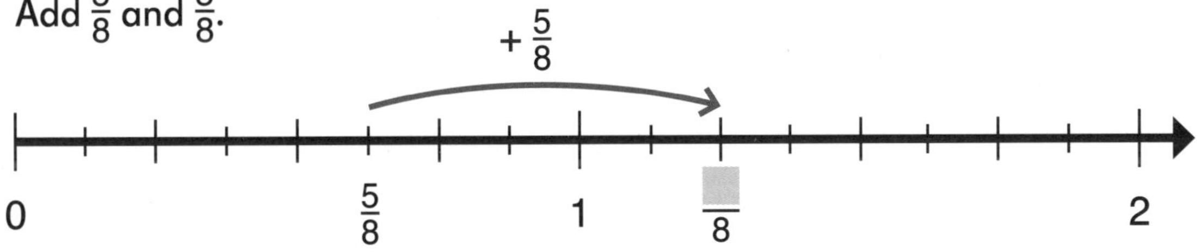

$\frac{5}{8} + \frac{5}{8} = \frac{\square}{8} = \frac{\square}{4} = \square\frac{\square}{4}$

4 Subtract $\frac{2}{5}$ from $\frac{9}{5}$.

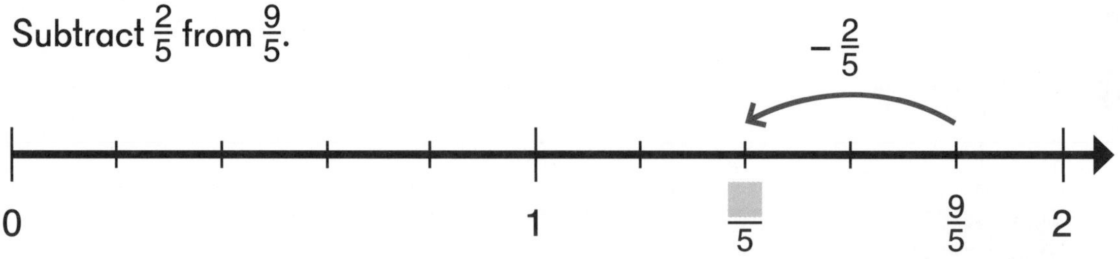

$\frac{9}{5} - \frac{2}{5} = \frac{■}{5} = ■\frac{■}{5}$

5 Add or subtract. Express each answer in its simplest form.

(a) $\frac{1}{7} + \frac{4}{7}$

(b) $\frac{5}{8} - \frac{2}{8}$

(c) $\frac{4}{9} - \frac{2}{9}$

(d) $\frac{5}{10} - \frac{3}{10}$

(e) $\frac{2}{7} + \frac{3}{7} + \frac{1}{7}$

(f) $\frac{7}{9} - \frac{3}{9} - \frac{1}{9}$

6 Add or subtract. Express each answer in its simplest form.

(a) $\frac{3}{5} + \frac{4}{5}$

(b) $\frac{11}{5} - \frac{7}{5}$

(c) $\frac{7}{12} + \frac{11}{12}$

(d) $\frac{7}{6} - \frac{5}{6}$

(e) $\frac{8}{3} - \frac{2}{3}$

(f) $\frac{3}{5} + \frac{4}{5} + \frac{2}{5}$

7 It took Mei $\frac{3}{4}$ of an hour to weed the garden and another $\frac{3}{4}$ of an hour to trim some bushes. How many hours did it take Mei to do both tasks in all?

Exercise 1 • page 151

Lesson 2
Adding and Subtracting Fractions — Part 2

2

Think

There is $\frac{1}{2}$ L of grapefruit juice in a carton and $\frac{1}{4}$ L of grapefruit juice in a glass. How many liters of grapefruit juice are there altogether?

Learn

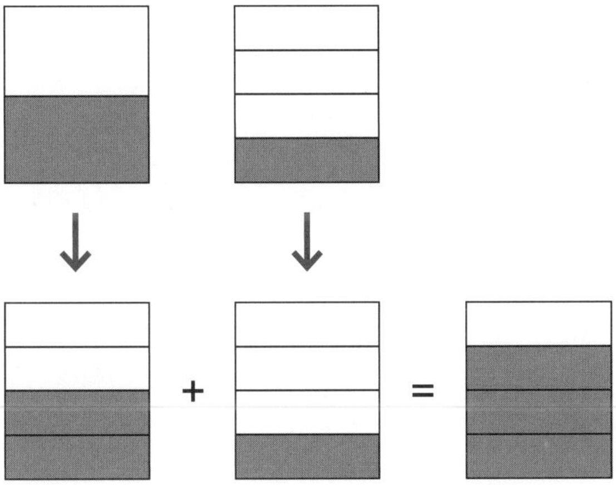

We cannot add halves and fourths together because they are different-sized units. If we change them to fractions with the same denominators, the units will be the same size.

$\frac{1}{2} + \frac{1}{4} = \frac{\square}{4} + \frac{1}{4}$

$= \frac{\square}{4}$

There are _______ L of grapefruit juice altogether.

Do

1 Add $\frac{3}{10}$ and $\frac{1}{5}$.

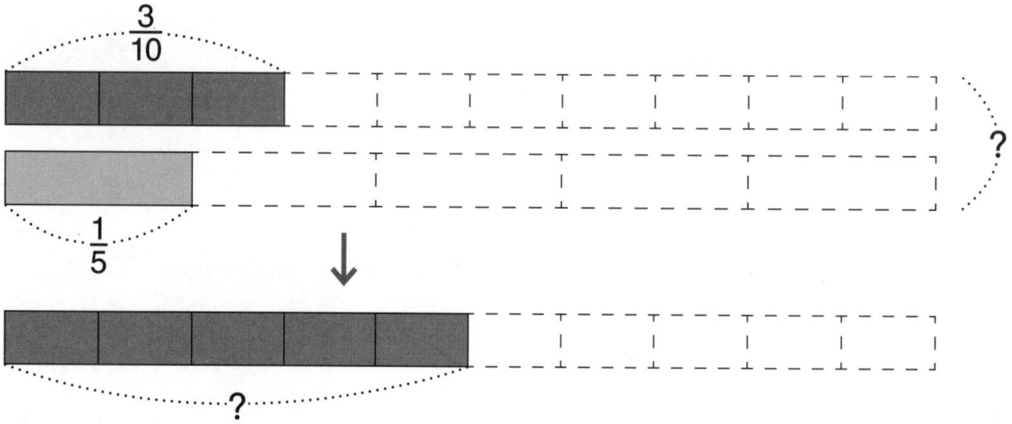

$$\frac{3}{10} + \frac{1}{5} = \frac{3}{10} + \frac{\square}{10} = \frac{\square}{10} = \frac{\square}{2}$$

2 Subtract $\frac{1}{2}$ from $\frac{5}{6}$.

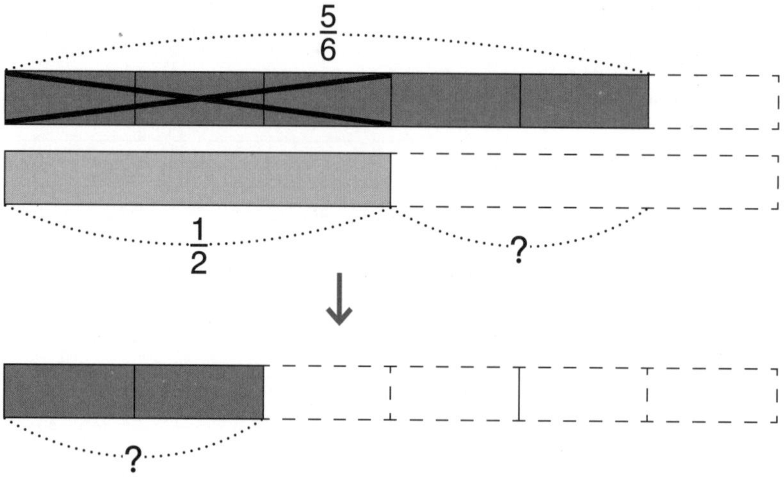

$$\frac{5}{6} - \frac{1}{2} = \frac{5}{6} - \frac{\square}{6} = \frac{\square}{6} = \frac{\square}{\square}$$

To add or subtract fractions, we need to have equal units.

3 Add $\frac{3}{4}$ and $\frac{7}{8}$.

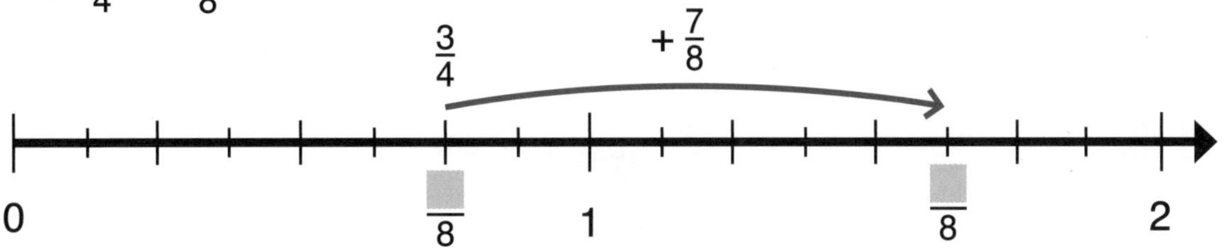

$$\frac{3}{4} + \frac{7}{8} = \frac{\square}{8} + \frac{7}{8} = \frac{\square}{8} = \square\frac{\square}{\square}$$

4 Subtract $\frac{8}{9}$ from $\frac{5}{3}$.

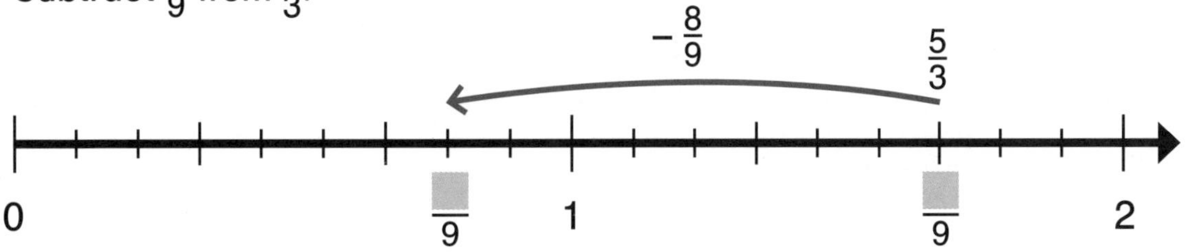

$$\frac{5}{3} - \frac{8}{9} = \frac{\square}{9} - \frac{8}{9} = \frac{\square}{9}$$

5 Add or subtract. Express each answer in its simplest form.

(a) $\frac{1}{9} + \frac{2}{3}$ (b) $\frac{1}{2} - \frac{1}{8}$ (c) $\frac{1}{6} + \frac{1}{2}$

(d) $\frac{3}{4} - \frac{7}{12}$ (e) $\frac{1}{5} + \frac{3}{10}$ (f) $\frac{2}{3} + \frac{7}{12}$

(g) $\frac{9}{8} - \frac{3}{4}$ (h) $\frac{1}{2} + \frac{1}{4} + \frac{1}{8}$ (i) $\frac{5}{12} + \frac{1}{2} + \frac{5}{6}$

6 Rope A is $\frac{7}{12}$ m long and Rope B is $\frac{2}{3}$ m long. What is the difference in length in meters between the two ropes?

Exercise 2 • page 154

Think

Sofia is making 2 kinds of playdough. She needs $1\frac{3}{4}$ cups of flour for the plain playdough and $\frac{3}{4}$ cups of flour for the silky playdough. How many cups of flour does she need in all?

Learn

$1\frac{3}{4} + \frac{3}{4}$

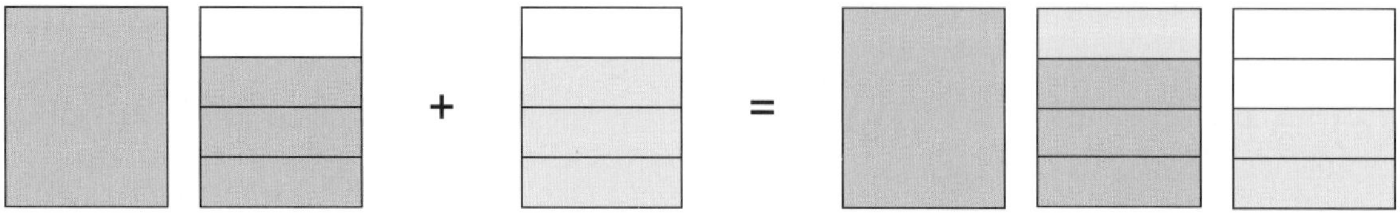

$$1\frac{3}{4} + \frac{3}{4} = 1\frac{6}{4}$$

$$= 2\frac{1}{2}$$

Sofia needs _______ cups of flour in all.

$$1\frac{6}{4} = 1 + \frac{6}{4} = 1 + 1 + \frac{2}{4}$$

Do

1 Add $2\frac{1}{4}$ and $\frac{1}{2}$.

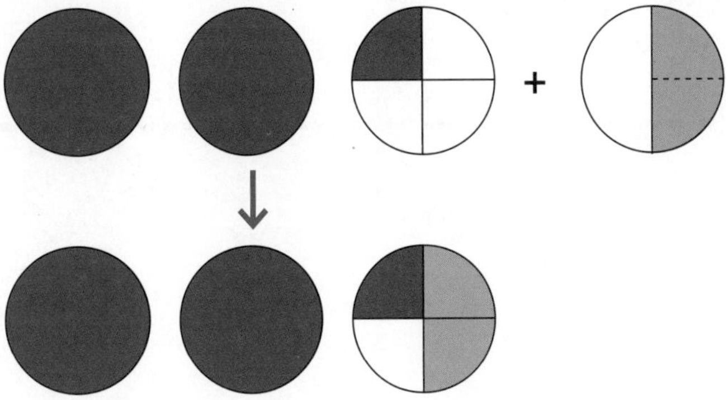

$2\frac{1}{4} + \frac{1}{2} = 2\frac{1}{4} + \frac{\square}{4}$

$= 2\frac{\square}{4}$

2 Add $1\frac{2}{3}$ and $\frac{7}{12}$.

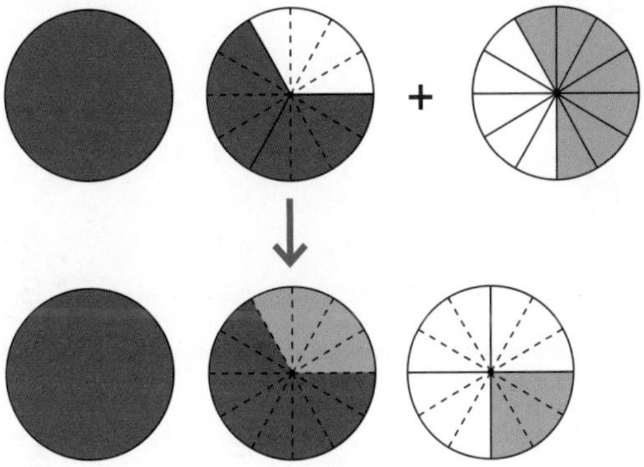

$1\frac{2}{3} + \frac{7}{12} = 1\frac{\square}{12} + \frac{7}{12}$

$= 1\frac{\square}{12}$

$= 2\frac{\square}{12}$

$= 2\frac{\square}{4}$

3 Add $1\frac{5}{6}$ and $\frac{5}{6}$.

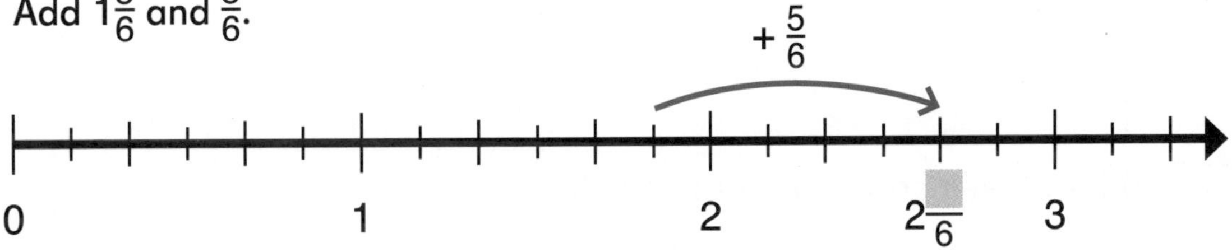

$1\frac{5}{6} + \frac{5}{6} = 1\frac{10}{6}$

$= 2\frac{\square}{6}$

$= 2\frac{\square}{3}$

4 Add $1\frac{5}{8}$ and $\frac{3}{4}$.

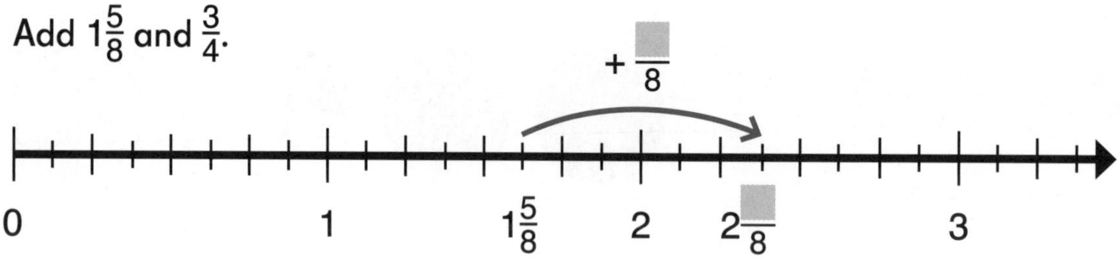

$$1\frac{5}{8} + \frac{3}{4} = 1\frac{5}{8} + \frac{\square}{8}$$

$$= 1\frac{\square}{8}$$

$$= 2\frac{\square}{8}$$

5 Add $2\frac{2}{3}$ and $\frac{5}{6}$.

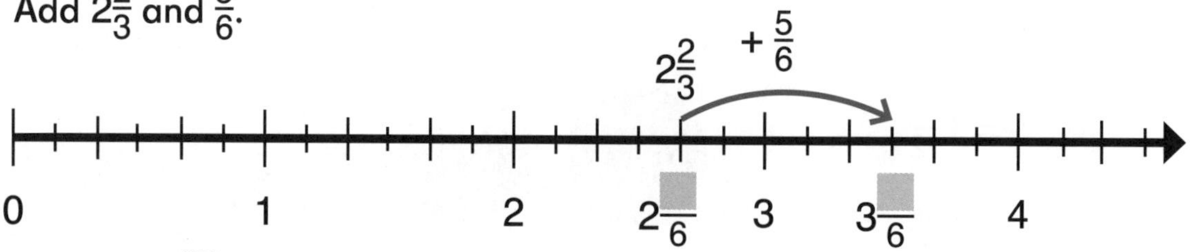

$$2\frac{2}{3} + \frac{5}{6} = 2\frac{\square}{6} + \frac{5}{6}$$

$$= 2\frac{\square}{6}$$

$$= 3\frac{\square}{2}$$

6 Add. Express each answer in its simplest form.

(a) $7\frac{5}{11} + \frac{3}{11}$ (b) $3\frac{1}{9} + \frac{5}{9}$ (c) $\frac{5}{12} + 1\frac{11}{12}$

(d) $6\frac{5}{8} + \frac{7}{8}$ (e) $7\frac{9}{14} + \frac{2}{7}$ (f) $3\frac{3}{10} + \frac{1}{5}$

(g) $9\frac{3}{4} + \frac{7}{12}$ (h) $\frac{1}{5} + \frac{2}{5} + 8\frac{3}{5}$ (i) $6\frac{1}{2} + \frac{1}{4} + \frac{3}{8}$

Exercise 3 • page 157

Lesson 4
Adding Mixed Numbers

4

Think

Dion's mother is making potato soup. She used $2\frac{3}{5}$ kg of white potatoes and $1\frac{4}{5}$ kg of russet potatoes.
How many kilograms of potatoes did she use in all?

Learn

$2\frac{3}{5} + 1\frac{4}{5}$

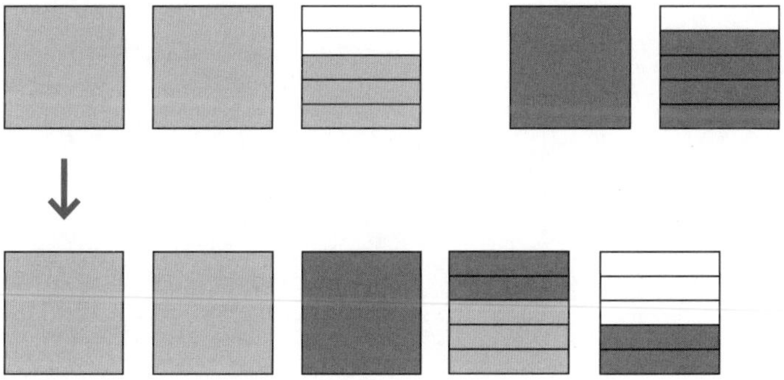

$2\frac{3}{5} \xrightarrow{+1} 3\frac{3}{5} \xrightarrow{+\frac{4}{5}} 3\frac{7}{5}$

$2 + 1 + \frac{3}{5} + \frac{4}{5} = 3\frac{7}{5}$

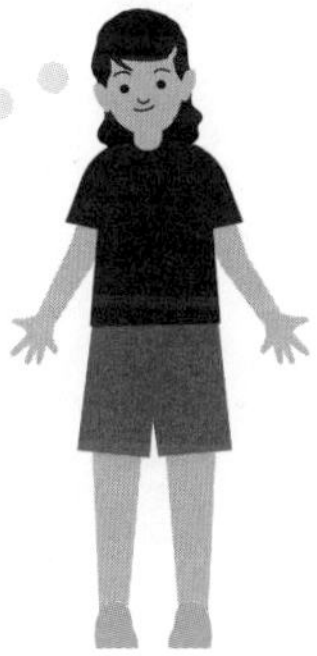

$2\frac{3}{5} + 1\frac{4}{5} = 3\frac{7}{5}$

$= 4\frac{2}{5}$

Dion's mother used _______ kilograms of potatoes in all.

Do

1 Add $1\frac{5}{6}$ and $2\frac{2}{3}$.

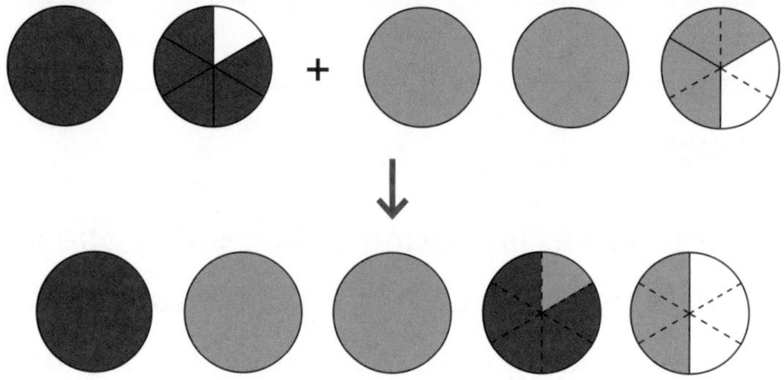

$1\frac{5}{6} + 2\frac{2}{3} = 3\frac{5}{6} + \frac{4}{6}$

$= 3\frac{\square}{6}$

$= 4\frac{\square}{2}$

2 Add $5\frac{2}{3}$ and $3\frac{5}{9}$.

$5\frac{2}{3} + 3\frac{5}{9} = 8\frac{2}{3} + \frac{5}{9}$

$= 8\frac{\square}{9} + \frac{\square}{9}$

$= 8\frac{\square}{9}$

$= 9\frac{\square}{9}$

3 Add. Express each answer in its simplest form.

(a) $6\frac{4}{5} + 2\frac{3}{5}$ (b) $8\frac{7}{10} + 1\frac{9}{10}$ (c) $3\frac{5}{9} + 8\frac{7}{9}$

(d) $4\frac{1}{6} + 4\frac{1}{2}$ (e) $8\frac{5}{6} + 4\frac{5}{12}$ (f) $3\frac{1}{2} + 1\frac{5}{8}$

(g) $1\frac{3}{4} + 6\frac{5}{12}$ (h) $\frac{1}{7} + 5\frac{2}{7} + 4\frac{3}{7}$ (i) $2\frac{1}{2} + \frac{3}{4} + 6\frac{5}{8}$

4 The drive from Ava's house to her grandmother's house takes $4\frac{3}{4}$ hours if there are no stops. Ava's family stopped for $1\frac{1}{2}$ hours for a meal and $\frac{1}{4}$ of an hour for a break. How long did the trip take in all?

Exercise 4 • page 160

Think

Alex made $2\frac{1}{5}$ L of coffee. He used $\frac{4}{5}$ L to make coffee mousse. How many liters of coffee does he have left?

Learn

$2\frac{1}{5} - \frac{4}{5}$

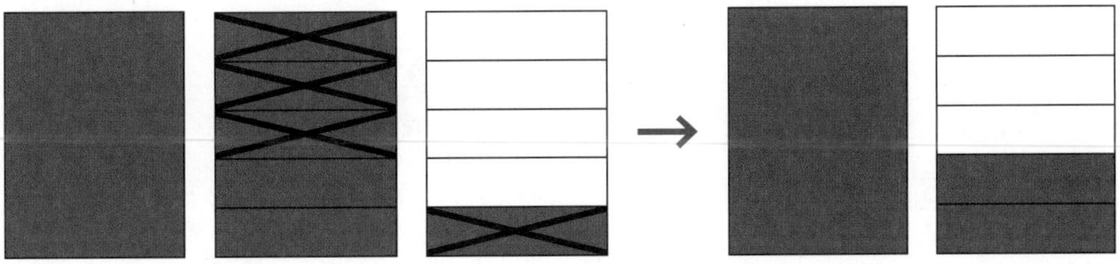

$2\frac{1}{5} - \frac{4}{5} = 1\frac{6}{5} - \frac{4}{5}$

$= 1\frac{2}{5}$

$\frac{4}{5}$ is greater than $\frac{1}{5}$. Express 1 as $\frac{5}{5}$.

$2\frac{1}{5} = 1 + \frac{5}{5} + \frac{1}{5} = 1\frac{6}{5}$

Alex has _______ L of coffee left.

Do

1 (a) Subtract $\frac{5}{7}$ from 1.

$1 - \frac{5}{7} = \frac{\square}{7} - \frac{5}{7}$

$= \frac{\square}{7}$

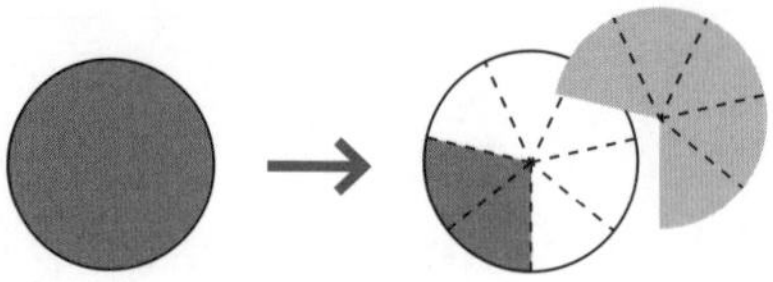

(b) Subtract $\frac{5}{7}$ from 2.

$2 - \frac{5}{7} = 1\frac{\square}{7} - \frac{5}{7}$

$= 1\frac{\square}{7}$

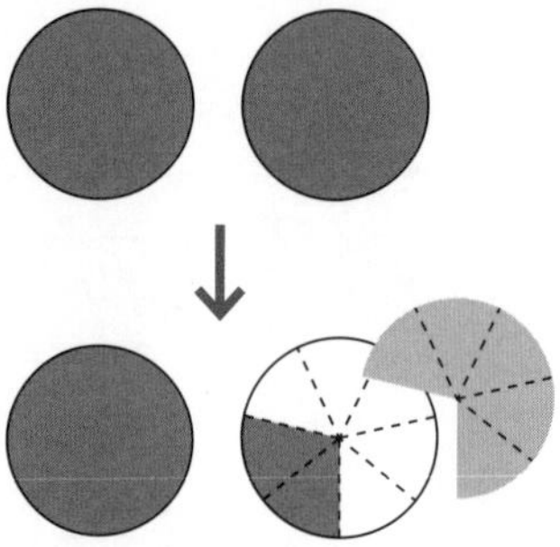

(c) Subtract $\frac{5}{7}$ from $2\frac{3}{7}$.

$2\frac{3}{7} - \frac{5}{7} = 1\frac{\square}{7} - \frac{5}{7}$

$= 1\frac{\square}{7}$

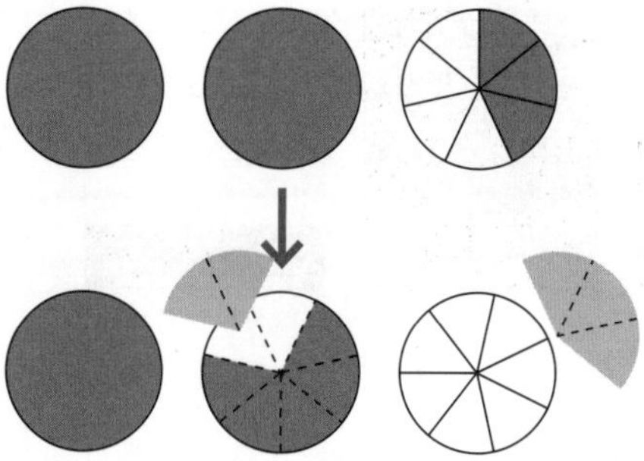

2 Subtract $\frac{2}{3}$ from $3\frac{1}{6}$.

$3\frac{1}{6} - \frac{2}{3} = 3\frac{1}{6} - \frac{\square}{6}$

$= 2\frac{\square}{6} - \frac{\square}{6}$

$= 2\frac{\square}{6}$

$= 2\frac{\square}{2}$

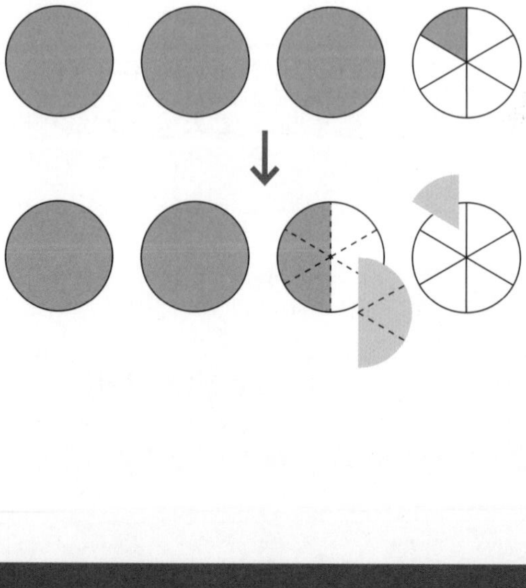

3 Subtract $\frac{5}{8}$ from $1\frac{1}{2}$.

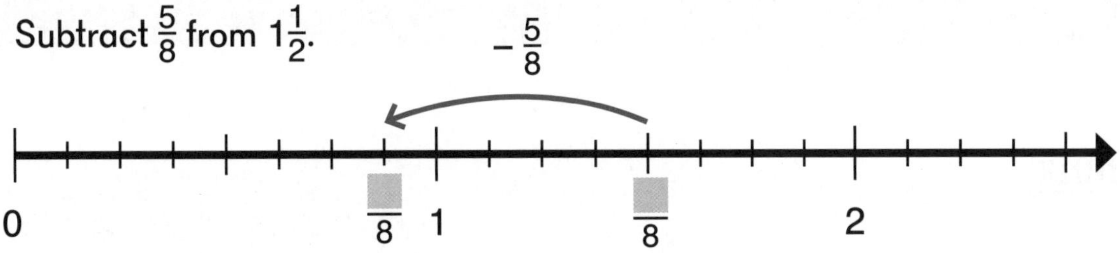

$1\frac{1}{2} - \frac{5}{8} = 1\frac{\square}{8} - \frac{5}{8}$

$= \frac{\square}{8} - \frac{\square}{8}$

$= \frac{\square}{8}$

4 $6\frac{5}{12} - \frac{3}{4} = 6\frac{5}{12} - \frac{\square}{12}$

$= 5\frac{\square}{12} - \frac{\square}{12}$

$= 5\frac{\square}{12}$

$= 5\frac{\square}{3}$

$6\frac{5}{12} = 5 + 1\frac{5}{12}$

$= 5 + \frac{17}{12}$

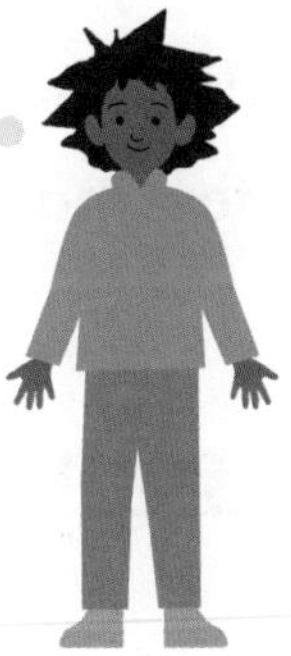

5 Subtract. Express each answer in its simplest form.

(a) $7\frac{5}{11} - \frac{3}{11}$ (b) $3\frac{1}{9} - \frac{5}{9}$ (c) $5\frac{3}{10} - \frac{7}{10}$

(d) $6\frac{5}{8} - \frac{7}{8}$ (e) $7\frac{9}{14} - \frac{2}{7}$ (f) $4\frac{3}{4} - \frac{7}{12}$

(g) $9\frac{3}{10} - \frac{1}{2}$ (h) $6\frac{1}{2} - \frac{7}{8}$ (i) $8\frac{1}{3} - \frac{4}{9}$

Exercise 5 • page 162

Lesson 6
Subtracting Mixed Numbers

6

Think

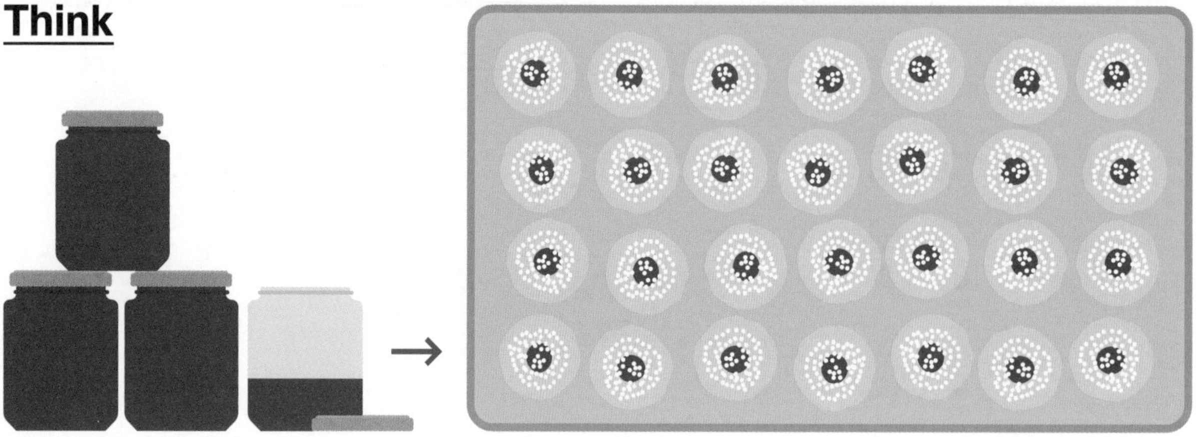

Mei has $3\frac{2}{5}$ jars of jam. She uses $1\frac{3}{5}$ jars of jam to make jelly donuts. How many jars of jam does she have left?

Learn

$3\frac{2}{5} - 1\frac{3}{5}$

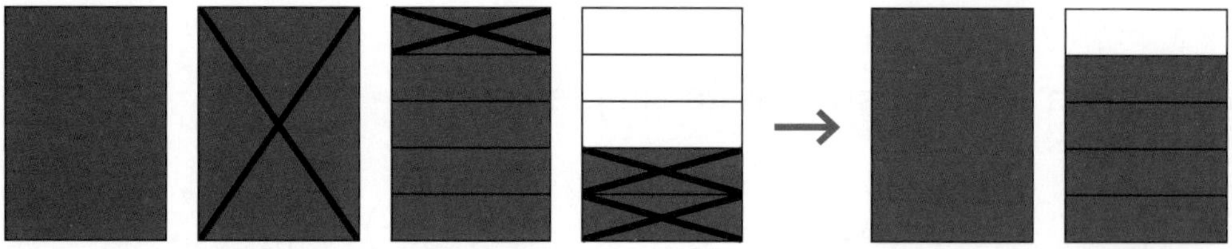

$$3\frac{2}{5} - 1\frac{3}{5} = 2\frac{2}{5} - \frac{3}{5}$$

$$= 1\frac{7}{5} - \frac{3}{5}$$

$$= 1\frac{4}{5}$$

$$3\frac{2}{5} \xrightarrow{-1} 2\frac{2}{5} \xrightarrow{-\frac{3}{5}} ?$$

Mei has ______ jars of jam left.

Do

1 Subtract 2 from $3\frac{3}{7}$.

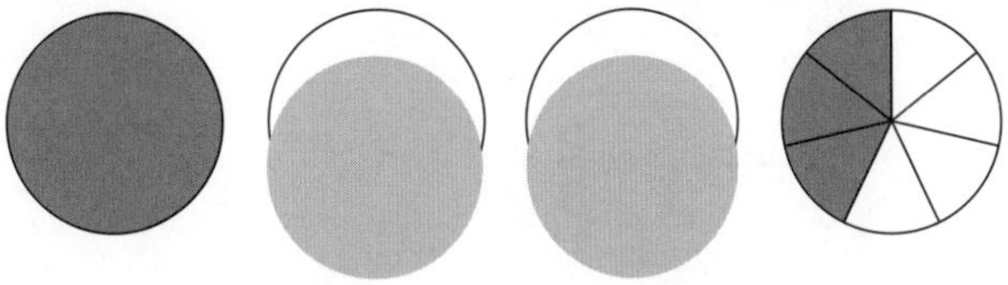

$3\frac{3}{7} - 2 = \square\,\frac{\square}{7}$

2 Subtract $2\frac{1}{5}$ from 4.

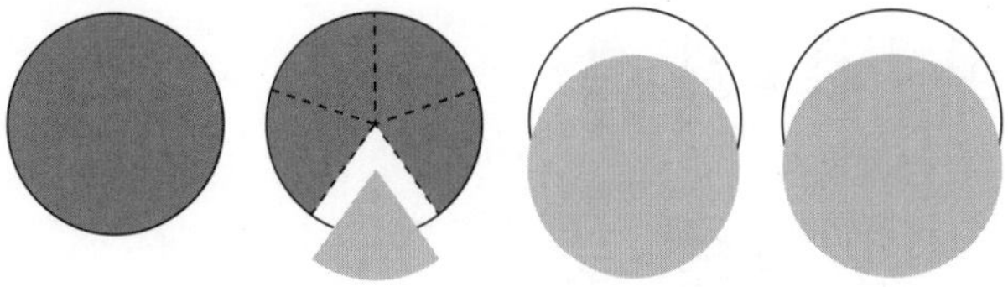

$4 - 2\frac{1}{5} = 4 - 2 - \frac{1}{5}$

$= \square\,\frac{\square}{5}$

3 Subtract $1\frac{3}{4}$ from $2\frac{3}{8}$.

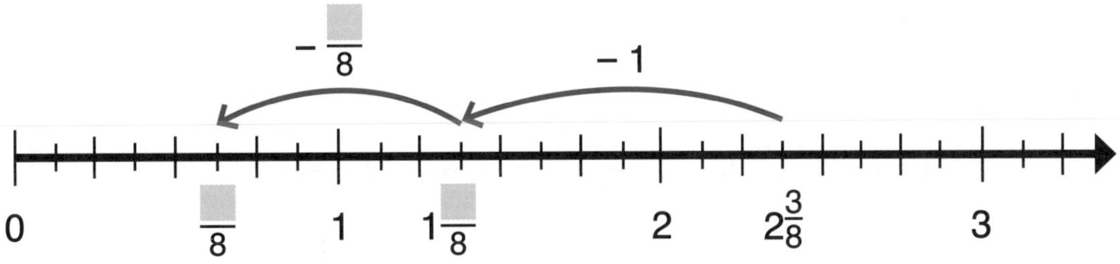

$2\frac{3}{8} - 1\frac{3}{4} = 1\frac{\square}{8} - \frac{3}{4}$

$= \frac{\square}{8} - \frac{\square}{8}$

$= \frac{\square}{8}$

4 $7\frac{1}{3} - 1\frac{2}{3} = 6\frac{1}{3} - \frac{2}{3}$

$= 5\frac{\square}{3} - \frac{2}{3}$

$= 5\frac{\square}{3}$

$6\frac{1}{3} = 5 + 1\frac{1}{3}$

$= 5 + \frac{4}{3}$

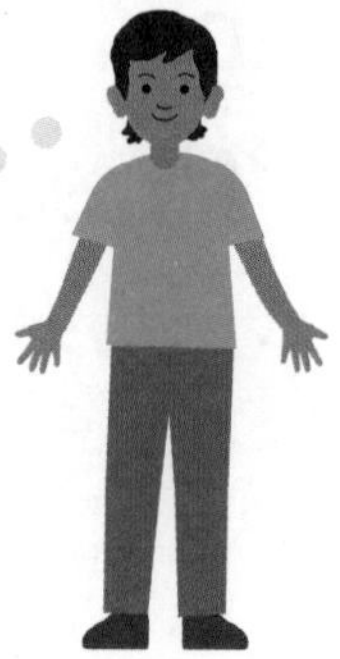

5 $9\frac{1}{6} - 4\frac{1}{2} = 5\frac{1}{6} - \frac{1}{2}$

$= 5\frac{1}{6} - \frac{\square}{6}$

$= 4\frac{\square}{6} - \frac{\square}{6}$

$= 4\frac{\square}{6}$

$= 4\frac{\square}{3}$

$5\frac{1}{6} = 4 + 1\frac{1}{6}$

$= 4 + \frac{7}{6}$

6 Subtract. Express each answer in its simplest form.

(a) $7\frac{7}{10} - 4$ (b) $9 - 6\frac{5}{9}$ (c) $12 - 7\frac{5}{6}$

(d) $6\frac{2}{5} - 4\frac{2}{5}$ (e) $9\frac{7}{8} - 3\frac{3}{8}$ (f) $8\frac{7}{9} - 5\frac{5}{9}$

(g) $6\frac{2}{5} - 4\frac{4}{5}$ (h) $9\frac{3}{8} - 3\frac{7}{8}$ (i) $8\frac{5}{9} - 5\frac{7}{9}$

(j) $7\frac{9}{12} - 2\frac{1}{3}$ (k) $6\frac{7}{8} - 3\frac{1}{4}$ (l) $8\frac{2}{3} - 7\frac{4}{9}$

(m) $7\frac{1}{3} - 2\frac{9}{12}$ (n) $6\frac{1}{4} - 3\frac{7}{8}$ (o) $8\frac{4}{9} - 7\frac{2}{3}$

Exercise 6 • page 165

Lesson 7
Practice

P 7

1 Add or subtract. Express each answer in its simplest form.

(a) $\frac{4}{9} + \frac{8}{9}$

(b) $\frac{11}{12} - \frac{7}{12}$

(c) $\frac{3}{7} + \frac{5}{7}$

(d) $\frac{2}{3} - \frac{2}{9}$

(e) $\frac{1}{6} + \frac{3}{12}$

(f) $\frac{5}{6} - \frac{2}{3}$

(g) $\frac{13}{16} - \frac{3}{8}$

(h) $\frac{17}{20} + \frac{3}{5}$

(i) $\frac{9}{10} + \frac{1}{2} + \frac{3}{5}$

2 Add or subtract. Express each answer in its simplest form.

(a) $12 - 7\frac{5}{9}$

(b) $5\frac{1}{8} + 3\frac{3}{8}$

(c) $4\frac{5}{12} + 5\frac{7}{12}$

(d) $4\frac{3}{5} - 1\frac{1}{10}$

(e) $9\frac{5}{8} - 3\frac{1}{4}$

(f) $8\frac{2}{3} - 5\frac{2}{9}$

(g) $7\frac{1}{6} - 4\frac{1}{2}$

(h) $9\frac{3}{8} - 3\frac{3}{4}$

(i) $10\frac{2}{3} - 4\frac{5}{6}$

3 Amanda ran $\frac{7}{10}$ km on Monday, the same distance on Tuesday, and $\frac{9}{10}$ km on Wednesday. How far did she run altogether?

4 Max and Lincoln are painting a fence. Max painted $\frac{1}{3}$ of it and Lincoln painted $\frac{4}{9}$ of it.

(a) How much of the fence did they paint altogether?

(b) How much more of the fence did Lincoln paint than Max?

5 A bag of red beans weighs $3\frac{7}{8}$ lb. A bag of white beans is $1\frac{3}{8}$ lb heavier than the bag of red beans. What is the total weight of both bags of beans?

6 It is $10\frac{1}{2}$ miles from Town A to Town B. Then it is another $8\frac{3}{4}$ miles from Town B to Town C.

(a) What is the total distance from Town A to Town C through Town B?

(b) How much farther is it from Town A to Town B than from Town B to Town C?

7 A white ribbon is $\frac{3}{4}$ m long. A red ribbon is $\frac{1}{8}$ m shorter than the white ribbon. A blue ribbon is $\frac{1}{2}$ m longer than the red ribbon.

(a) How much longer is the blue ribbon than the white ribbon?

(b) What is the total length of all three ribbons?

8 A bucket contains $4\frac{3}{5}$ L of water. After $1\frac{7}{10}$ L of water was poured from a pail into the bucket, the pail had $2\frac{1}{2}$ L less water than the bucket.

(a) How much water is in the bucket now?

(b) If the capacity of the bucket is 8 L, how much more water could it hold?

(c) How much water is left in the pail?

Exercise 7 • page 167

Chapter 8

Multiplying a Fraction and a Whole Number

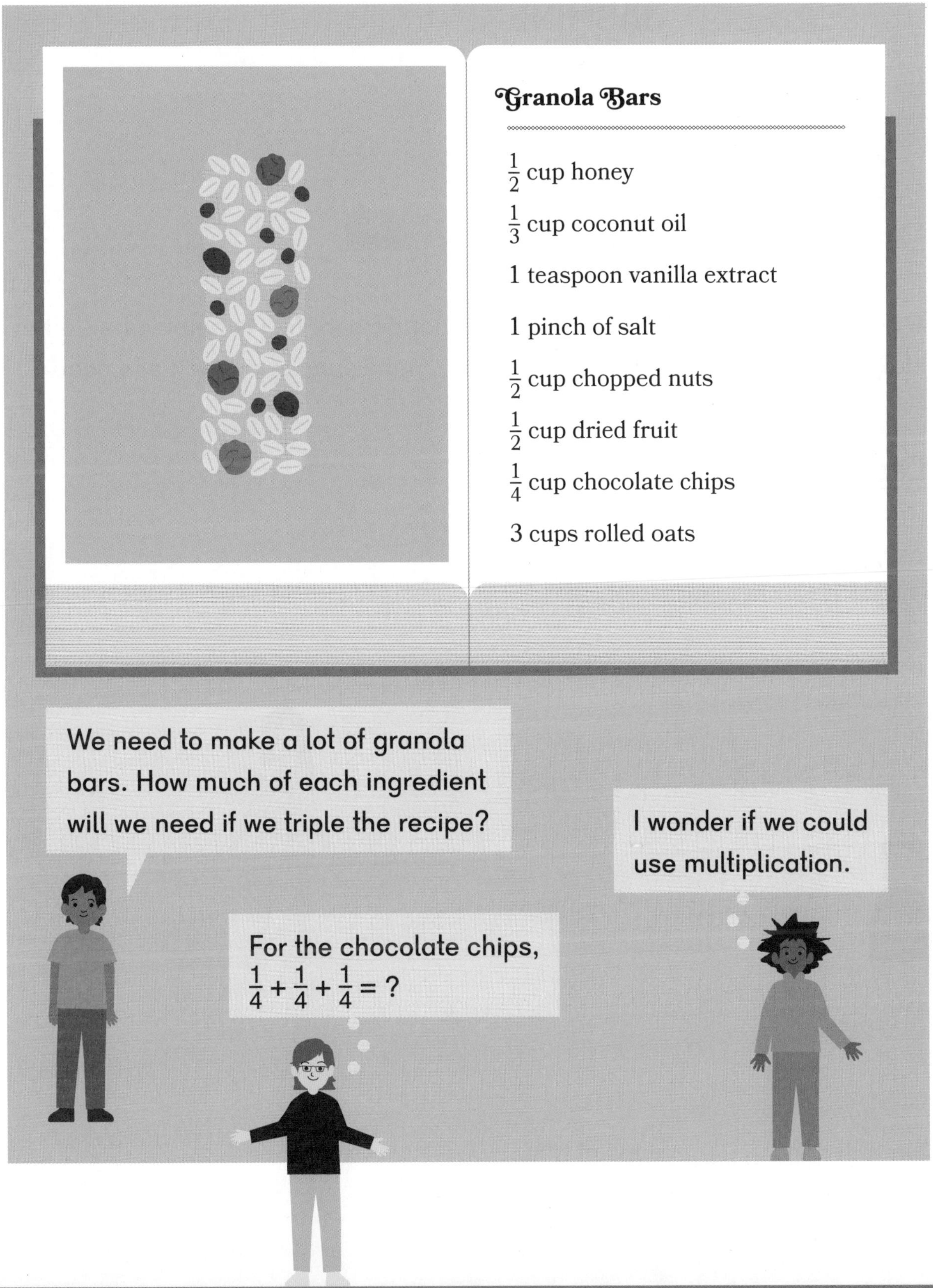

Lesson 1
Multiplying a Unit Fraction by a Whole Number

1

Think

A rice pilaf recipe calls for $\frac{1}{8}$ cup of rice per person. Mei is helping her father make enough rice pilaf for 5 people. How many cups of rice will she need?

Learn

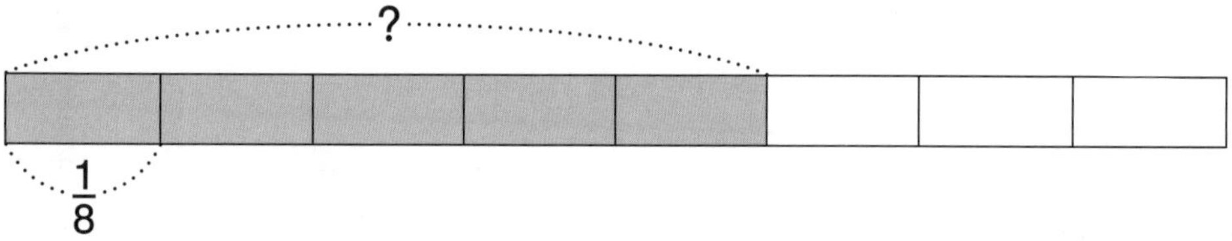

$5 \times \frac{1}{8} = \frac{5 \times 1}{8} = \frac{\square}{8}$

$\frac{1}{8} + \frac{1}{8} + \frac{1}{8} + \frac{1}{8} + \frac{1}{8} = \frac{?}{8}$

5 × 1 eighth = 5 eighths

She will need _______ cups of rice.

Do

1 (a)

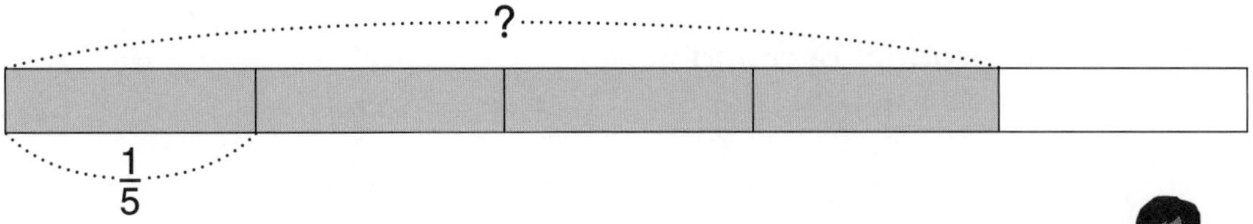

$\frac{\square}{5} = \frac{1}{5} + \frac{1}{5} + \frac{1}{5} + \frac{1}{5}$

How many $\frac{1}{5}$s are in $\frac{4}{5}$?

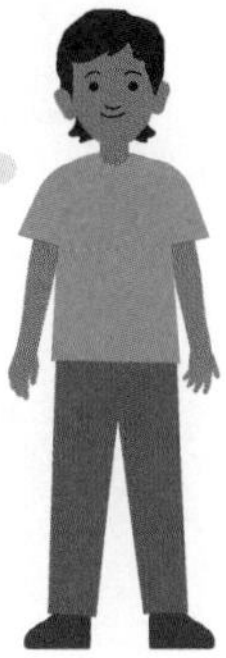

$\frac{4}{5} = \square \times \frac{1}{5}$

(b)

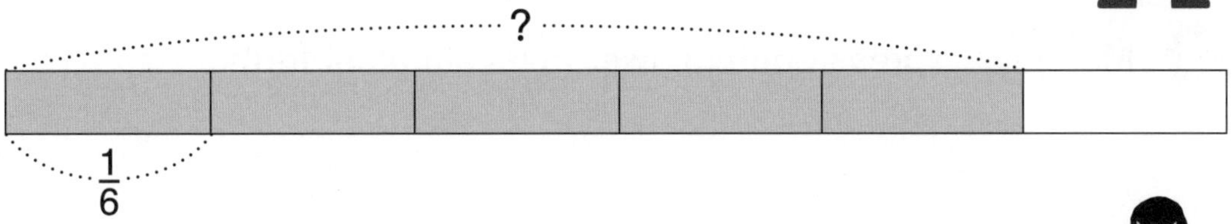

$\frac{5}{6} = \frac{\square}{\square} + \frac{\square}{\square} + \frac{\square}{\square} + \frac{\square}{\square} + \frac{\square}{\square}$

How many $\frac{1}{6}$s are in $\frac{5}{6}$?

$\frac{5}{6} = \square \times \frac{\square}{6}$

2 Find the products.

(a) $3 \times \frac{1}{4} = \frac{3 \times 1}{4} = \frac{\square}{4}$

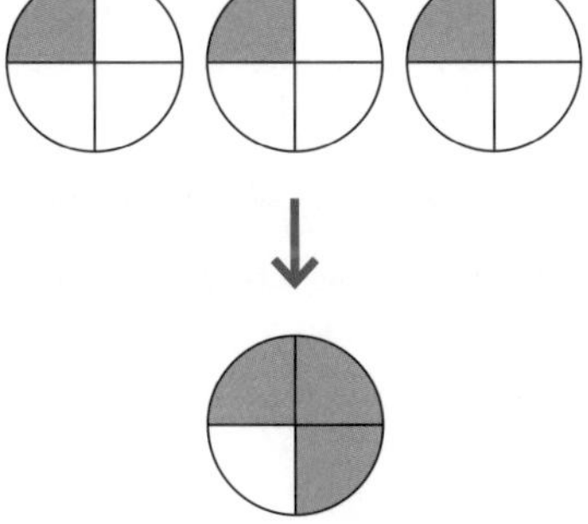

(b) $4 \times \frac{1}{2} = \frac{\square \times 1}{2} = \frac{\square}{2} = \square$

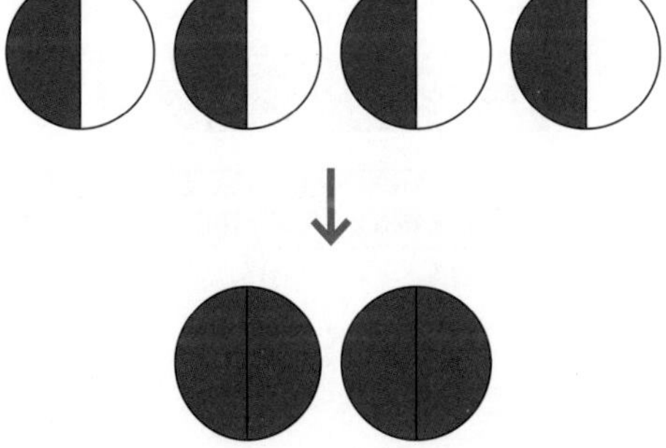

3 Find the product of 5 and $\frac{1}{3}$.

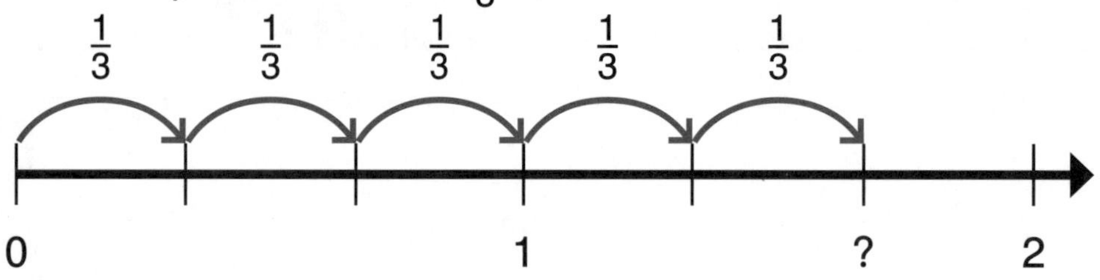

$5 \times \frac{1}{3} = \frac{\square \times 1}{\square} = \frac{\square}{\square} = \square\frac{\square}{\square}$

4 Multiply. Express each answer in its simplest form.

(a) $5 \times \frac{1}{7}$

(b) $3 \times \frac{1}{5}$

(c) $6 \times \frac{1}{8}$

(d) $4 \times \frac{1}{4}$

(e) $9 \times \frac{1}{3}$

(f) $6 \times \frac{1}{12}$

(g) $10 \times \frac{1}{4}$

(h) $9 \times \frac{1}{6}$

5 A red ribbon is $\frac{1}{3}$ m long. A blue ribbon is 3 times as long as the red ribbon. What is the total combined length of the two ribbons in meters?

Exercise 1 • page 171

Multiplying a Fraction by a Whole Number — Part 1

2

Think

Alex drank $\frac{2}{7}$ L of water. Sofia drank 3 times as much water as Alex. How much water did Sofia drink?

Learn

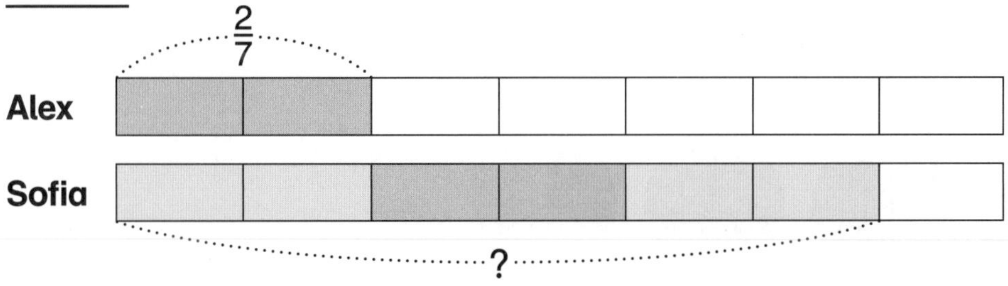

Method 1

$3 \times \frac{2}{7} = \frac{3 \times 2}{7} = \frac{\square}{7}$

$\frac{2}{7} + \frac{2}{7} + \frac{2}{7} = \frac{?}{7}$

3 × 2 sevenths = ? sevenths

Method 2

$3 \times \frac{2}{7} = 3 \times 2 \times \frac{1}{7}$

$= 6 \times \frac{1}{7}$

$= \frac{\square}{7}$

$\frac{2}{7} = 2 \times \frac{1}{7}$

Sofia drank _______ L of water.

Do

1 Find the product of 4 and $\frac{2}{9}$.

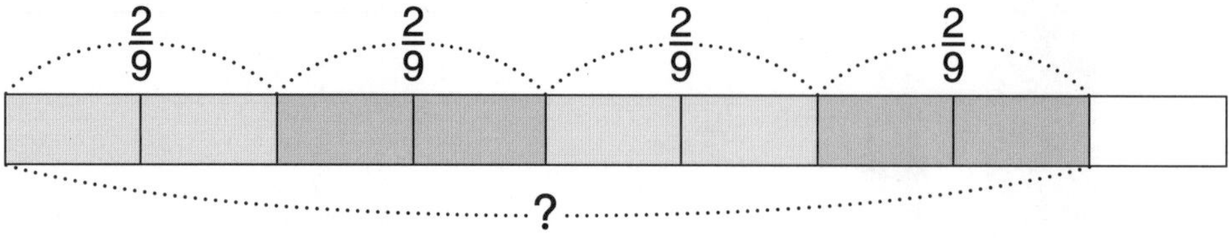

$$4 \times \frac{2}{9} = \frac{4 \times 2}{9} = \frac{\square}{9}$$

2 Find the product of 5 and $\frac{2}{3}$.

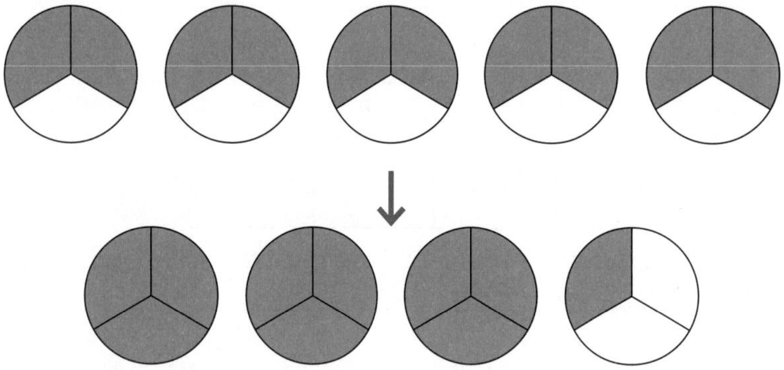

$$5 \times \frac{2}{3} = \frac{\square \times 2}{3} = \frac{\square}{\square} = \square\frac{\square}{\square}$$

3 Find the product of 4 and $\frac{3}{4}$.

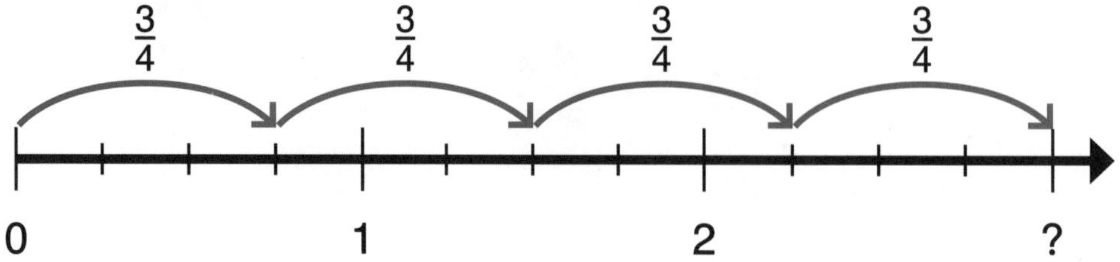

$$4 \times \frac{3}{4} = \frac{\square \times 3}{\square} = \frac{\square}{\square} = \square$$

4 Mei is stapling 5 paper rectangles end-to-end on a bulletin board to make a border. Each rectangle is $\frac{7}{8}$ inches long. How long is the border?

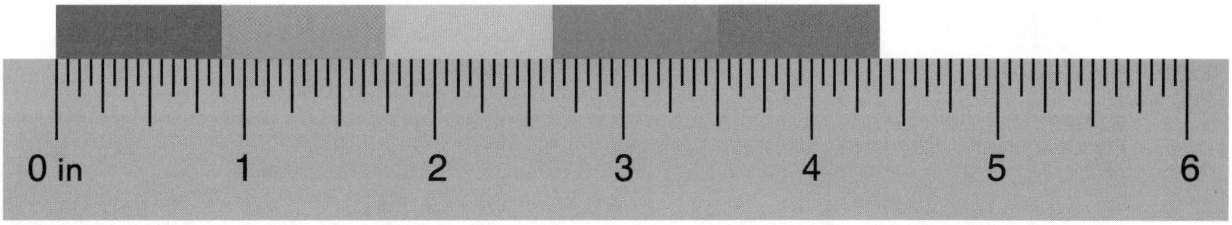

$5 \times \frac{7}{8} = \frac{5 \times \square}{\square} = \frac{\square}{\square} = \square\frac{\square}{\square}$

5 Multiply. Express each answer in its simplest form.

(a) $2 \times \frac{2}{5}$

(b) $2 \times \frac{3}{7}$

(c) $3 \times \frac{2}{9}$

(d) $5 \times \frac{3}{4}$

(e) $2 \times \frac{4}{8}$

(f) $3 \times \frac{5}{2}$

(g) $6 \times \frac{3}{4}$

(h) $3 \times \frac{4}{5}$

6

A bag of broccoli weighs $\frac{3}{4}$ lb. Janice bought 3 bags of broccoli. How many pounds of broccoli did she buy?

Exercise 2 • page 174

Think

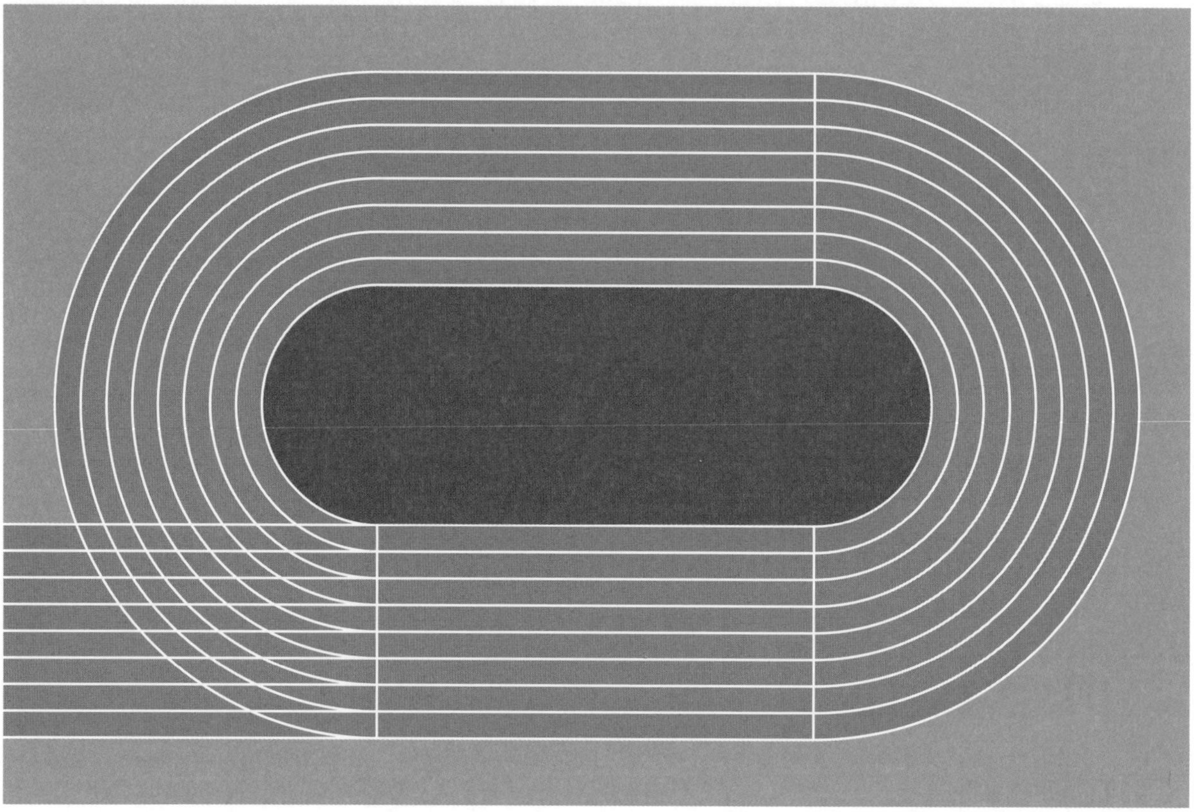

The distance around a running track is $\frac{3}{8}$ mile. Dion ran around the track twice. How far did he run?

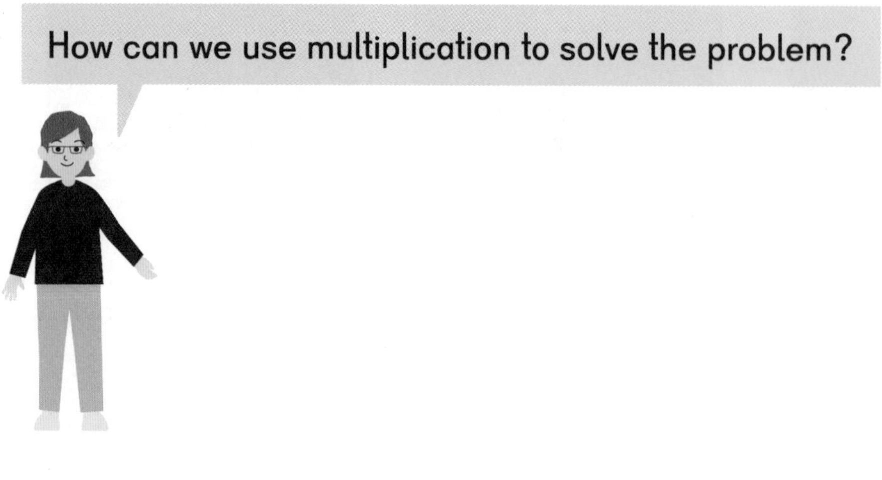

Learn

Method 1

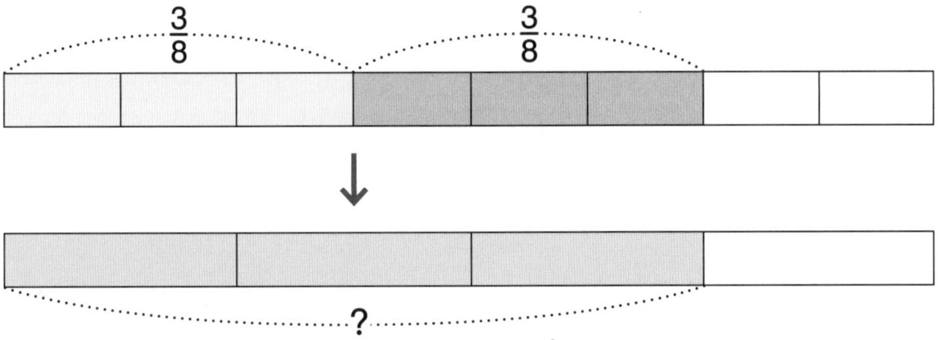

$$2 \times \frac{3}{8} = \frac{2 \times 3}{8} = \frac{\square}{8} = \frac{\square}{4}$$

Method 2

$$2 \times \frac{3}{8} = \frac{\overset{1}{\cancel{2}} \times 3}{\underset{4}{\cancel{8}}} = \frac{\square}{4}$$

We can simplify the calculation by dividing the numerator and the denominator by a common factor in the same way we simplify fractions.

$$\frac{2 \times 3}{8} = \frac{1 \times 3}{4}$$

Factors of 2 ⟶ 1, **2**
Factors of 8 ⟶ 1, **2**, 4, 8

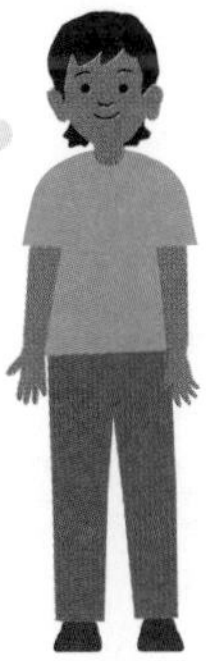

He ran ________ mile.

Do

1 Find the product of 3 and $\frac{2}{9}$.

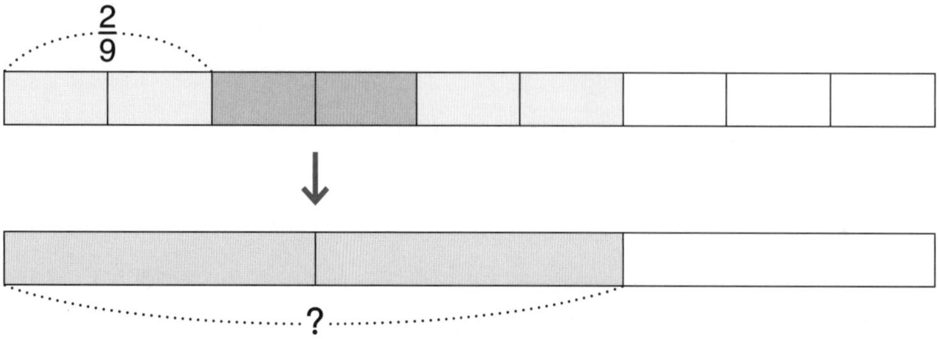

$$3 \times \frac{2}{9} = \frac{\overset{1}{\cancel{3}} \times 2}{\underset{3}{\cancel{9}}} = \frac{\square}{\square}$$

Simplify the calculation first.
Factors of 3 ⟶ 1, **3**
Factors of 9 ⟶ 1, **3**, 9

We could also show it this way:
$\overset{1}{\cancel{3}} \times \frac{2}{\underset{3}{\cancel{9}}}$

2 Find the product of 5 and $\frac{3}{5}$.

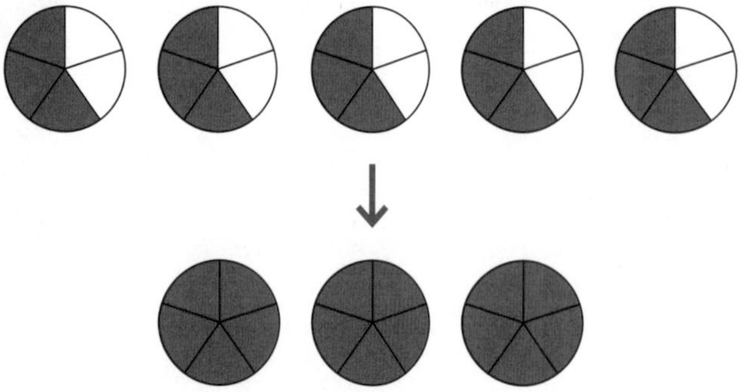

$$5 \times \frac{3}{5} = \frac{\overset{1}{\cancel{5}} \times 3}{\underset{1}{\cancel{5}}} = \square$$

3 Find the product of 6 and $\frac{5}{8}$.

$$6 \times \frac{5}{8} = \frac{\overset{\square}{\cancel{6}} \times 5}{\underset{4}{\cancel{8}}} = \frac{\square}{\square} = \square\frac{\square}{\square}$$

Factors of 6 ⟶ 1, **2**, 3

Factors of 8 ⟶ 1, **2**, 4, 8

4 Find the product of 8 and $\frac{5}{12}$.

$$\overset{\square}{\cancel{8}} \times \frac{5}{\underset{\square}{\cancel{12}}} = \frac{\square}{\square} = \square\frac{\square}{\square}$$

Factors of 8 ⟶ 1, **2**, **4**, 8

Factors of 12 ⟶ 1, **2**, 3, **4**, 6, 12

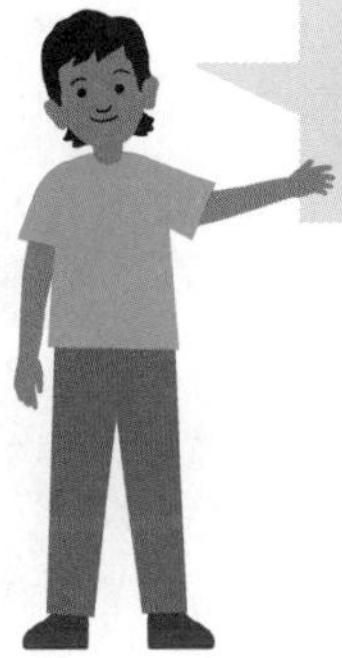

We can also simplify in more than one step:

$$\overset{\overset{2}{\cancel{4}}}{\cancel{8}} \times \frac{5}{\underset{\underset{3}{\cancel{6}}}{\cancel{12}}}$$

5 Find the values by simplifying the calculation first. Express each answer in its simplest form.

(a) $3 \times \frac{2}{9}$ (b) $2 \times \frac{3}{10}$ (c) $5 \times \frac{2}{15}$

(d) $8 \times \frac{7}{8}$ (e) $2 \times \frac{3}{4}$ (f) $6 \times \frac{5}{8}$

(g) $4 \times \frac{5}{6}$ (h) $4 \times \frac{7}{10}$ (i) $8 \times \frac{7}{20}$

6 The directions on an instant oatmeal package say, "Combine 1 package of instant oatmeal with $\frac{2}{3}$ cup of hot water." Sofia wants to use 6 packages. How much water should she use?

Exercise 3 • page 176

Think

There are 8 potatoes in a basket. 6 are yellow and 2 are red. What fraction of the potatoes are yellow? What fraction of the potatoes are red?

Learn

$\square$ out of 8 potatoes are yellow.

$\frac{\square}{8}$ of the potatoes are yellow.

$\square$ out of 8 potatoes are red.

$\frac{\square}{8}$ of the potatoes are red.

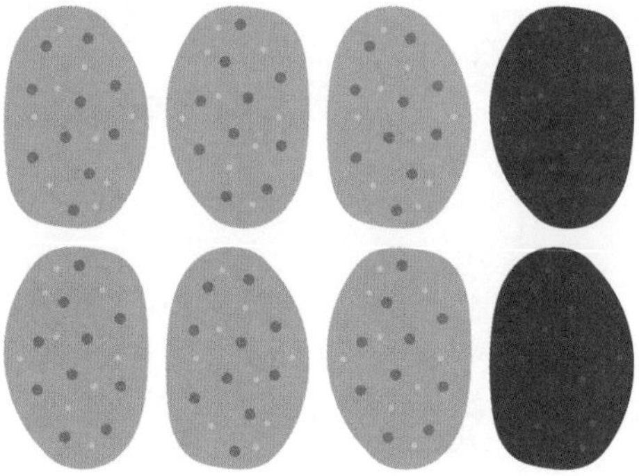

$\square$ out of 4 equal groups of potatoes are yellow.

$\frac{\square}{4}$ of the potatoes are yellow.

$\square$ out of 4 equal groups of potatoes are red.

$\frac{\square}{4}$ of the potatoes are red.

We can make equal groups of 2 potatoes. $\frac{6}{8} = \frac{3}{4}$

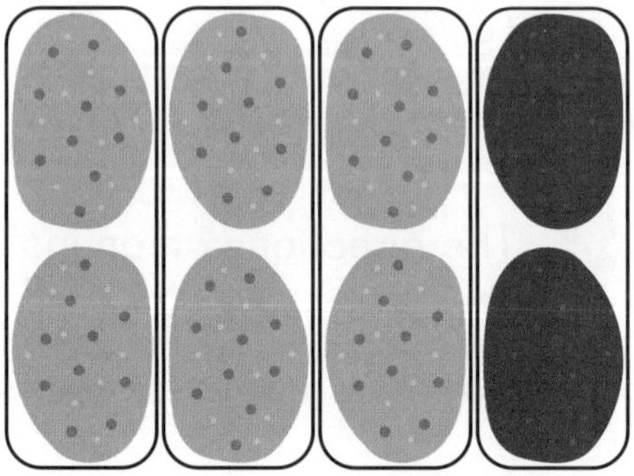

Do

1 What fraction of the animals are owls?

(a)

☐ out of 5 animals are owls.

$\frac{☐}{5}$ of the animals are owls.

(b)

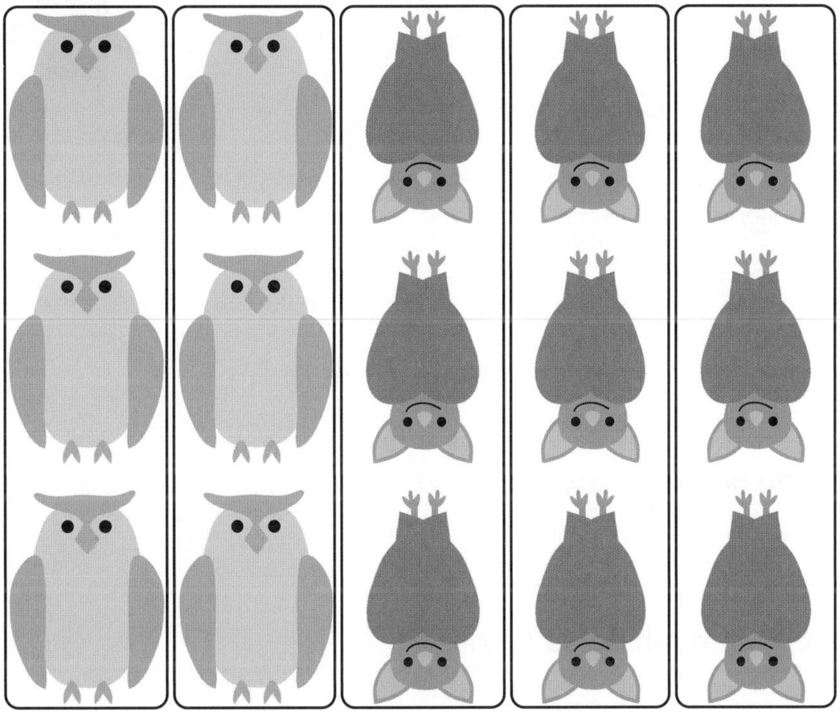

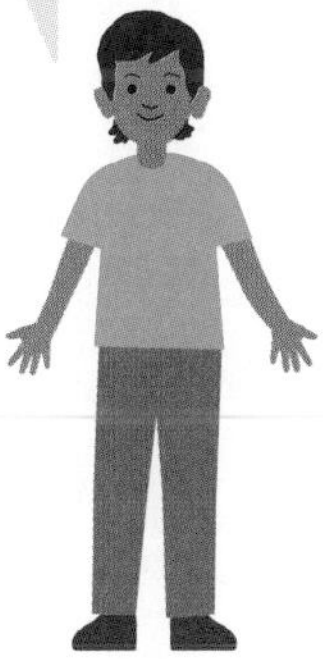

☐ out of 5 equal groups of animals are owls.

$\frac{☐}{5}$ of the animals are owls.

2 What fraction of each set of counters is red?

(a) 

___ out of ___ counters are red.

$\frac{\square}{\square}$ of the counters are red.

(b) 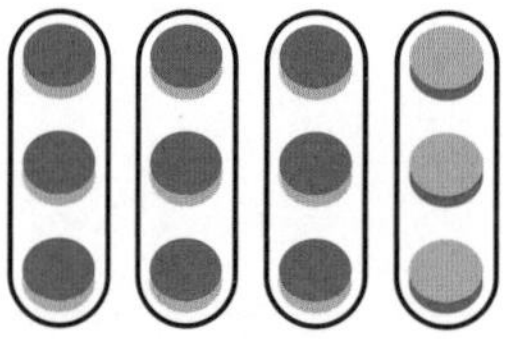

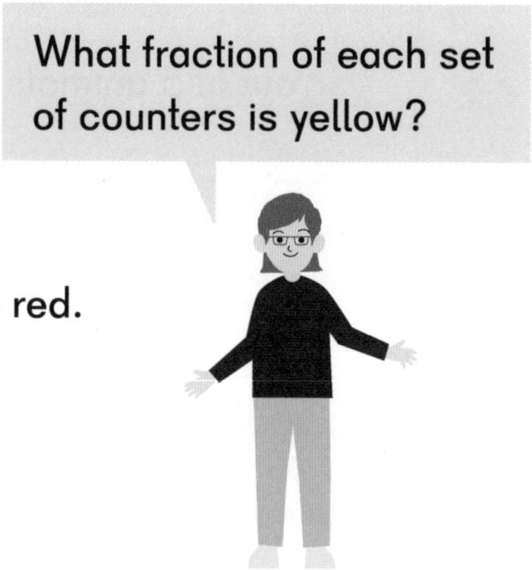

___ out of ___ groups of counters are red.

$\frac{\square}{\square}$ of the counters are red.

(c) 

___ out of ___ groups of counters are red.

$\frac{\square}{\square}$ of the counters are red.

3 What fraction of each set is colored?

(a) 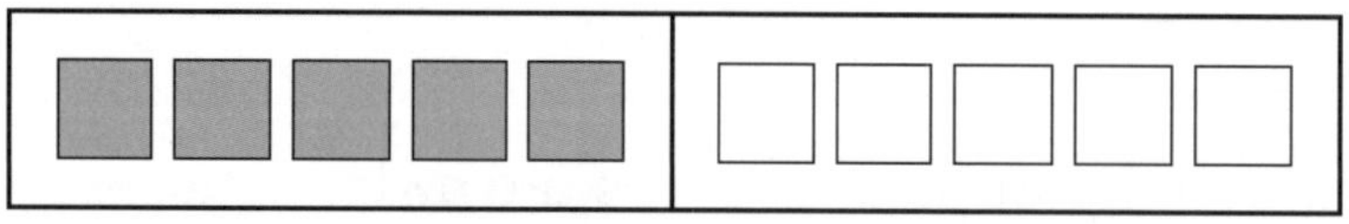

(b) 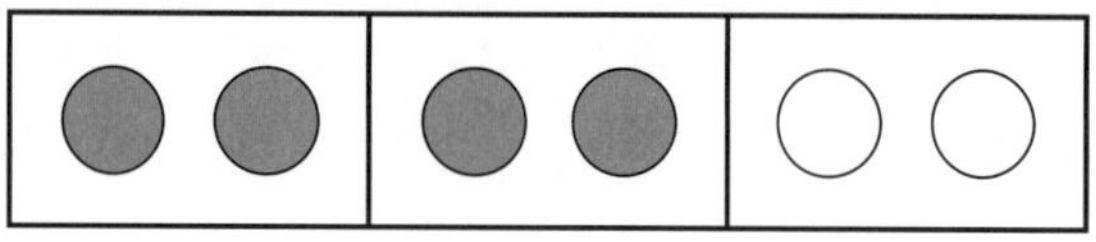

(c) 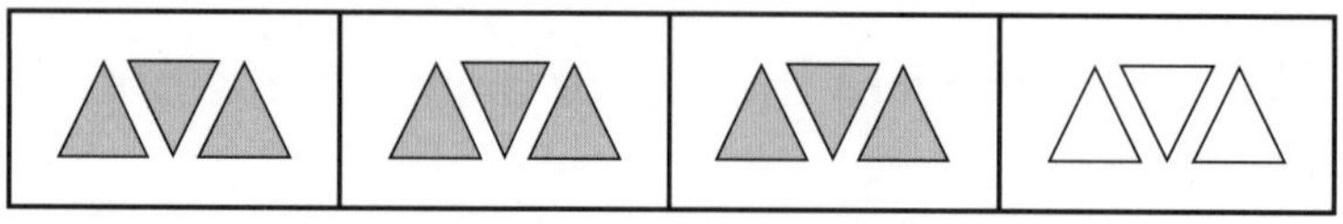

4 There are 8 toasters in a store. 6 are purple toasters and 2 are yellow toasters.

(a) What fraction of the toasters are purple?

$\frac{\square}{\square}$ of the toasters are purple.

6 out of 8 is $\frac{6}{8}$. $\frac{6}{8}$ in simplest form is...

(b) What fraction of the toasters are yellow?

$\frac{\square}{\square}$ of the toasters are yellow.

5 There are 100 oranges at a market. 25 of them are mandarin oranges and the rest are navel oranges.

(a) What fraction of the oranges are mandarin oranges?

(b) What fraction of the oranges are navel oranges?

Write your answers in simplest form.

Exercise 4 • page 179

Lesson 5
Multiplying a Whole Number by a Fraction — Part 1

5

Think

Emma has 16 coins in her collection. $\frac{3}{4}$ of them are silver-colored coins and the rest are copper-colored coins. How many silver-colored coins are there?

Will the answer be more than or less than 16?

Learn

Method 1

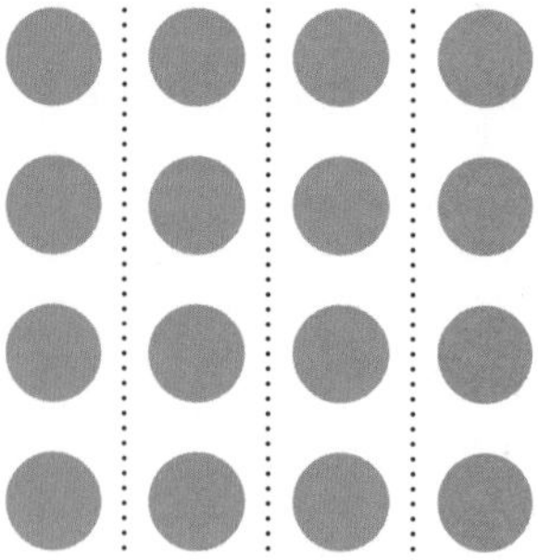

If we divide 16 into 4 equal groups, how many coins are in each group? How many coins are in 3 groups?

$\frac{1}{4}$ of 16 $\longrightarrow$ $\frac{16}{4} = 16 \div 4 = 4$

$\frac{3}{4}$ of 16 $\longrightarrow$ $3 \times \frac{16}{4} = 3 \times 4 = \square$

Method 2

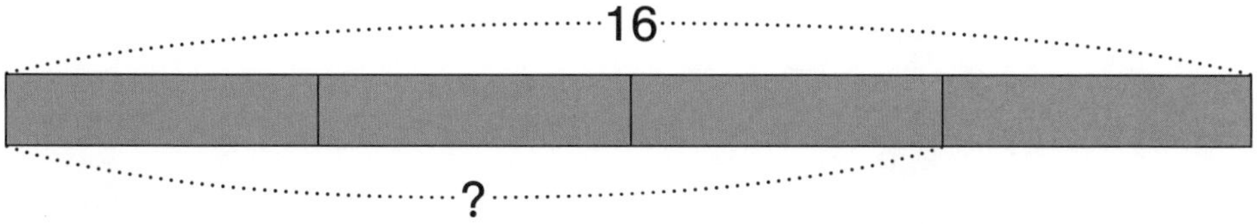

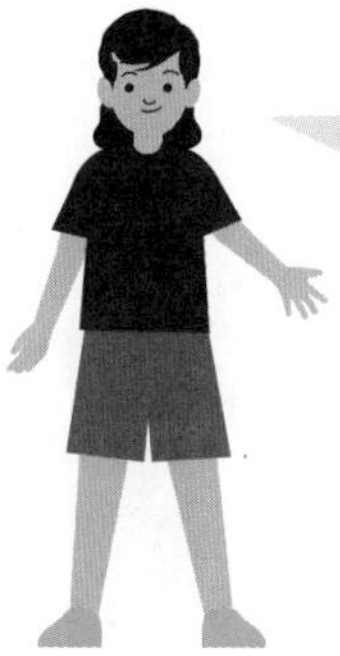

$\frac{3}{4}$ of 16 is the number that is $\frac{3}{4}$ times as much as 16.

The answer will be less than 16.

4 units $\longrightarrow$ 16

1 unit $\longrightarrow$ $\frac{16}{4} = 4$

3 units $\longrightarrow$ $3 \times 4 =$ ☐

Method 3

$\frac{3}{4} \times 16 = 16 \times \frac{3}{4}$, so I can use the same method as when I multiplied a fraction by a whole number.

$$\frac{3}{4} \times 16 = \frac{3 \times \overset{4}{\cancel{16}}}{\underset{1}{\cancel{4}}}$$

$$= \square$$

There are ________ silver-colored coins.

Do

1 (a) Find $\frac{1}{3}$ of 12.

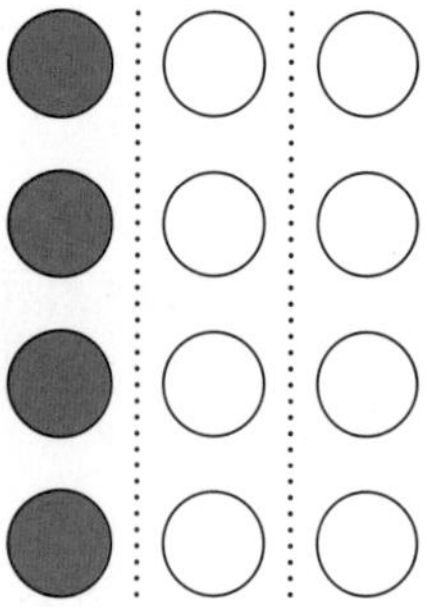

$12 \div 3 =$ ____

$\frac{1}{3} \times 12 =$ ____

(b) Find $\frac{2}{3}$ of 12.

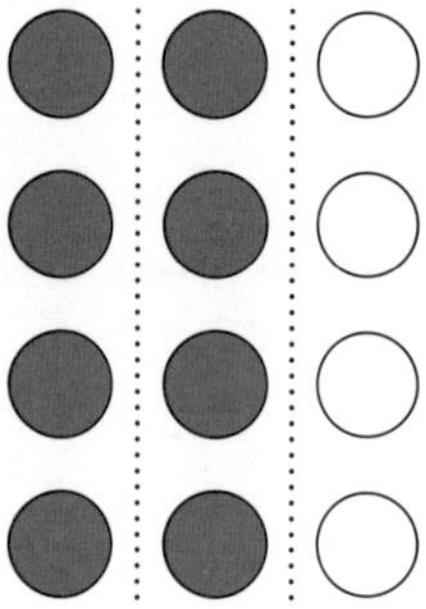

$\frac{1}{3} \times 12 = \frac{12}{3} = 4$

$\frac{2}{3} \times 12 = 2 \times \frac{12}{3}$

$=$ ____

2 (a) Find $\frac{1}{6}$ of 18.

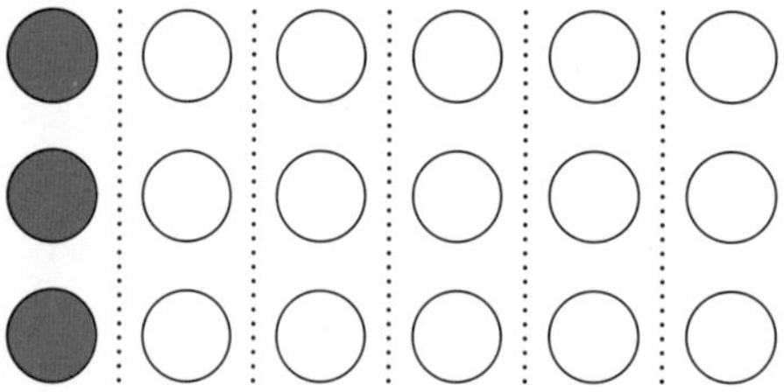

$\frac{1}{6} \times 18 = \frac{1 \times 18}{6}$

$=$ ____

(b) Find $\frac{5}{6}$ of 18.

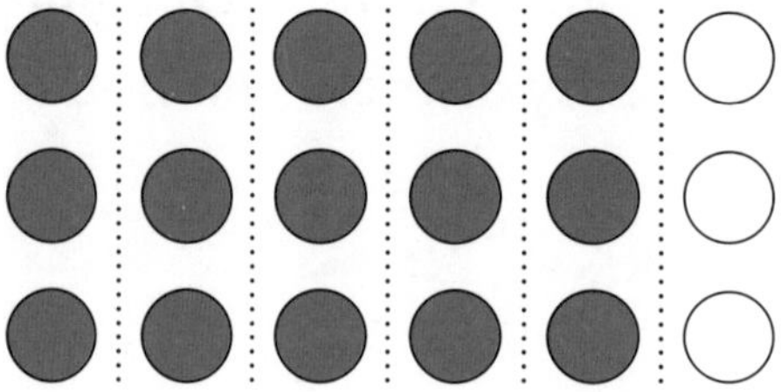

$\frac{5}{6} \times 18 = 5 \times \frac{18}{6}$

$=$ ____

3 (a) Find $\frac{3}{4}$ of 24.

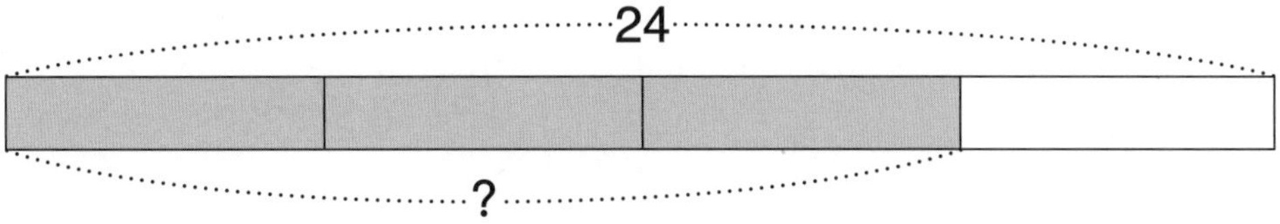

4 units $\longrightarrow$ 24

1 unit $\longrightarrow \frac{24}{4} = \square$

3 units $\longrightarrow 3 \times 6 = \square$

(b) $\frac{3}{4} \times 24 = \frac{3 \times 24}{4} = \square$

4 Find $\frac{4}{5}$ of 15.

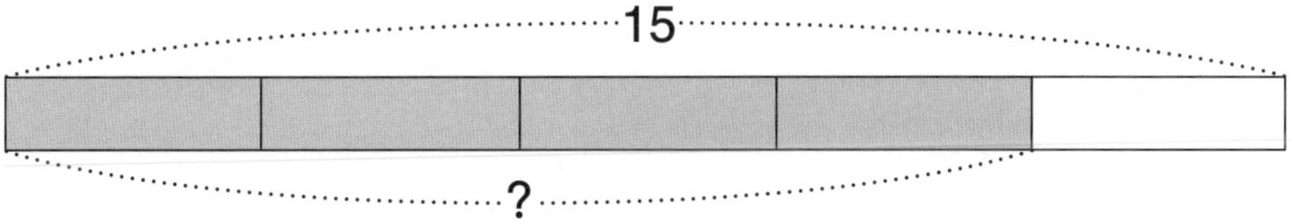

(a) 5 units $\longrightarrow \square$

1 unit $\longrightarrow \frac{15}{5} = \square$

4 units $\longrightarrow 4 \times \square = \square$

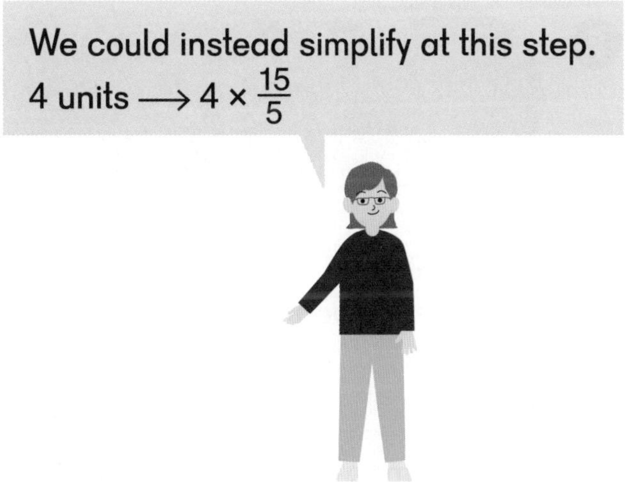

(b) $\frac{4}{5} \times 15 = \frac{\square \times \square}{5} = \square$

5 Find the value.

(a) $\frac{1}{5}$ of 10

(b) $\frac{1}{6}$ of 30

(c) $\frac{3}{5}$ of 10

(d) $\frac{5}{6}$ of 30

(e) $\frac{1}{3}$ of 18

(f) $\frac{2}{7}$ of 14

(g) $\frac{2}{3} \times 24$

(h) $\frac{3}{8} \times 16$

(i) $\frac{4}{6} \times 9$

(j) $\frac{4}{5} \times 60$

6 There are 15 dogs at an animal shelter. $\frac{2}{3}$ of them are puppies. How many puppies are there?

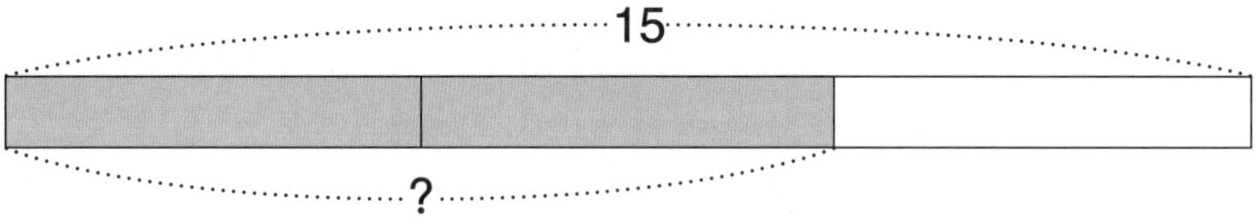

7

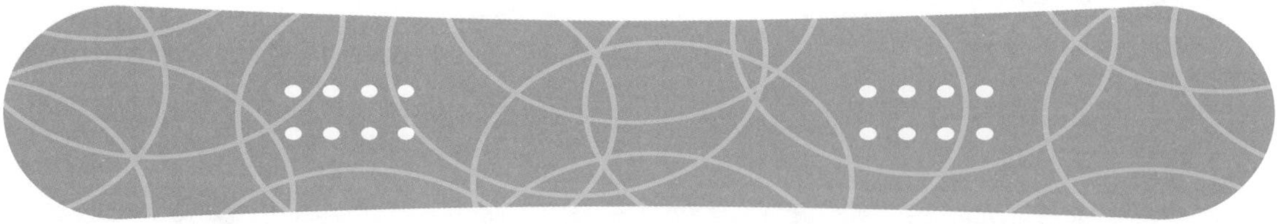

Caleb saved $100. He spent $\frac{3}{4}$ of his savings on a snowboard. How much did the snowboard cost?

8 The distance around a track is 400 m. Camila ran $\frac{5}{8}$ of the distance around and walked the rest of the way. How far did she run in meters?

Exercise 5 • page 182

Lesson 6
Multiplying a Whole Number by a Fraction — Part 2

6

Think

6 pizzas were delivered for a Pizza and Play night. $\frac{3}{4}$ of the pizzas were eaten. How many pizzas were eaten?

Learn

Method 1

$\frac{1}{4}$ of 6 $\longrightarrow \frac{6}{4}$

$\frac{3}{4}$ of 6 $\longrightarrow 3 \times \frac{6}{4} = \frac{18}{4}$

$= \frac{9}{2}$

$= 4\frac{1}{2}$

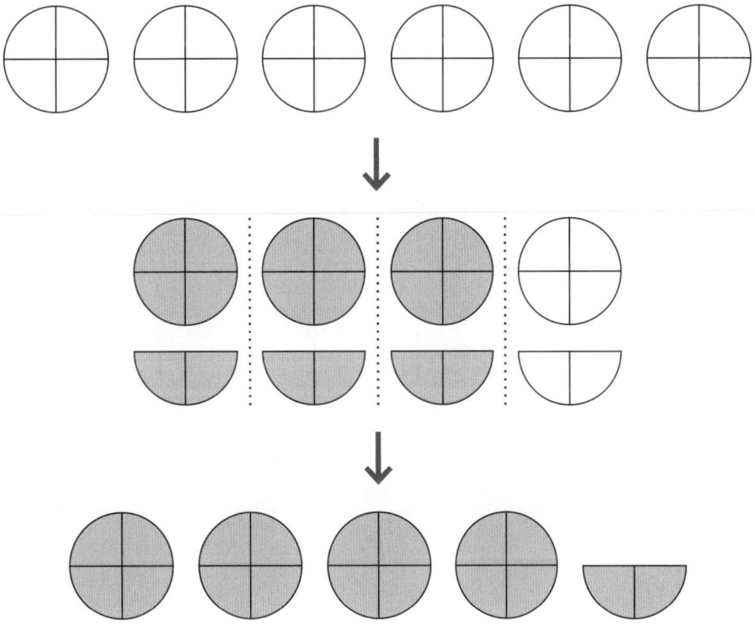

Method 2

$\frac{3}{4} \times 6 = \frac{3 \times \overset{3}{\cancel{6}}}{\underset{2}{\cancel{4}}}$

$= \frac{9}{2}$

$= 4\frac{1}{2}$

________ pizzas were eaten.

Do

1 (a) Find $\frac{1}{3}$ of 10.

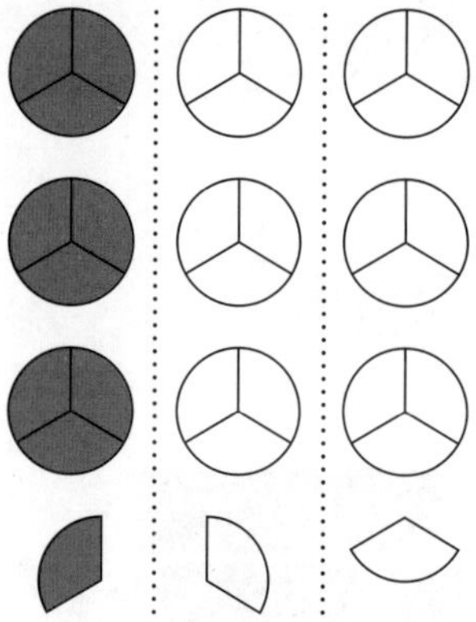

$10 \div 3 = \frac{\square}{3}$

$\frac{1}{3} \times 10 = \frac{\square}{3}$

$= \square \frac{\square}{3}$

(b) Find $\frac{2}{3}$ of 10.

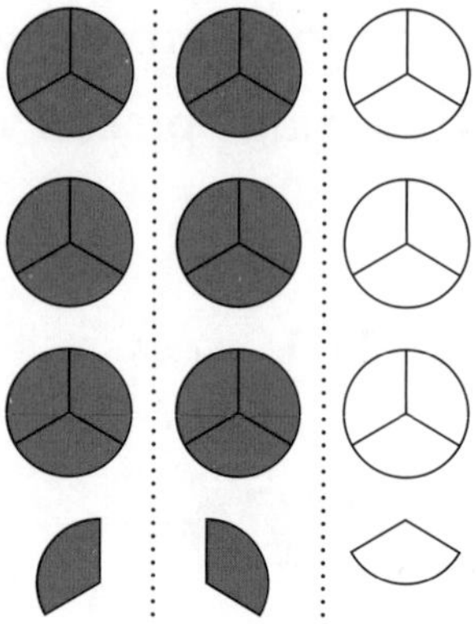

$\frac{2}{3} \times 10 = 2 \times \frac{\square}{3}$

$= \frac{\square}{3}$

$= \square \frac{\square}{\square}$

2 A board is 4 m long. $\frac{3}{5}$ of it is sawed off. How long is the sawed-off piece in meters?

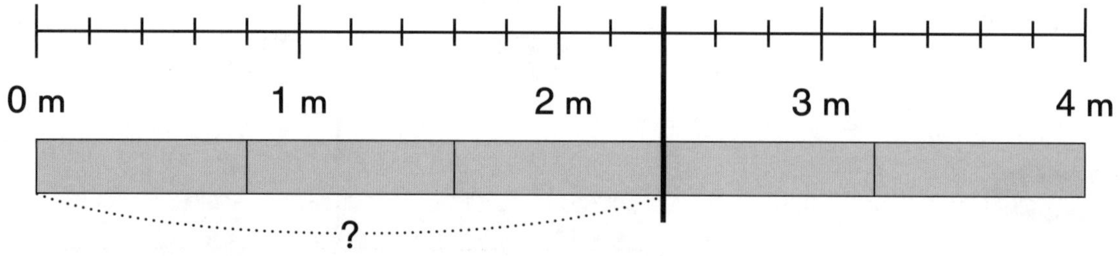

5 units $\longrightarrow$ 4

1 unit $\longrightarrow \frac{4}{5}$

3 units $\longrightarrow \square \times \frac{4}{5} = \frac{\square \times 4}{5} = \frac{\square}{5} = \square \frac{\square}{5}$

The sawed-off piece is ________ m long.

3 Find $\frac{2}{3}$ of 8.

$\frac{2}{3} \times 8 = \frac{\square \times \square}{3} = \frac{\square}{3} = \square\frac{\square}{\square}$

4 Find $\frac{5}{6}$ of 9.

$\frac{5}{6} \times 9 = \frac{5 \times \cancel{9}^{3}}{\cancel{6}_{2}} = \frac{\square}{2} = \square\frac{\square}{\square}$

5 Find the value. Express each answer in its simplest form.

(a) $\frac{1}{2}$ of 15

(b) $\frac{1}{3}$ of 25

(c) $\frac{4}{5} \times 9$

(d) $\frac{5}{8} \times 20$

(e) $\frac{2}{6} \times 16$

(f) $\frac{4}{5} \times 12$

(g) $\frac{5}{12} \times 20$

(h) $\frac{1}{3} \times 100$

6 Dion has a board that is 8 ft long. He cuts off $\frac{2}{3}$ of its length. How long in feet is the piece he cut off?

Exercise 6 • page 185

Think

There are 20 people at a school play. $\frac{3}{5}$ of them are children and the rest are adults. How many adults are there?

Learn

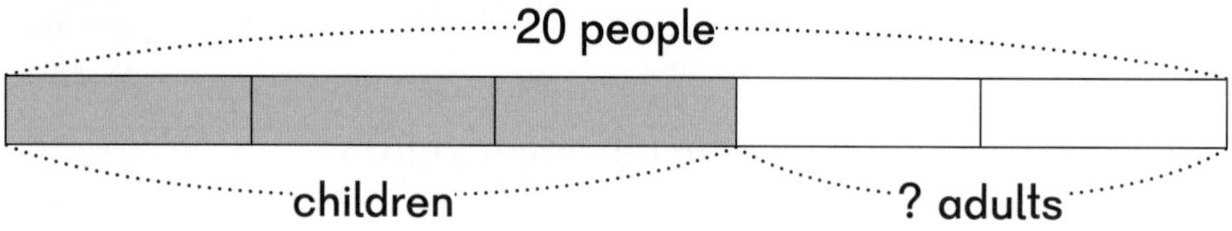

Method 1

5 units $\longrightarrow$ 20

1 unit $\longrightarrow \frac{20}{5} = 4$

2 units $\longrightarrow 2 \times 4 = \square$

Method 2

$\frac{3}{5} \times 20 = \square$

$20 - 12 = \square$

Method 3

$1 - \frac{3}{5} = \frac{\square}{5}$

$\frac{2}{5} \times 20 = \square$

There are ________ adults.

Do

1 Emma spent $\frac{2}{5}$ of her money on a puzzle. The puzzle cost \$12. How much money did she have at first?

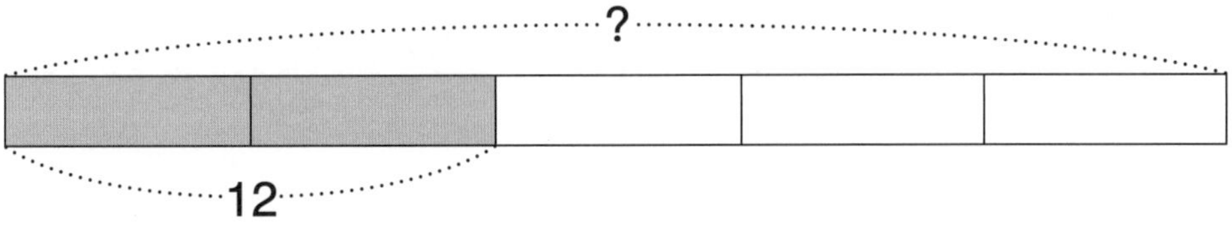

2 units $\longrightarrow$ 12

1 unit $\longrightarrow \frac{12}{2} = 6$

5 units $\longrightarrow 5 \times 6 =$ ____

She had \$________ at first.

2

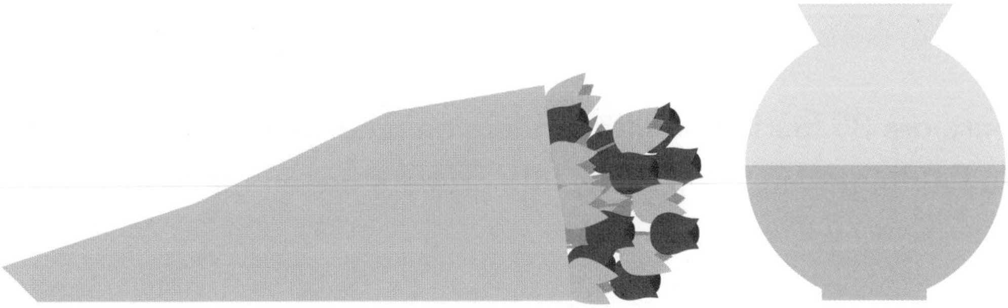

$\frac{3}{5}$ of the flowers in a bouquet are roses and the rest are tulips. There are 36 roses.

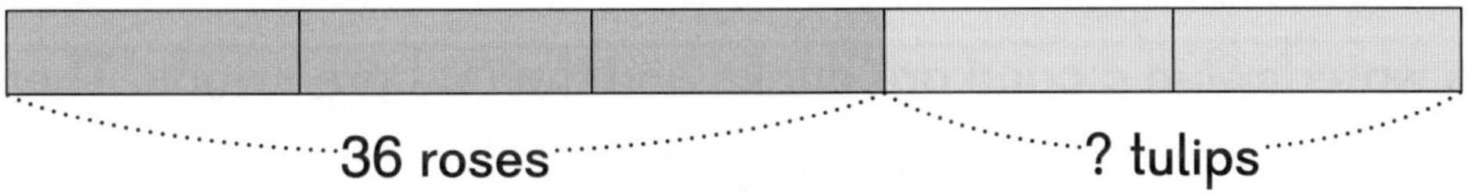

(a) What fraction of the flowers are tulips?

(b) How many tulips are there?

(c) How many flowers are there in all?

3 Dion had \$40. He used $\frac{3}{8}$ of it to buy a game. How much money did he have left?

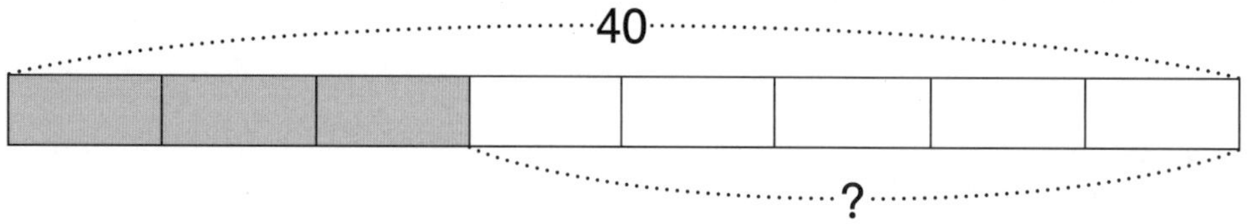

4 In a coin collection, $\frac{1}{3}$ of the coins are silver coins and the rest are gold coins. If there are 14 gold coins, how many coins are there altogether?

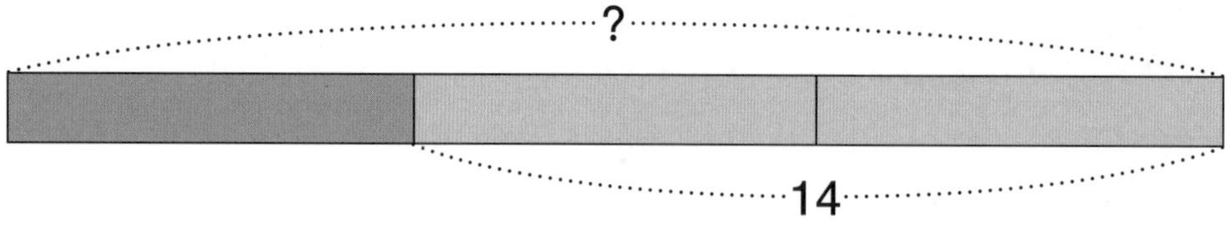

5 There are 30 fourth and fifth graders on a basketball team. $\frac{5}{6}$ of them are fourth graders. How many fifth graders are on the team?

6 $\frac{5}{8}$ of the fourth graders ride the bus to school and the rest walk to school. If 45 fourth graders walk to school, how many ride the bus to school?

7 $\frac{4}{7}$ of the waterfowl in a pond are ducks and the rest are swans. There are 21 swans. How many waterfowl are in the pond?

Exercise 7 • page 188

Lesson 8
Word Problems — Part 2

8

Think

Alex has 24 envelopes. 16 of them are green and the rest are yellow. What fraction of his envelopes are yellow?

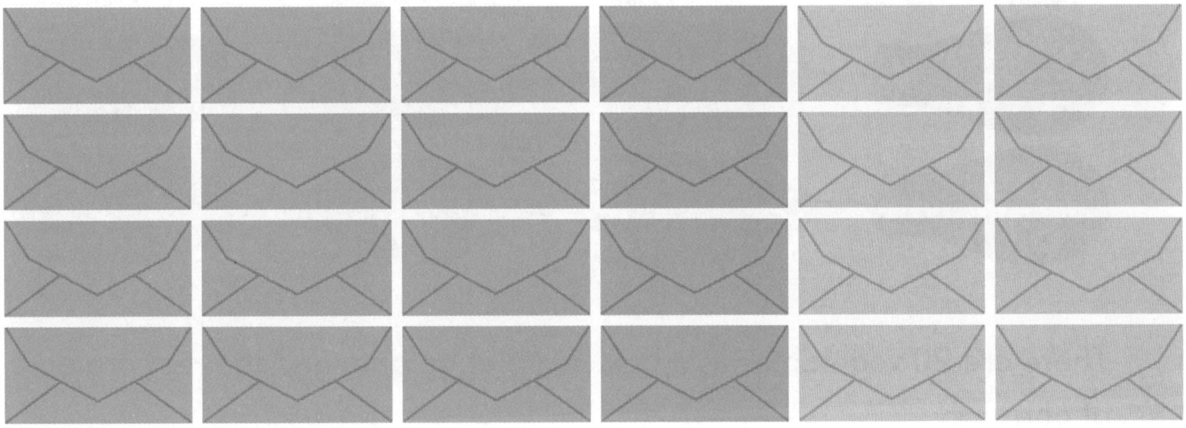

Learn

Method 1

$24 - 16 = 8$

$\frac{8}{24} = \frac{1}{3}$

Method 2

$\frac{16}{24} = \frac{2}{3}$

$1 - \frac{2}{3} = \frac{1}{3}$

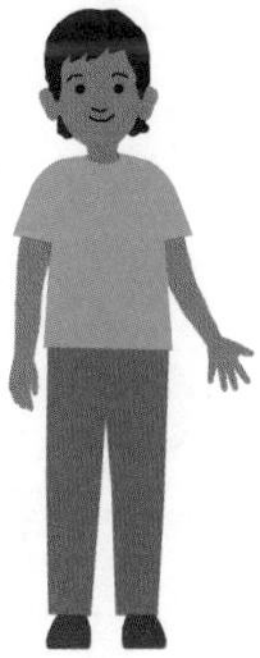

________ of the envelopes are yellow.

Do

1

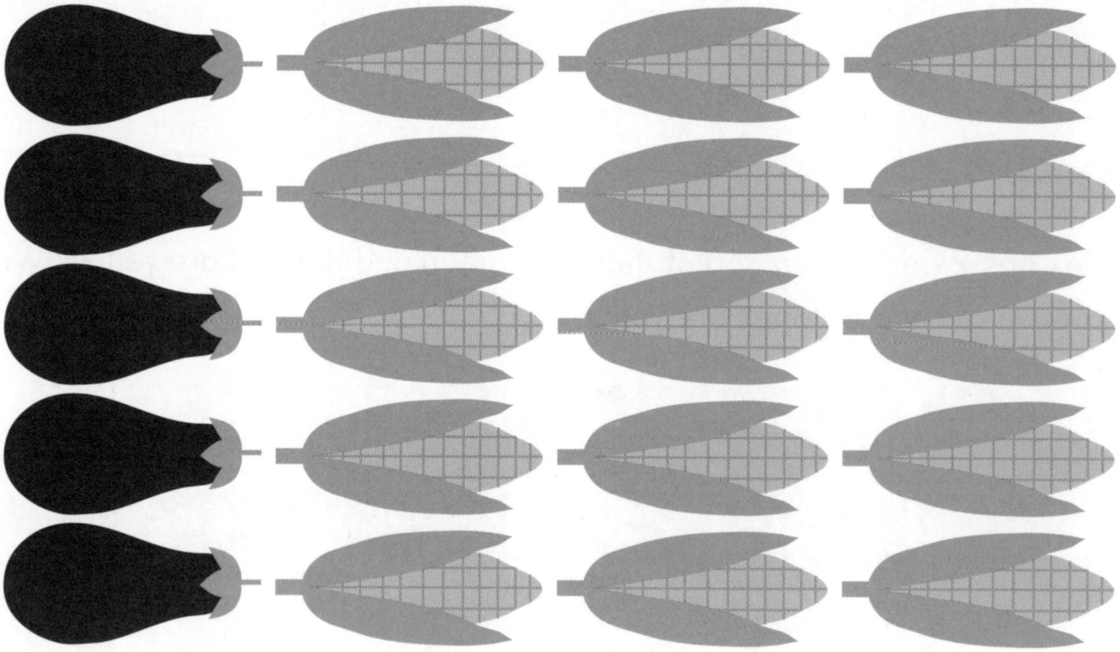

There are 20 vegetables in a box. 5 are eggplants and the rest are ears of corn.

(a) What fraction of the vegetables are eggplants?

(b) What fraction of the vegetables are ears of corn?

2 There are 40 children in the garden club. 25 of them are wearing hats. What fraction of the children are not wearing hats?

3 Karina had $75. She spent $15 and saved the rest. What fraction of her money did she save?

4 There are 48 pieces of fruit in a basket. 8 are peaches and 16 are apples. The rest are oranges. What fraction of the pieces of fruit are oranges?

5 Alex made 175 granola bars. He gave 25 of them to his friends. He sold $\frac{3}{5}$ of the remaining granola bars at a bake sale. How many granola bars did he have left?

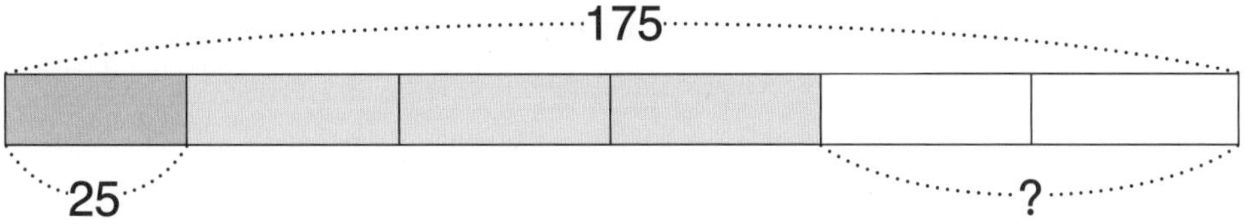

6 Mei has \$12. She spent $\frac{1}{2}$ of her money on a book and $\frac{1}{4}$ of it on a pen. How much money did she have left?

7 There were 245 books at a library sale. On the first day, 85 books were sold. On the second day, 40 books were sold. On the third day, $\frac{3}{5}$ of the remaining books were sold.

(a) How many books were sold on the third day?

(b) How many books were left?

8 There were 24 L of water in an outdoor tub. $\frac{2}{5}$ of the water evaporated. How many liters of water are left in the tub?

Exercise 8 • page 192

Lesson 9
Practice

P 9

1 Multiply. Express each answer in its simplest form.

(a) $2 \times \frac{1}{3}$

(b) $\frac{2}{7} \times 3$

(c) $6 \times \frac{1}{8}$

(d) $\frac{4}{9} \times 15$

(e) $\frac{2}{5} \times 5$

(f) $8 \times \frac{3}{4}$

2 A bread recipe calls for $\frac{3}{4}$ cups of flour to make one loaf of bread. Chad wants to make 3 loaves of bread. How much flour should he use?

3 There are 28 students in a fourth grade class. 16 of them are wearing sneakers. What fraction of the students are not wearing sneakers?

4 Johnathan earned some money gardening. He spent $\frac{1}{4}$ of the money he earned on a board game that cost $11. How much money did he earn gardening?

5 Ashna had 8 ft of ribbon. She used $\frac{3}{5}$ of it to wrap presents. How many feet of ribbon does she have left?

6 $\frac{2}{5}$ of the students in the Language Club are learning Spanish, $\frac{3}{10}$ of them are learning Mandarin, and the rest are learning French. If 30 students are learning Mandarin, how many students are in the club?

Exercise 9 • page 196

Chapter 9

Line Graphs and Line Plots

These are some different kinds of graphs.

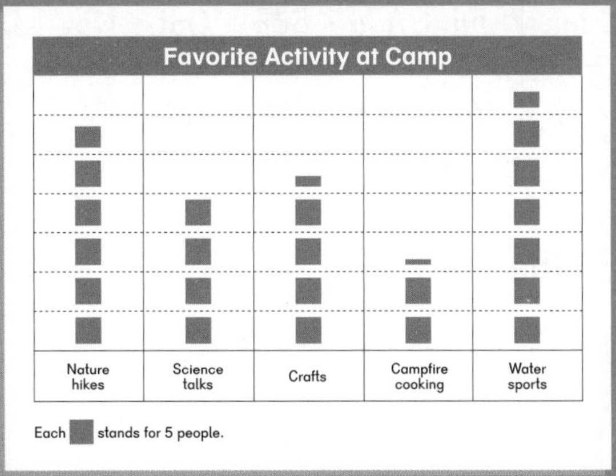

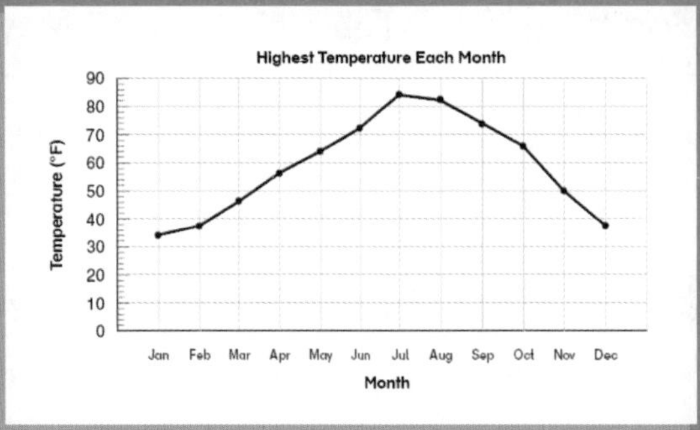

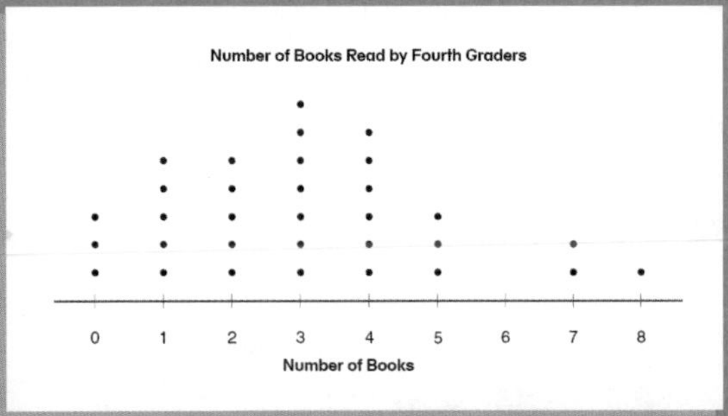

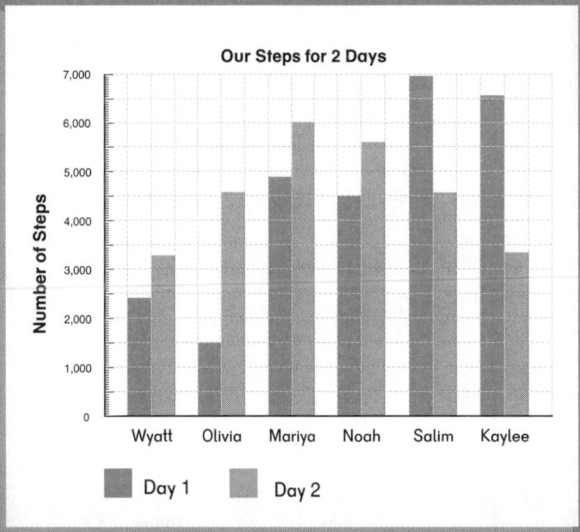

Which of the types of graphs shown here have we learned about already?

Think

This table shows the highest temperature in Dion's city in each month.

Month	Jan	Feb	Mar	Apr	May	Jun	Jul	Aug	Sep	Oct	Nov	Dec
Temp (°F)	34	38	46	56	64	72	84	82	74	66	50	38

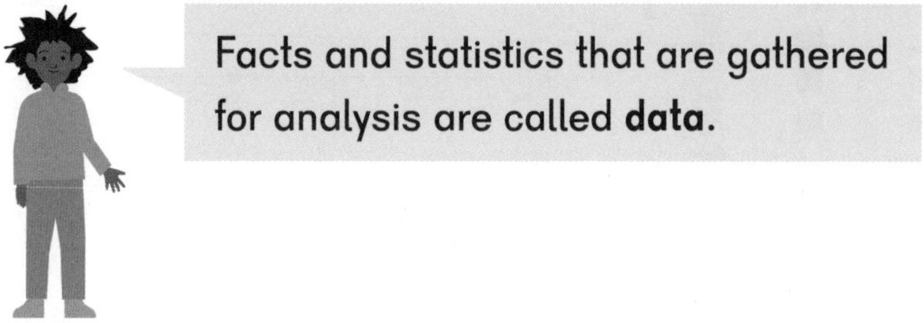

This shows the same data displayed in a bar graph.

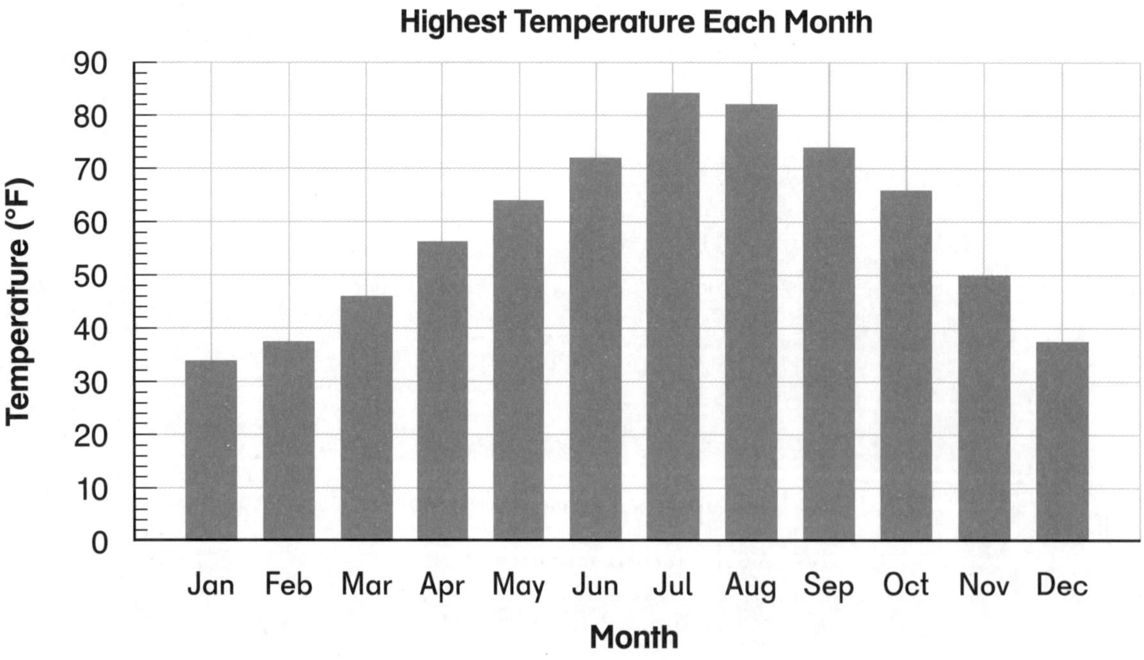

What do you notice about how the high temperature changes from month to month and during the whole year?

Learn

We can draw points at the top of each bar and connect them with a line.

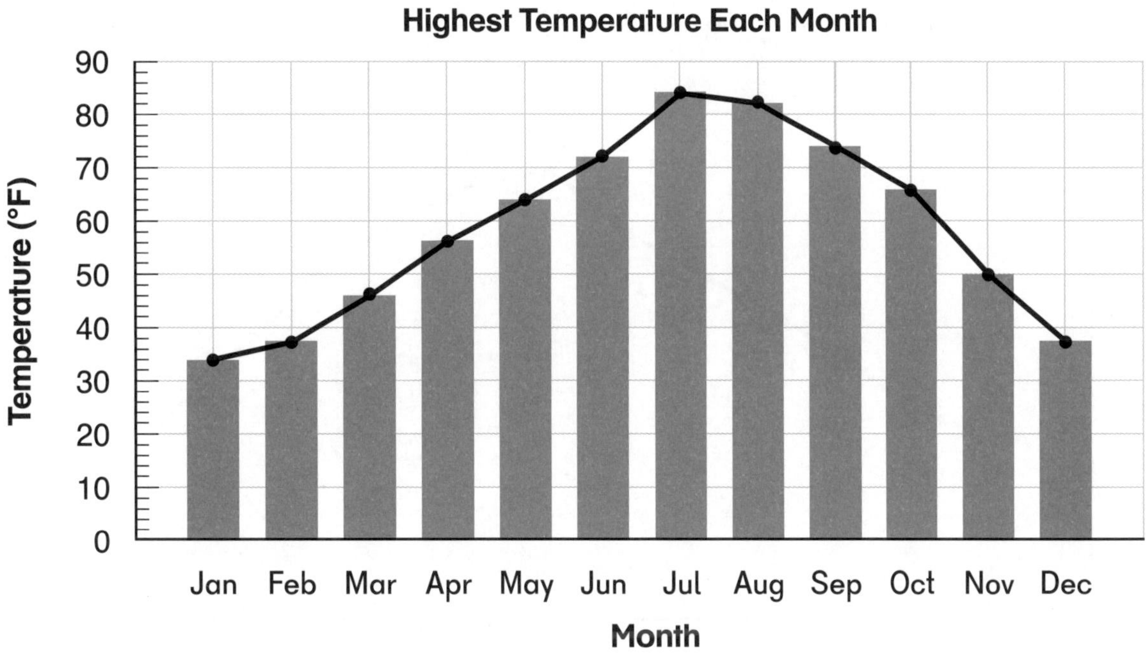

If we remove the bars we have a **line graph**.

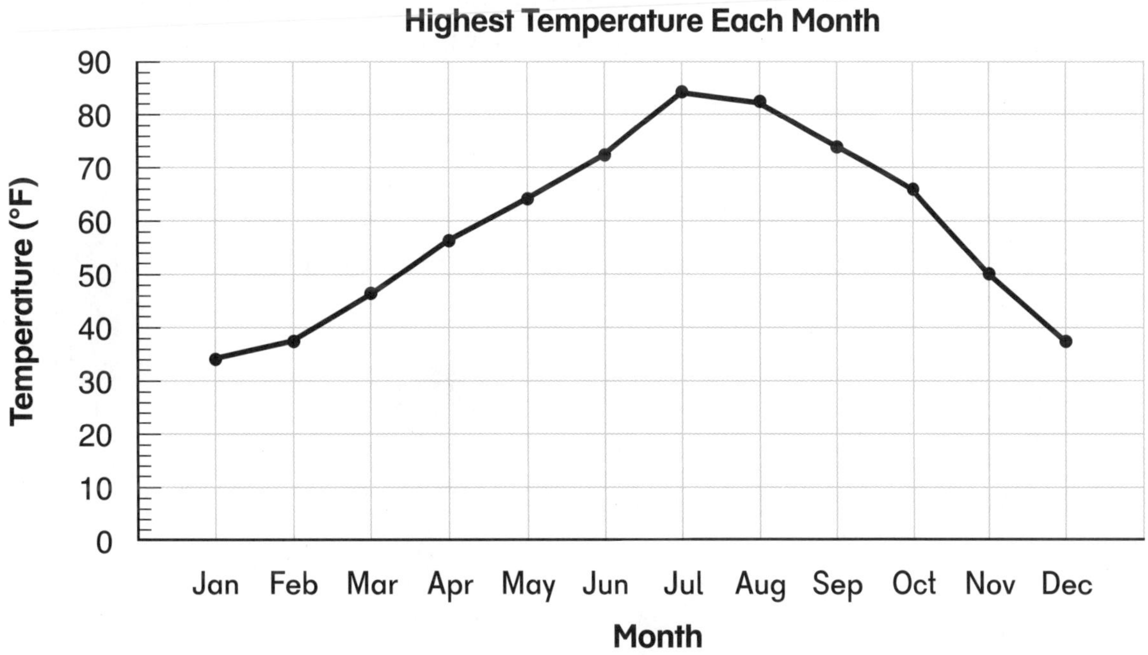

Highest Temperature Each Month

Month	Jan	Feb	Mar	Apr	May	Jun	Jul	Aug	Sep	Oct	Nov	Dec
Temp (°F)	34	38	46	56	64	72	84	82	74	66	50	38

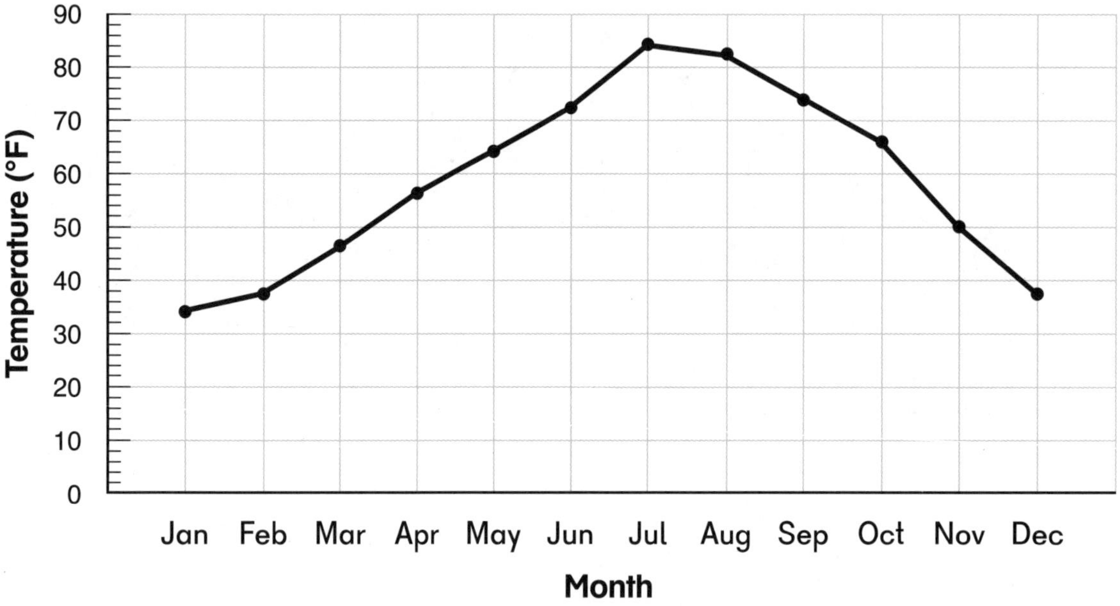

The line at the bottom is called the **horizontal axis**. The line along the side is called the **vertical axis**. Graphs usually show the categories along the horizontal axis. The values are shown along the vertical axis.

Line graphs help us to see changes and trends in data over time. To show the actual data values, it is better to use a table.

I can easily see from the graph that the temperature rises from January to July, and then drops from July to December.

The day with the highest temperature was in July.

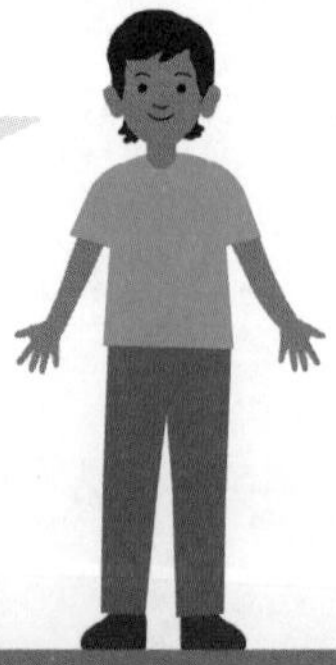

Do

1 Use the graph or table on the preceding page to answer the following questions.

(a) What does the horizontal axis represent?

(b) What does the vertical axis represent?

(c) What is the increment in degrees between each tick mark?

(d) Which months had the same highest temperature and what is that temperature?

(e) By how many degrees did the highest temperature rise from January to February?

(f) Between which two months was the sharpest rise in temperature?

(g) By how many degrees did the highest temperature drop from November to December?

(h) Between which two months was the sharpest drop in temperature?

(i) By how many degrees did the highest temperature fall from July to December?

(j) Dion's grandmother wants to visit for two months in a row. She does not like really hot or really cold weather. Which two months do you think she should visit and why?

2 The line graph shows the amount of rainfall in a certain city each month from April to September.

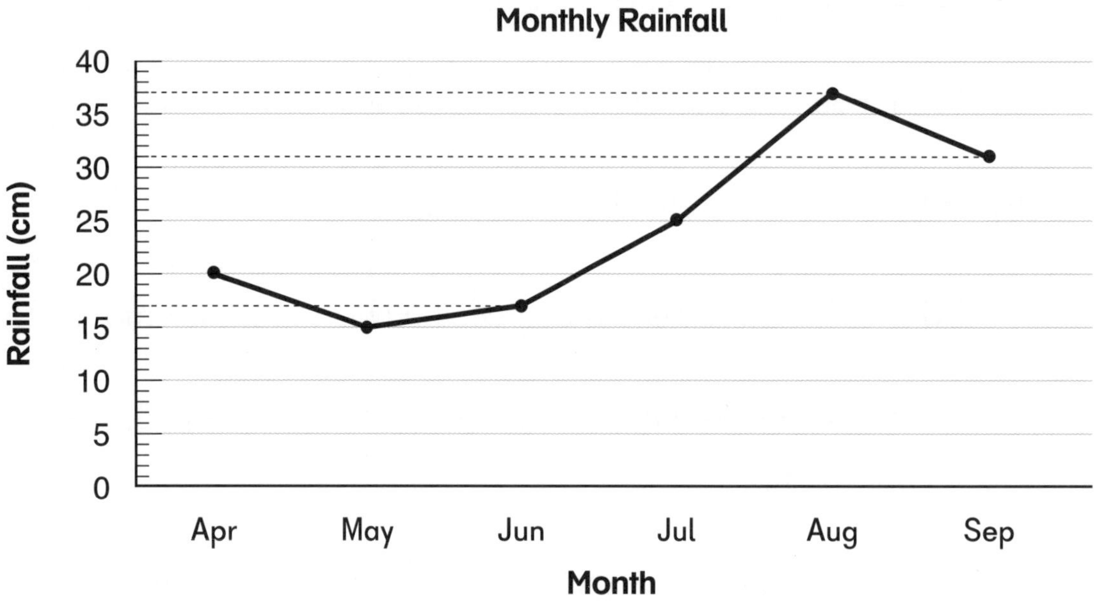

(a) Which month had the greatest amount of rainfall? How much did it rain? Which month had the least amount of rainfall? How much did it rain? In which month was there 17 cm of rainfall?

(b) Between which months was there a continuous rise in rainfall? Between which two months was the sharpest rise in rainfall and by how much?

(c) Between which months was there a decrease in rainfall? Between which two months was the sharpest decrease in rainfall and by how much?

(d) A family wants to visit this city to sightsee and go to the beach. Which month do you think they should plan on going and why?

3 The table shows the water temperature of a koi pond in degrees Fahrenheit at different times on a certain day.

Time	7:00 a.m.	10:00 a.m.	1:00 p.m.	4:00 p.m.	7:00 p.m.
Temp (°F)	60	65	72	81	68

Which line graph shows the trends in this data correctly?

Graph A

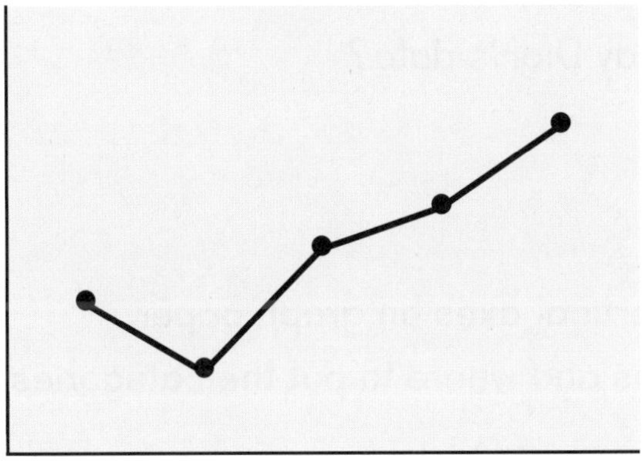

Graph B

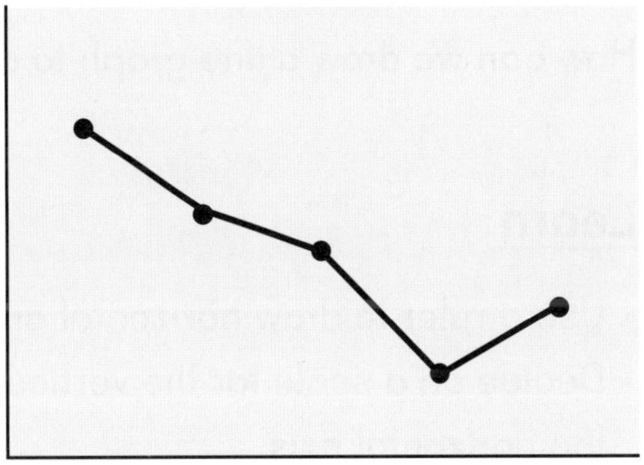

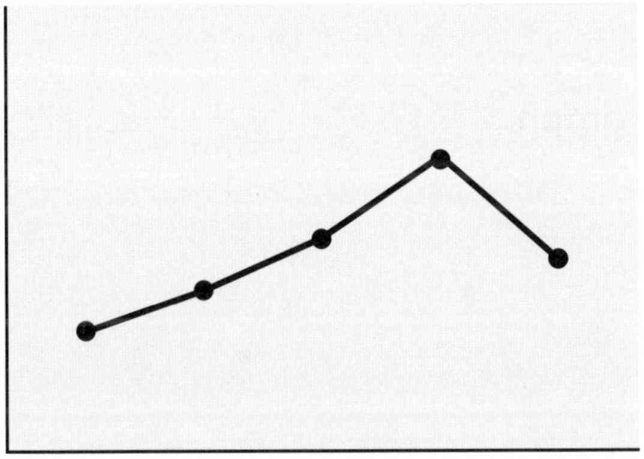

Graph C

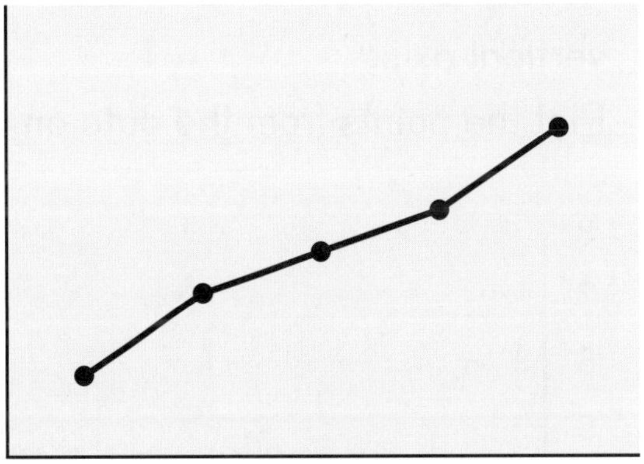

Graph D

Exercise 1 • page 201

Lesson 2
Drawing Line Graphs

2

Think

Dion collected data about the total rainfall where he lives over a six-month period.

Month	Jan	Feb	Mar	Apr	May	Jun
Rainfall (cm)	2	3	4	7	6	4

How can we draw a line graph to display Dion's data?

Learn

- Use a ruler to draw horizontal and vertical axes on graph paper.
- Decide on a scale for the vertical axis and where to put the categories on the horizontal axis.
- Label the axes. Include the units of measurement in the label for the vertical axis.
- Plot the points from the data on your graph.

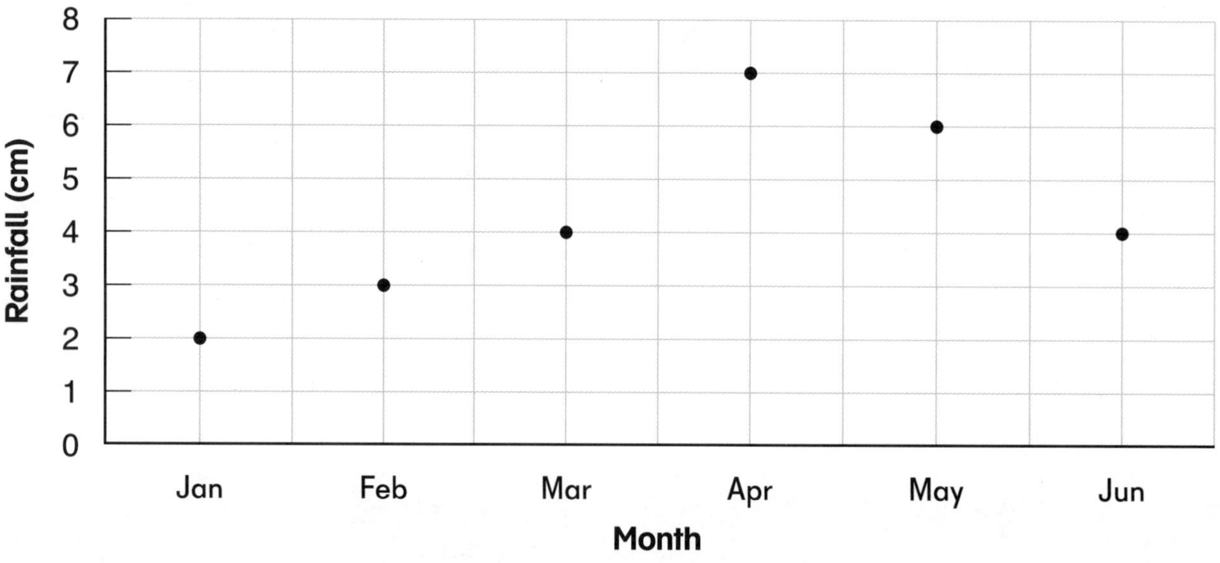

- Using a ruler, draw lines to connect the points, one after the other.
- Give your graph a title.

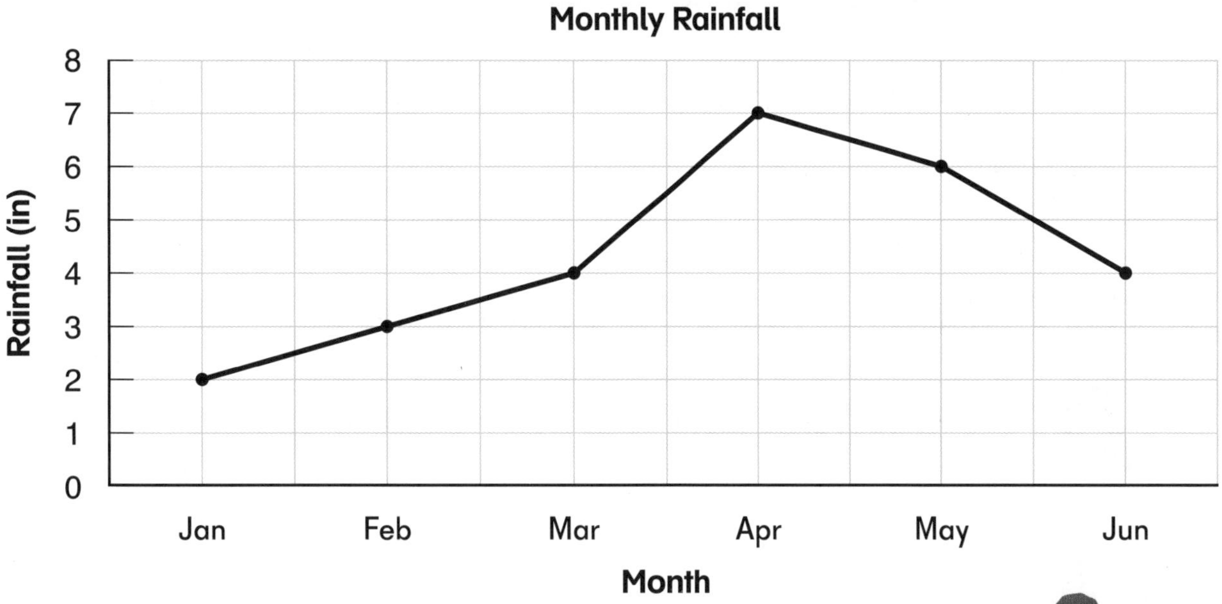

We could also use a **spreadsheet** program such as the one shown here, or a graphing program to graph data.

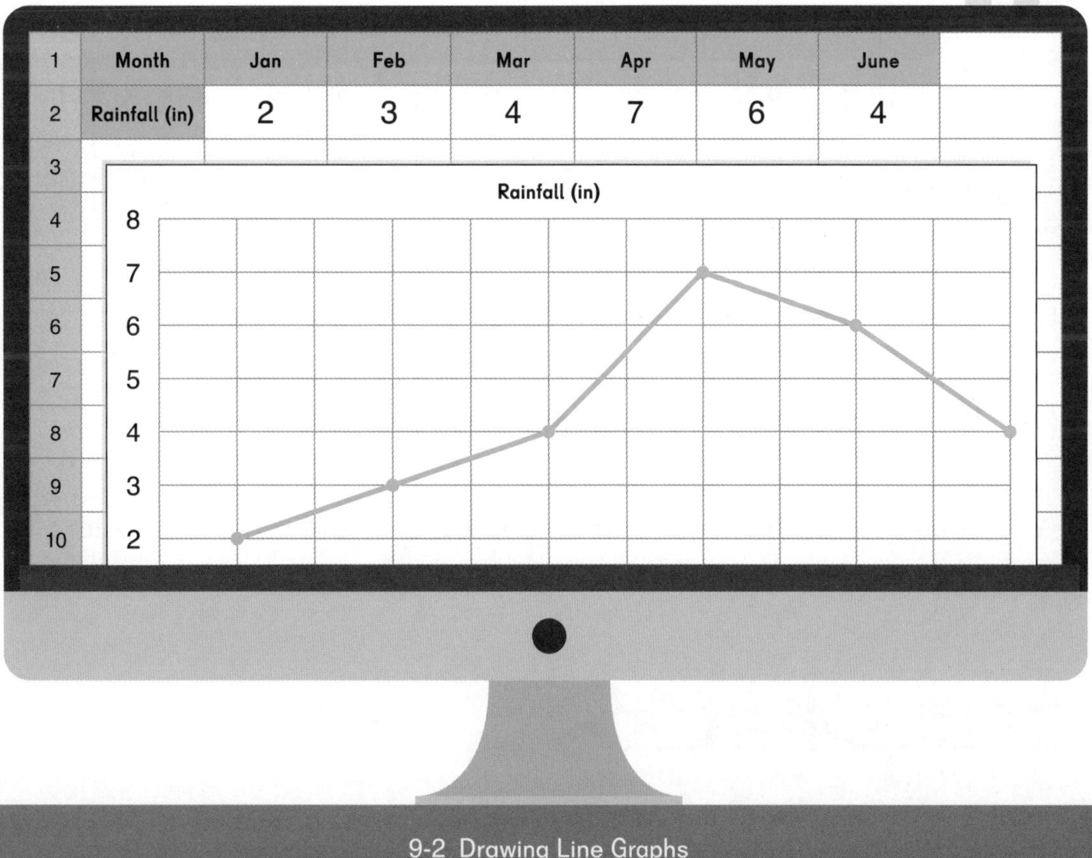

1	Month	Jan	Feb	Mar	Apr	May	June
2	Rainfall (in)	2	3	4	7	6	4

Do

1 The table below shows the temperature in degrees Fahrenheit in a certain town from 6:00 a.m. to 9:00 p.m.

Time	6:00 a.m.	9:00 a.m.	12:00 noon	3:00 p.m.	6:00 p.m.	9:00 p.m.
Temp (°F)	55	60	70	75	65	50

Draw a line graph on graph paper to display the data.

What scale should we use on the vertical axis?

2 The table below shows the number of shoppers at a store during each hour.

	a.m.					p.m.							
Time	7	8	9	10	11	12	1	2	3	4	5	6	7
Shoppers	19	36	28	52	69	86	73	52	47	55	68	34	23

(a) Draw a line graph on graph paper to display the data.

(b) When does the store need the most cashiers?

(c) When would be a good time to shop to avoid a crowded store?

Exercise 2 • page 205

Think

The table below shows the names and ages of children at Mei's birthday party.

Name	Age (years)
Dion	9
Pablo	6
Kawai	10
Emma	9
Alex	10
Kaitlyn	7
Sofia	9
Mei	10
Ximena	12
Tomas	9

(a) How many children are at the party?

(b) What is the difference between the age of the youngest child and the age of the oldest child?

(c) What ages are the most common?

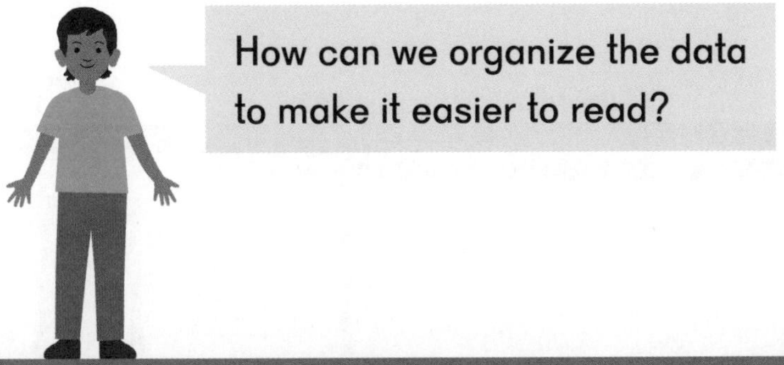

Learn

We can use a **line plot** to organize the data.

Ages of Children at Mei's Birthday Party

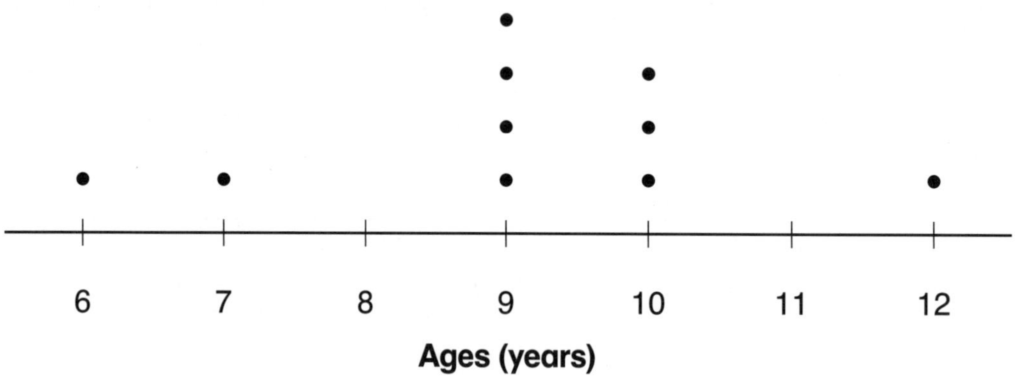

(a) There were ____ children at the party.

(b) The youngest child is ____ years old.

The oldest child is ____ years old.

The difference between the age of the youngest child and the age of the oldest child is ____ years.

(c) The most common ages are ____ and ____.

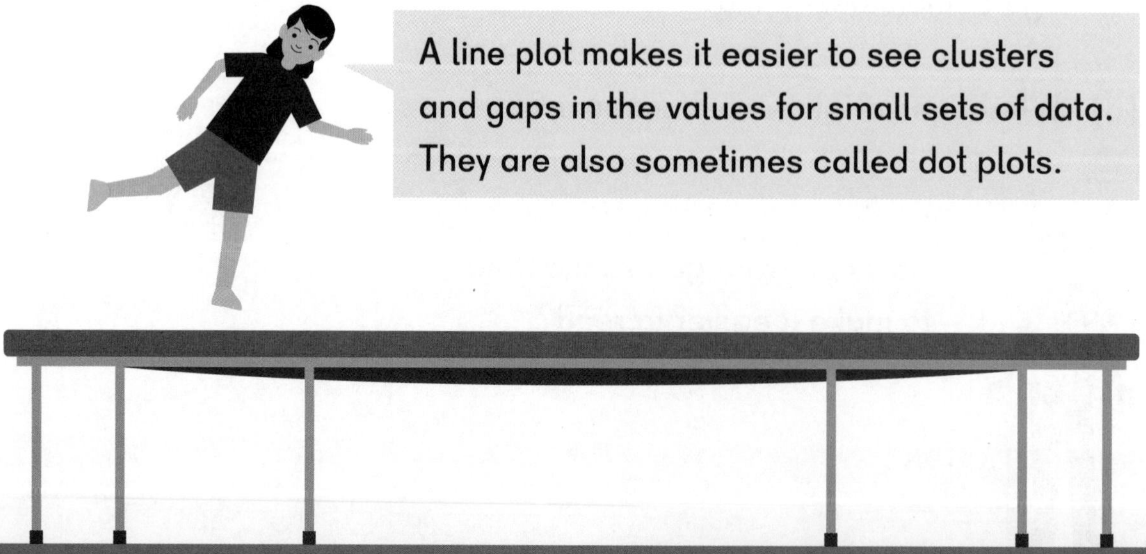

Do

1 The line plot shows the number of books read by fourth grade students in Alex's class last month.

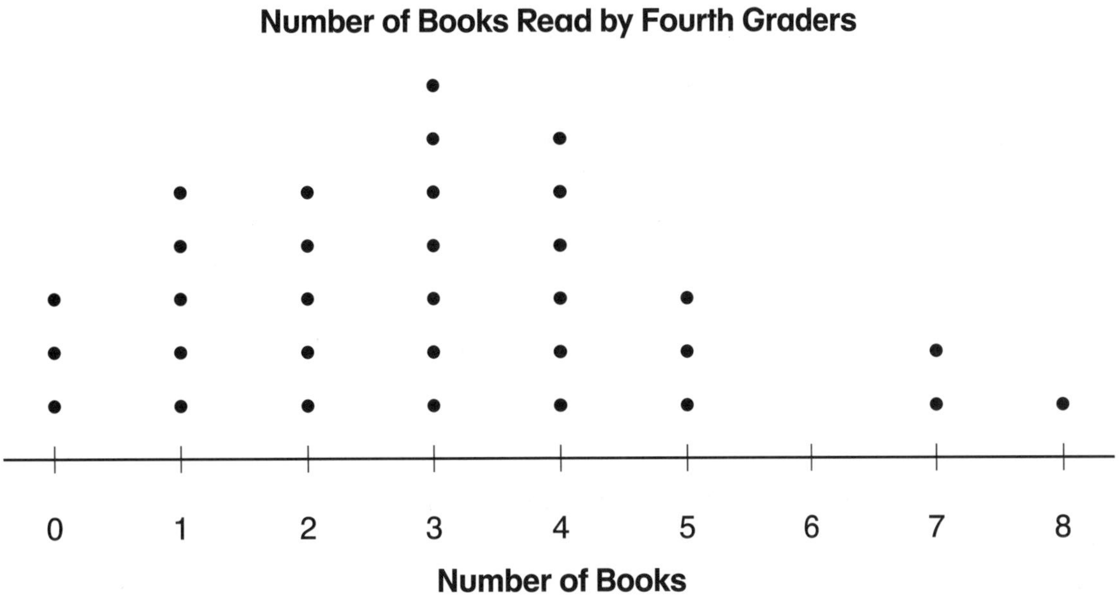

(a) How many students are included in the data set?

(b) How many students read more than 2 books?

(c) How many students read fewer than 2 books?

(d) What is the difference between the greatest and least number of books read?

(e) What is the most common number of books read by these children?

2 Emma collected data on how far her friends live from her house to the nearest quarter mile and recorded the data in a line plot.

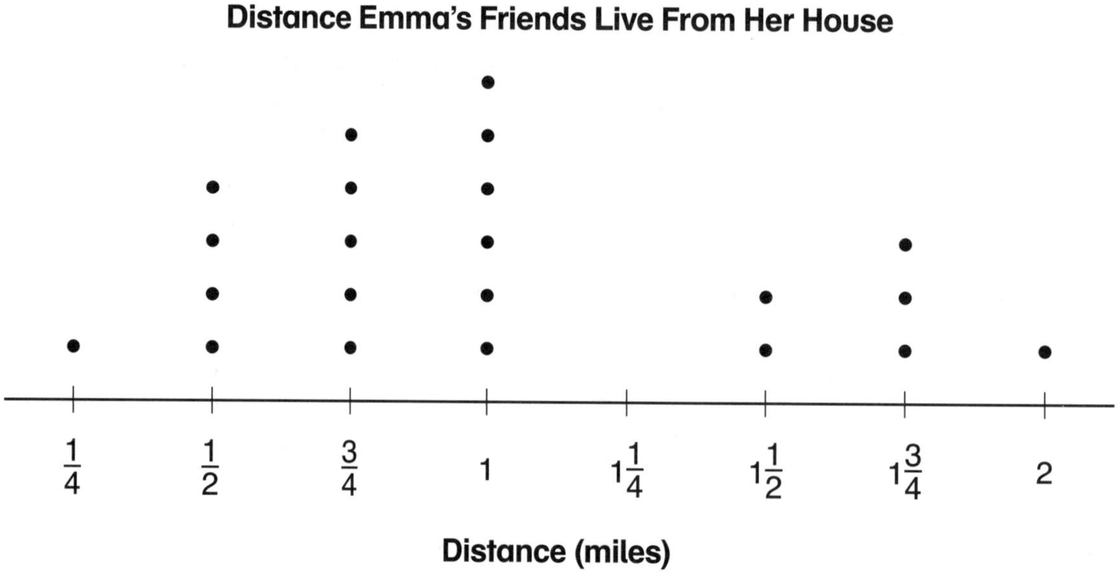

(a) How far from her house do the greatest number of her friends live?

(b) How far from her house do the fewest number of her friends live?

(c) How many friends live $\frac{3}{4}$ mile from her house?

(d) How many friends live less than a mile from her house?

(e) How many more friends live 1 mile from her house than $\frac{1}{2}$ mile from her house?

(f) What is the difference between the greatest distance and the least distance her friends live from her house?

(g) Do more of her friends live less than or more than a mile from her house?

3 Mei collected data on the amount of rainfall each day in May. She measured up to each $\frac{1}{4}$ inch interval.

Number of Inches of Rainfall in May

		2	2	$1\frac{3}{4}$	$\frac{1}{2}$	$\frac{1}{4}$
$\frac{1}{2}$	$\frac{1}{2}$	$\frac{1}{4}$	$\frac{3}{4}$	0	0	0
0	1	1	2	$1\frac{1}{2}$	$\frac{1}{2}$	$\frac{1}{2}$
$\frac{1}{2}$	1	$2\frac{1}{2}$	$1\frac{1}{4}$	1	$1\frac{1}{2}$	0
$1\frac{1}{4}$	$1\frac{1}{4}$	$1\frac{3}{4}$	0	0		

(a) Draw a line plot on graph paper to show the information. First draw a horizontal axis. Find the least and greatest values and decide on a scale along the axis. Then draw dots for each data value. Write a title for your graph.

(b) On how many days did it rain?

(c) On how many days did it rain 1 or more inches?

(d) On how many days did it rain less than 1 inch?

(e) What was the most common amount of rain in a day when it did rain?

Exercise 3 • page 208

1

The table shows the monthly high temperatures from January to December in a given year in Seattle, Washington, rounded to the nearest 5 degrees Fahrenheit.

Month	Jan	Feb	Mar	Apr	May	Jun	Jul	Aug	Sep	Oct	Nov	Dec
Temp (°F)	45	50	55	60	65	70	80	85	75	60	50	45

Create a line graph to show the data.

(a) Which month had the hottest day?

(b) Which months had the lowest high temperature?

(c) What is the difference in the highest temperature and the lowest temperature?

(d) How many months had a day with a high temperature above 60 degrees?

(e) How many months had no days warmer than 60 degrees?

2

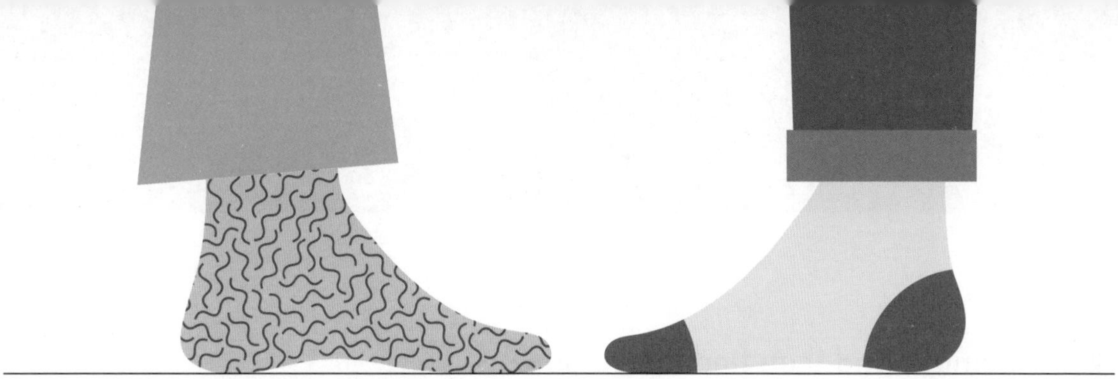

Some fourth grade students measured the length of their feet to the nearest $\frac{1}{4}$ inch.

Foot Length (inches)							
$9\frac{1}{2}$	$9\frac{1}{4}$	$8\frac{3}{4}$	$9\frac{3}{4}$	9	$9\frac{1}{2}$	$8\frac{3}{4}$	$9\frac{1}{4}$
$9\frac{1}{4}$	$9\frac{1}{2}$	9	$7\frac{3}{4}$	$8\frac{1}{2}$	$10\frac{1}{4}$	$9\frac{1}{4}$	9
10	$8\frac{1}{2}$	$9\frac{1}{4}$	$9\frac{1}{4}$	$9\frac{1}{2}$			

Draw a line plot to show the data.

(a) How many measurements were recorded?

(b) What is the length of the longest foot?

(c) What is the length of the shortest foot?

(d) What is the difference between the length of the longest foot and the length of the shortest foot?

(e) Sock sizes 3–5 fit feet that are from $8\frac{1}{2}$ to $9\frac{1}{8}$ inches long. How many of these students would wear these sizes?

(f) Sock sizes 5–7 fit feet that are from $9\frac{1}{8}$ to $9\frac{13}{16}$ inches long. How many of these students would wear these sizes?

Exercise 4 • page 211

Review 2

R 2

1 Estimate and then find the values.

(a) $8{,}684 + 44{,}907$

(b) $82{,}120 - 5{,}555$

(c) 269×52

(d) $1{,}908 \times 63$

(e) $7{,}435 \div 6$

(f) $25{,}025 \div 7$

2 Find the values.

(a) $30{,}000 - 6{,}924$

(b) $5{,}278 + 998$

(c) $9{,}410 - 29$

(d) 6×199

(e) $37{,}000 \times 4$

(f) $76{,}000 \div 8$

3 Which of the following numbers have 8 as a factor?

96	218	6,279	23,408	52,215

4 Which of the following numbers are common multiples of 4 and 9?

36	117	540	2,016	16,218

5 What sign, >, <, or =, goes in each ◯?

(a) $\frac{3}{7}$ ◯ $\frac{5}{8}$

(b) $\frac{2}{3}$ ◯ $\frac{5}{6}$

(c) $\frac{9}{7}$ ◯ $\frac{7}{9}$

(d) $1\frac{3}{8}$ ◯ $\frac{11}{8}$

(e) $\frac{17}{3}$ ◯ $5\frac{2}{5}$

(f) $\frac{24}{8}$ ◯ $\frac{18}{9}$

6 Express each of the following as a proper fraction or mixed number. Express each answer in its simplest form.

(a) $8 \div 10$

(b) $12 \div 18$

(c) $38 \div 7$

(d) $21 \div 6$

(e) $36 \div 8$

(f) $100 \div 30$

7 Find the value. Express each answer in its simplest form.

(a) $\frac{6}{7} - \frac{2}{7}$

(b) $4 - \frac{3}{8}$

(c) $\frac{5}{6} + \frac{5}{6}$

(d) $\frac{7}{12} + \frac{3}{4}$

(e) $3\frac{5}{9} + \frac{7}{9}$

(f) $6\frac{5}{8} - \frac{1}{4}$

(g) $8\frac{5}{6} + 4\frac{5}{12}$

(h) $7\frac{1}{6} - 3\frac{2}{3}$

(i) $2\frac{3}{5} + \frac{1}{10} + 4\frac{1}{5}$

8 Find the product. Express each answer in its simplest form.

(a) $2 \times \frac{1}{5}$

(b) $6 \times \frac{1}{8}$

(c) $\frac{2}{3} \times 3$

(d) $\frac{3}{4} \times 12$

(e) $\frac{4}{5} \times 20$

(f) $15 \times \frac{3}{9}$

(g) $\frac{2}{9} \times 6$

(h) $\frac{2}{3} \times 20$

(i) $\frac{5}{3} \times 10$

9 There are 25 waterfowl in a pond. 10 of them are ducks and the rest are geese. What fraction of the waterfowl are geese? (Give your answer in simplest form.)

10 Shoshana had $\frac{8}{9}$ m of ribbon. She cut off two $\frac{1}{3}$ m long pieces to wrap two presents. How long is the piece she has left?

11 James earned some money cutting lawns. He spent $\frac{3}{4}$ of his money on a bicycle and $\frac{1}{8}$ of it on a helmet. What fraction of the money does he have left?

12 On Tuesday, Jamel ran $2\frac{3}{5}$ km in the morning. In the evening, he ran $1\frac{7}{10}$ km farther than in the morning. How many kilometers did he run on Tuesday?

13 Melanie put $\frac{1}{4}$ L of water into each of 10 jars to mix paint. How many liters of water did she use altogether?

14 A baker had 75 lb of flour. He used $\frac{3}{4}$ of it to make bread. How many pounds of flour does he have left?

15 $\frac{5}{8}$ of the vehicles in a parking lot are vans. If there are 60 vans, how many vehicles are in the parking lot?

16 100 concert tickets were sold on Monday and Tuesday altogether. 10 fewer tickets were sold on Tuesday than on Monday. $\frac{2}{3}$ as many concert tickets were sold on Wednesday as on Tuesday. How many tickets were sold those three days altogether?

Exercise 5 • page 215